MESOAMERICAN VOICES

Mesoamerican Voices presents a collection of indigenous-language writings from the colonial period, translated into English. The texts were written from the sixteenth through the eighteenth centuries by Nahuas from central Mexico, Mixtecs from Oaxaca, Mayas from Yucatan, and other groups from Mexico and Guatemala.

The volume gives college teachers and students access to important new sources for the history of Latin America and Native Americans. It is the first collection to present the translated writings of so many native groups and to address such a wide variety of topics, including conquest, government, land, household, society, gender, religion, writing, law, crime, and morality.

Matthew Restall is Professor of Latin American History at Pennsylvania State University. He is the author of more than thirty articles and essays and seven books, including *The Maya World* (1997) and *Seven Myths of the Spanish Conquest* (2003).

Lisa Sousa is Assistant Professor of Latin American History at Occidental College in Los Angeles. She has coedited and translated *The Story of Guadalupe* (1998), with James Lockhart and Stafford Poole, and is completing a book manuscript on indigenous culture and gender in colonial Mexico.

Kevin Terraciano is Associate Professor of Latin American History at the University of California, Los Angeles. He studies the Nahuatl, Mixtec, and Zapotec languages of central and southern Mexico and is the author of many published writings on colonial Mexico, including *The Mixtecs of Colonial Oaxaca* (2001).

MESOAMERICAN VOICES

Native-Language Writings from Colonial Mexico, Oaxaca, Yucatan, and Guatemala

Edited by

MATTHEW RESTALL
Pennsylvania State University

LISA SOUSA
Occidental College

KEVIN TERRACIANO
University of California, Los Angeles

CAMBRIDGE
UNIVERSITY PRESS

CAMBRIDGE UNIVERSITY PRESS
Cambridge, New York, Melbourne, Madrid, Cape Town, Singapore, São Paulo

Cambridge University Press
40 West 20th Street, New York, NY 10011-4211, USA

www.cambridge.org
Information on this title: www.cambridge.org/9780521812795

First published 2005

Printed in the United States of America

A catalog record for this publication is available from the British Library.

Library of Congress Cataloging in Publication Data

Mesoamerican voices : Native-Language Writings from Colonial Mexico, Oaxaca, Yucatan,
and Guatemala / edited by Matthew Restall, Lisa Sousa, Kevin Terraciano.
p. cm.
Includes bibliographical references and index.
ISBN-13: 978-0-521-81279-5 (hardback)
ISBN-10: 0-521-81279-8 (hardback)
ISBN-13: 978-0-521-01221-8 (pbk.)
ISBN-10: 0-521-01221-X (pbk.)
1. Indian literature – Mexico – History and criticism. 2. Indian literature – Guatemala –
History and criticism. 3. Nahuatl literature. 4. Maya literature.
I. Restall, Matthew, 1964– II. Sousa, Lisa, 1962– III. Terraciano, Kevin, 1962– IV. Title.
⌐ PM3055.M47 2005
897'.0972 – dc22   2005012969

ISBN-13 978-0-521-81279-5 hardback
ISBN-10 0-521-81279-8 hardback

ISBN-13 978-0-521-01221-8 paperback
ISBN-10 0-521-01221-X paperback

CONTENTS

DOCUMENTS AND IMAGES

Chapter 7. Crime and Punishment

Chapter 8. Religious Life

Chapter 9. Rhetoric and Moral Philosophy

PREFACE AND ACKNOWLEDGMENTS

This volume evolved over more than a dozen years from the collections of documents that we assembled for undergraduate students in courses on colonial Mexican and Latin American history. Such collections began with documents translated from Nahuatl by James Lockhart, which we three were required to read as graduate students at UCLA. In fact, all three of us took his upper-division class on the Indians of colonial Mexico in the spring of 1988. The collections grew as we added materials that we had found and translated for use in our doctoral dissertations and other projects, and as we began to teach our own courses. We continued to swap materials, exchange ideas, and discuss approaches to using such documents in the classroom. Eventually, we three editors and authors combined our efforts and contributed equally to this volume.

We are thus very grateful to James Lockhart for the various roles he has played in the evolution of this project. First, he introduced us to the labor and pleasure of translating and analyzing native-language texts for the purposes of writing history. Second, he generously allowed us to use his course reader for our classes and now is allowing us to use his original transcriptions and translations of several Nahuatl-language documents, which we have left unaltered or have modified only slightly because we do not pretend to be able to produce better translations. Finally, we thank Jim for his careful reading of the manuscript, his comments on every chapter, and his advice on how to proceed at many stages of the process. This volume clearly would not exist without him.

Also, we would like to acknowledge several other scholars who preceded us in working with these types of native-language texts, some of which were published in transcription and translation, making it possible for us to access and translate them here – especially Arthur J. O. Anderson, Frances Berdan, Pedro Carrasco, S. L. Cline, Charles Dibble, Wigberto Jiménez Moreno, Frances Karttunen, Miguel León-Portilla, Jesús Monjarás-Ruiz, Stafford Poole, Luis Reyes García, Ralph Roys, Susan Schroeder, and Gunter Zimmermann.

We also would like to thank the directors and staff of the various archives where the original Mesoamerican sources were located, most notably the Archivo General de la Nación in Mexico City and the state and local archives of Oaxaca and Yucatan. We also thank the undergraduate and graduate students who have read and discussed many of the sixty sources presented in this volume. Finally, we are grateful to Frank Smith and his colleagues at Cambridge University Press for their many contributions to the finished product.

Let us comment briefly on our method. We have tried to provide idiomatic modern English translations that correspond closely to the meaning of the texts while retaining some of the conventions and style of the original language. As a result, a range of colonial Mesoamerican literary styles has been partially preserved, some dry and legalistic, others vividly conversational, stilted and awkward, or poetic and steeped in metaphor. We seek to retain some of the repetitive, rhetorical aspects of the writings and to convey a sense of their eloquence. For example, in the Nahuatl formal texts, especially those from the Florentine Codex, we provide the intended meaning of many (but not all) metaphorical expressions rather than translating the metaphors literally.

We italicize and define the first usage of significant native- and Spanish-language concepts, and then define them in parentheses and in the glossary. For example, rather than translating the Nahuatl word *altepetl* as "city" or "town," we prefer to retain the original word in the translation and thereby challenge the reader to learn an important indigenous concept. The glossary at the back of this volume contains brief definitions for most of the Spanish, Nahuatl, Maya, and Mixtec terms retained in the documents. Nearly all the native-language texts in this collection contain Spanish loanwords, some more than others. We have translated the loanwords into English, retaining them (and defining them in parentheses) when they seem to represent a significant introduction to the material culture or conceptual vocabulary of the period. In general, loanwords refer to introduced items or concepts that have no ready indigenous equivalent; the number of loanwords in a text reflects the writer's familiarity with Spanish. Texts that include an inordinate number of loanwords are identified in the document's introduction.

The punctuation and organization of the texts into sentences and paragraphs conform to conventional standards and often do not exist in the original documents. We reserve brackets for implicit or understood, but unstated or unreadable, material in the original texts; information in parentheses should be explanatory. In general, we have tried to avoid both brackets and parentheses as much as possible, to make the texts more readable and less confusing. Also, we try to resolve the ambiguities in a translation by simply choosing one possible meaning rather than presenting various possibilities.

Finally, in the introductions to each chapter and to each document, we have attempted to address some of the issues or questions that the particular text raises, rather than creating endnotes or explanatory apparatus in the actual translation. The documents are arranged according to prominent topics, but almost all the texts illustrate multiple themes and patterns. We have made references to some of these overlaps in the chapter introductions, while leaving readers to make use of the index to explore further cross-references.

MR, *State College, Pennsylvania*
LS & KT, *Los Angeles, California*

Colonial Mesoamerica

COLONIAL MESOAMERICA

YUCATAN

Gulf of Mexico

Motul
Mérida
Ebtun
Mani
Caikini
Tekax
Campeche

Acalan-Tixchel

Coban

Totonicapan
Santiago (Antigua)

GUATEMALA

Rostoll '04

PART ONE

1

MESOAMERICANS AND SPANIARDS IN THE SIXTEENTH CENTURY

"Here I shall write a few histories of our first fathers and ancestors, those who engendered the men of ancient times, before these mountains and valleys were inhabited, when there were only hares and birds."

Thus begins one of the great native histories of Mesoamerica, the Annals of the Cakchiquels (excerpted further in Chapter 3). The quote evokes three important introductory topics. The first and second, discussed in this chapter, are that of the geography and settlement of Mesoamerica. The third theme, which stems from the simple fact that Mesoamericans wrote, is the subject of Chapter 2.

Mesoamerican Diversity

The term "Mesoamerica" describes a geographical and culture area stretching from present-day central and southern Mexico down through much of Central America, tapering out in Honduras and Nicaragua. The geography of Mesoamerica features a remarkable diversity of environments, from the volcanoes of highland central Mexico and Guatemala to the tropical Pacific and Atlantic coasts, from the rain forests of Chiapas to the subtropical flatlands of Yucatan. Such environmental diversity made Mesoamerica not only one of the richest and most varied regions of the planet in terms of its plant and animal life but also determined a complex and varied pattern of human settlement.

Many tens of thousands of years ago, there were indeed "only" animals in Mesoamerica, as throughout the Americas; but by the time Spaniards arrived in the sixteenth century, the region had developed an array of cultures and language groups that can be as bewildering to us as it was to those early European invaders. Despite differences of language, culture, and sociopolitical organization, Mesoamerican societies had so many cultural traits and practices in common that modern scholars and students may consider them as part of a single civilization. This was especially true of those who lived in the fully sedentary societies of the Mesoamerican core. In general, most peoples of the area lived in temperate climates, where water and rich soils made the practice of permanent agriculture possible. Most of the population cultivated the soil on a regular basis, utilizing terraces, irrigation, and land reclamation techniques. Mesoamericans lived in ethnic states ruled by hereditary nobilities. They had well-organized markets, marked social distinctions, writing or recordkeeping systems and calendars, systems of taxation, military organizations, state religions, and priesthoods. The sedentary peoples of Mesoamerica also practiced monumental architecture and metalworking and produced fine textiles, ceramics, and sculptures, among many other crafts.

Although Europeans tended to lump native peoples together as "Indians" (as the Americas were called "the Indies" by Spaniards in this period), and in this volume we make some general comments about "Mesoamericans," in fact the peoples of Mesoamerica were neither unified politically nor shared a common identity. Mesoamericans' geographical awareness tended to be limited to the particular regions in which they lived, with the exception of a few long-distance traders, and individuals primarily identified themselves with their local ethnic state. Mesoamericans never adopted the term "*indio*" ("Indian") imposed by the Spanish. They did, however, share the experience of Spanish conquest and its consequences and developed comparable strategies of living under colonial rule.

The native men and women featured in this volume lived in the core regions of Mesoamerica; we shall be reading words written by Nahuas from central Mexico, Mixtecs from Oaxaca, and Mayas from Yucatan, as well as a few contributions from Zapotecs of Oaxaca and Mayas from highland Guatemala. The Nahuas were the dominant ethnic group in central Mexico. They spoke the Nahuatl language, as they continue to do so today. They lived in thousands of ethnic states called *altepeme* (*altepetl*, singular). Each altepetl consisted of several constituent parts called *calpolli* or *tlaxilacalli*, which were important in organizing and delivering on a rotational basis tribute payments of goods and labor to the dynastic ruler (called a *tlatoani*) and in managing lands within its borders. Perhaps the most famous altepetl was the home of the Aztecs, called Mexico-Tenochtitlan, located on an island in Lake Tetzcoco in the Valley of Mexico. Although they are best known as the Aztecs, in reference to their legendary origins from a place called Aztlan ("place of the white heron"), the people who lived on the island altepetl of Mexico-Tenochtitlan (a double name, sometimes referred to as "Mexico" and other times as "Tenochtitlan") when the Spaniards arrived called themselves Mexica ("people from Mexico") or Tenochca ("people from Tenochtitlan"). But the Mexica were just one group of Nahuatl-speaking peoples. Other prominent altepetls in or near the Valley of Mexico included Xochimilco, Tlatelolco, Tetzcoco, Chalco, Amecameca, Tlaxcala, Huexotzinco, and Cholula.

In the Mixteca region of western Oaxaca, the local state was called a *ñuu*. Like the Nahua altepetl, the Mixtec ñuu was further subdivided into different parts called *siqui* (in some regions called *siña* or *dzini*). Mixtec refers to both the people and the language that they spoke (there are approximately three hundred thousand Mixtec speakers today). Actually, "Mixtec" is a term derived from the Nahuatl word for the people of the region *mixteca*, meaning "people of the cloud place." But in their own language, people referred to themselves as *tay ñudzahui* "people of the rain place" or "people from the place of *Dzahui*," the rain deity. Both males and females could rule and represent a ñuu; a male ruler was called an *yya toniñe* and a female was called an *yya dzehe toniñe*. When a male and female ruler married, they temporarily united their two ñuu in an alliance called a *yuhuitayu*.

In Yucatan, the Maya called their ethnic state a *cah*. Like each Nahua altepetl or Mixtec ñuu, each cah had a specific name, ruling nobility, tribute system, market, origin legend, deity, and separate identity. However, unlike the altepetl or ñuu, the cah was not further subdivided into constituent parts. The Yucatec Maya (which refers to both the people and their language) lived in many hundreds of *cahob* (plural of cah) when Spaniards first arrived; there were about two hundred in colonial Yucatan. The cah was ruled by a hereditary ruler called a *batab*. Other prominent language groups in Mesoamerica included the Otomis of central Mexico, the Zapotecs of Oaxaca, the Purépechas of Michoacan, the Tzeltal and Tzotzil Mayas of Chiapas, and the Quiché and Cakchiquel Mayas of Guatemala.

Over the centuries a number of ethnic states in central and southern Mexico and Guatemala achieved impressive size and economic and political influence over large regions. But none came close to imposing political unity on Mesoamerica, including the last of them, the Aztec empire. What we refer to as the Aztec empire was more accurately a loose confederation of a patchwork of territories across central and southern Mexico that were conquered between 1428 and 1521 by the Triple Alliance of the three altepetls of Mexico-Tenochtitlan, Tetzcoco, and Tlacopan. Those subject to the Triple Alliance paid tribute and provided troops and supplies for further conquests. In this way the Triple Alliance, headed by the Mexica, built a power base that extended into southern Mexico and unified the regional economy to a large extent. However, in most cases, peoples of the ethnic states conquered by the Triple Alliance continued to rule themselves and retained their own local identity. Furthermore, some large altepetls, like Tlaxcala, were never conquered by the Triple Alliance and forced to join their empire.

There are therefore two themes that were central to the colonial period in Mesoamerica and are central to the documents presented here: (1) Mesoamerican diversity and the persistence of local identity; and (2) the historical experiences and ways of doing things that were common to Nahuas, Mixtecs, and Mayas alike. For centuries, Spaniards and other Europeans, including professional historians, argued that the Conquest and colonial rule of what became New Spain was possible because Mesoamericans were either barbarians or, at the very least, less civilized than Europeans. It is now clear, however, that it was the very depth and diversity of Mesoamerican civilization that made the colonial period possible, and that New Spain was as much indigenous as it was Spanish – if not more so. This volume is testimony to that fact.

The Spanish Invasion

For thousands of years, human societies on either side of the Atlantic remained isolated from each other and unaware of each other's existence. In the fifteenth century, southern Europeans, led by the Portuguese, explored and expanded into the Atlantic, partly with a view to finding a sea route to Asia. The Americas were discovered as an accidental by-product of this process, but whereas the Portuguese continued to focus primarily on Asia and Africa, a newly formed Spanish state made the Americas a target of its imperial ambitions.

In the wake of the transatlantic voyages of Columbus and others in the 1490s, Spaniards established a network of colonies in the Caribbean. After the first Spanish settlement in Santo Domingo, on the island of Española, Cuba became the base for a series of exploratory expeditions in the 1510s, culminating in the 1519 expedition led by Hernando Cortés. Motivated more by the desire for profit than a commitment to spread Christianity, Spaniards under Cortés initiated a bloody war against the Mexica and their allies as they made their way from the Gulf Coast to Mexico-Tenochtitlan. The Spaniards had distinct advantages that allowed them quickly to subdue the indigenous resistance that they encountered. Steel, horses, and gunpowder gave the Spaniards tremendous military advantages. Indigenous weapons, which consisted mainly of obsidian-blade clubs, bows and arrows, and spear throwers, could not seriously harm someone equipped with a sword, helmet, and body armor; horsemen with lances were unstoppable because they could fight for hours without tiring. Native fatalities often numbered in the thousands, whereas the Spaniards escaped with minor injuries. Firearms were used mostly for effect but were especially important in the siege of Tenochtitlan, when cannons were rigged to boats and guns were fired into crowds. Mesoamericans also had different military tactics than the European invaders; rather than kill their enemies on the battlefield as the Spaniards did, indigenous warriors customarily took captives. In addition, the Spaniards, who were few in number, also benefited from the aid of thousands of native allies that they drew from enemies of the Mexica (such as the Tlaxcalans) and from the places that they conquered as they marched toward Tenochtitlan. Finally, the Spaniards brought new diseases, including smallpox, to the Americas, which ravaged the native population. By the time the Spaniards reached Mexico-Tenochtitlan, epidemics had already weakened the Mexica. In 1521, after two years of stiff resistance and very near defeat after having been driven out of Mexico-Tenochtitlan, the Spaniards and their native allies finally defeated the Mexica. The Spaniards founded their own capital city of Mexico, but it was Mexicas and other Nahuas who rebuilt the city and were the majority of its residents; within Mexico City, Tenochtitlan survived, although in a very different form.

Over the two decades following 1521, the Spanish presence in Mesoamerica increased slowly but surely, as Cortés and others who had fought with him against the Mexica, such as Pedro de Alvarado and Francisco de Montejo, sought to consolidate and spread colonial control throughout the region. In relay fashion, each conquered place became a source of spoils, funds, and supplies, and a base for future expeditions. Because Mesoamericans did not share a common political identity – even groups within Mesoamerica, such as the Yucatec Mayas, lacked such an identity – there was little precedent for adopting a common front against the foreign enemy. Thus, for most of Mesoamerica, the fall of Tenochtitlan in 1521 was the beginning, not the end, of a protracted Conquest period. The central Mexican valley and especially Tenochtitlan/Mexico City remained the most important Spanish settlement in Mesoamerica, but it was gradually joined by regions to the north and south – most notably, and most relevant to this volume, the southern areas of Oaxaca, highland Guatemala, and Yucatan.

One of the crucial factors that permitted Spaniards to establish permanent footholds in Mesoamerica was disease. Mesoamericans had little or no immunity to epidemic diseases that had not been present in the Americas before 1492. Such epidemics were immediately devastating, reducing native populations dramatically and hindering their ability to organize resistance. We shall never know exactly how many people lived in Mesoamerica before Europeans arrived there, but it is estimated that a century after smallpox and other diseases were introduced into the region the native population had been reduced by as much as 90 percent, from as many as twenty-five million to about five million.

As tragic as this demographic disaster was, however, native peoples still vastly outnumbered Europeans in New Spain. As the documents in this volume demonstrate, Mesoamerican communities and cultures were far from destroyed by the events of the sixteenth century. On the contrary, for most of the colonial period, most Mesoamericans lived in their own communities and continued to do many things as they had done before the arrival of the Europeans – even though they were forced to adapt to colonial circumstances, to convert to Christianity, and to face the growing demands and influence of the Spanish-speaking population.

Colonialism in Mesoamerica

Conquest and settlement went hand in hand in Mesoamerica. The conquerors were not merely fighting men, but immigrants and businessmen. Those who participated in the conquest of a given region were rewarded with *encomiendas*, grants of tribute and labor (but not land) from one or more indigenous communities to a particular Spaniard.

Representatives of Spain's two major institutions – the Crown and the Church – arrived quickly on the scene of newly conquered regions to establish their presence. Mexico City served as the capital of the Viceroyalty of New Spain, which would eventually encompass the territory of the present-day U.S. southwest, California, Mexico, and all of Central America. Central Mexico, and especially Tenochtitlan / Mexico City, attracted the greatest number of Spaniards because of densely settled and wealthy native populations. For the most part, native populations were the basis of Spanish settlements. Spaniards gravitated to central Mexico, especially after the discovery of incredibly rich silver mines to the north of Mexico City.

The Spaniards brought to the Americas an incredible tradition of legalism based on Roman law, which depended heavily on a collection of competing agencies united under the rule of the Crown in Madrid. At the head of the viceregal government was a viceroy, who served as the Crown's representative in New Spain. His power was held in check by a high court (*audiencia*), which acted on local matters but was responsible to the Council of Indies (in Seville) and the King of Spain. Cities had municipal councils called *cabildos*, staffed with elected officials from the Spanish nobility. Spanish officials with wide-ranging administrative and judicial powers (*alcaldes mayores* and *corregidores*) bought offices, usually for a five-year period, to collect taxes and act as judges (with access to legal advisors) within jurisdictions in the largely indigenous countryside.

Despite the visible presence of the Crown, especially in Mexico City, the Spanish system of ruling the indigenous population was indirect. Mesoamericans so vastly outnumbered the Spaniards that they had little choice but to rely on the well-structured organization and traditions of the local ethnic state and its ruling nobility. Native communities established their own town councils or cabildos, based loosely on the Spanish model, headed by a native governor who was often descended from a local dynasty that had ruled before the Conquest. The community elected local noblemen (never women) as *alcaldes* (judges) and *regidores* (councilmen), according to the Spanish model; these political titles can easily be found in the documents in Part Two. But local indigenous traditions and practices influenced the election process, the number of such offices, their relationship to sociopolitical units based on pre-Conquest settlements, and the responsibilities and privileges of office. The cabildo was responsible for organizing and paying tribute to the alcalde mayor and reporting major crimes or disputes to him. The cabildo also functioned as a judicial body in its own right, solving local disputes and dispensing justice. Mesoamerican communities, represented by the cabildo, had access to the colonial legal system, which they used, for example, to pursue cases against local Spaniards for some perceived abuses or against neighboring communities over land disputes. When they received an unfavorable judgment, they could appeal cases to the audiencia. The colonial legal system acknowledged native cabildos as legal and judicial bodies, recognized documents written by notaries in Mesoamerican languages, and under some circumstances provided legal counsel.

Friars and secular priests lived in urban and rural parishes, following in the footsteps of the conquistadors. They referred to the work of evangelizing the indigenous peoples as the "spiritual conquest." Parishes were organized based on the local native communities. Thus, a Nahua altepetl, Mixtec ñuu, or Maya cah would become the basis of a parish, just as it was the basis of an encomienda. A percentage of the community's labor and tribute was directed toward building the church and maintaining the priest – an issue that often divided friars and encomenderos over who would get what, especially as the population began to decline. Local native authorities were expected to oversee church construction and attendance, but they could not become priests or nuns. All the lesser church and parish posts were filled by local native men – usually from the same families who controlled the cabildo. Churches were located right in the middle of native communities, often built from the same stones and on the same site as the preconquest temple. And because the Mesoamericans had a great tradition of building temples and pyramids, they also had the resources and skills to build magnificent churches in the colonial period.

The vast majority of Spanish officials, including priests, did not live in native communities, nor were there Spanish feudal lords. Rather, Spanish administrators had regional jurisdictions and tended to congregate and live in the few Spanish cities founded in New Spain. The colonial economy was exploitative; native governors collected tribute and other taxes from their own people, keeping some of it for community expenses and for the maintenance of the local nobility but passing much of it on to Spanish officials and priests.

The encomienda system, and the separation of Spaniards and Mesoamericans in their own communities, began to dissolve within a generation after the Conquest – quickest in and around Mexico City, slower in the rural hinterland of Oaxaca, Yucatan, and Guatemala. As the colonists grew in number, more Spaniards demanded access to native labor, leading to other arrangements including a system of temporary labor grants of native workers called the *repartimiento*. As native men and women migrated into Spanish cities and towns to live and work, Spaniards also began to make individual wage labor arrangements. Spanish urban households soon became centers of cultural contact not only between Spaniards and Mesoamericans but also between them and the thousands of Africans brought into the colonies as slaves. Cultural interaction and change occurred initially in the cities and eventually in smaller towns and villages as *mestizos* (persons of mixed European and indigenous descent), mulattoes (persons of mixed African and European descent), Africans (both enslaved and free), and small numbers of Spaniards became part of the rural, mainly indigenous population. Nevertheless, these changes did not destroy the integrity of the colonial Mesoamerican community. Each altepetl, ñuu, and cah maintained a distinct native and local identity; as the documents here reveal, in the vast majority of cases, the Mesoamerican cabildo neither included nor represented people of Spanish or African descent – or even native peoples from outside that particular community.

The sixty documents presented in this volume bear witness to the numerous ways in which Mesoamericans interacted with nonnatives, accommodated the demands and innovations of conquest and colonialism, and persisted in doing things according to custom while also absorbing Spanish influences. This can be seen in material culture, for example, in the types of household possessions, tools, and properties that Mesoamericans sold, inherited, and sometimes fought over in the colonial courts (see Chapters 5 and 6). It can be seen in the way that Mesoamericans participated in a global money economy while also maintaining aspects of local trade (see Chapters 4–6). It also can be seen in naming patterns, as Mesoamericans adopted Christian names and, in some regions (such as central Mexico), Spanish surnames, too, making Nahuas look at first glance like Spaniards (see Chapter 6). And it can be seen in the ways that Mesoamericans expressed their views on the Spanish invaders of the sixteenth century (Chapter 3), on religious matters (Chapter 8), and on the moral conduct and responsibilities of children, politicians, and priests (Chapters 4 and 7–9).

It is also important to recognize that Mesoamericans and Spaniards had a great deal in common. Many of the characteristic Mesoamerican cultural traits and modes of organization discussed earlier had close parallels in Europe. Despite many significant differences, Mesoamericans and Europeans saw a number of similarities that they would immediately recognize. This recognition was crucial for many types of interactions between both sides and for the continuity of many Mesoamerican lifeways in altered but still recognizable forms.

No civilization or culture is static; for Mesoamerican cultures, processes of change were profoundly influenced by the Spanish invasion. We may lament the burning of native codices and the leveling of ancient pyramids, and we should be aware of the exploitative nature of a colonial system that chiefly benefited the colonizers – an awareness aided by some of the petitions presented in this volume. But colonial Mesoamerica cannot be properly understood if viewed through an entirely negative lens, as if all the people in this part of the world succumbed to European hegemony. In this long period of more than three centuries, Mesoamericans lived and toiled under varied and complex circumstances and conditions. This volume presents glimpses of Mesoamerican experiences under colonial rule, relying primarily on their own written words, carefully translated into English. These writings represent Mesoamerican voices that deserve to be heard.

2

LITERACY IN COLONIAL MESOAMERICA

By the 1530s, Franciscan, Dominican, and Augustinian friars were beginning to teach the art of alphabetic writing to members of the indigenous elite. Between the 1540s and the end of the colonial period in the early nineteenth century, Mesoamericans produced great quantities of written records in their own languages using the Roman alphabet.

The first group to adopt the alphabet were the Nahuas of central Mexico, but they were soon followed by the Mixtecs, Yucatec Mayas, and other Mesoamericans. Nahuatl has survived in greater quantities than sources in other languages, but significant numbers of documents also have been found in Mixtec, Zapotec, Chocho, and the Mayan languages of Yucatec, Chontal, Cakchiquel, and Quiché. Otomí, Purépecha and no doubt other Mesoamerican languages also were written in colonial times. This chapter primarily discusses the nature and content of only those sources that to date have been studied in detail – those in Nahuatl, Mixtec, and Maya.

Pre-Conquest Precedents

The indigenous peoples of Mesoamerica had their own systems of written communication, ranging from the hieroglyphs of the Maya and Zapotec to the pictographs and painted codices of the Mixtec and Nahua. The earliest examples of such writing are painted or carved on stone and pottery; those from the immediate pre-Conquest period are also painted on deer hide or native paper. The texts recorded everything from histories and origin legends to divinatory and cosmological information and approached an extended narrative form of expression. Literacy was presumably a privilege of the priestly and noble classes.

Indigenous writing combined pictorial representation (direct depiction by images) with a numerical and calendrical system, logograms or images (which conveyed a word or idea), and phonetic representation of individual syllables or roots of words. The possibilities of phonetic expression were expanded by the use of homonyms or "tone puns." All three fundamental techniques often operated simultaneously in the codices of the postclassic period (c. 1000–1500 A.D.). No Mesoamerican group had developed a full syllabary by the time of the conquest; the Mayan systems at their classic-period height came the closest to producing sentences as fully as alphabetic writing.

The style and method of interpreting pre-Conquest–style codices could be extremely subtle and complex. They were likely not "read" in the conventional sense of reading to oneself silently but were rendered in a more public setting, like scores for performance; the meaning of the texts was elaborated orally and was subject to extrapolation with each recounting. Thus, there was probably never one "proper" reading, performance, or interpretation. It is unclear how interpretive the writing system was and to what extent memory and context guided the speaker/reader. Its rendition was flexible but not entirely subjective and definitely not random. Many of the texts were designed to be displayed visibly in a public setting before an informed audience.

The well-developed writing tradition in Mesoamerica did not preclude the primarily oral transmission of potential texts such as speeches, chronicles, and perhaps even testaments before the introduction of the alphabet. Pre-Conquest writing always complemented the oral tradition. Likewise, this oral tradition surfaces in the style and content of much post-Conquest indigenous documentation. Whereas Mesoamerican writing may have eased the transition to the many genres of Spanish legal documentation, it proved difficult to reconcile this primarily pictorial writing with the exacting requirements of the Spanish legal system. As Spaniards began to demand that writing employ the alphabet, native writers came to terms with the genres of writing that they would need to defend their interests in the colonial legal system.

Clearly, the existence of a time-honored and sophisticated writing system facilitated the adoption of the alphabet, which was surely seen as a great innovation because it could capture speeches and narratives of the oral tradition. One could now record speech verbatim. The precedent of writing in Mesoamerica and the innovation that the alphabet offered helps explain the readiness with which many groups took to generating documentation in their own languages using the Roman alphabet after the Spanish Conquest. The connection between the two systems was so clear that terminology for the instruments and act of reading and writing is drawn from the earlier tradition; for example, the indigenous word for "paper" continued to be used throughout the colonial period: *amatl* (Nahuatl); *tutu* (Mixtec); *quichi* (Zapotec); *hun* (Yucatec Maya); and *vuh* (Cakchiquel Maya).

Post-Conquest Literacy

In the 1520s, friars in central Mexico began to experiment with pictorial communication but concentrated on rendering spoken Nahuatl in alphabetic form. Beginning in the 1540s, documents of many types and styles were

produced in central Mexico as alphabetic writing in Nahuatl spread rapidly
to become the dominant form of expression in the latter half of the century. In
Oaxaca, the first extant Mixtec documents did not appear until the late 1560s.
The early use of Nahuatl as a *lingua franca* in the Mixteca (the Mixtec region
of Oaxaca), the friars' difficulty with the tonality and variants of Mixtecan
languages, and the relatively small number of Dominicans in the area – all
contributed to the delay in Mixtec alphabetic writing. In fact, the pictorial
tradition remained strong in this region. With significant regional variation
throughout highland central and southern Mexico, alphabetic text at first
shared space with and eventually displaced pictorial text; essentially, pictorial text represented the visual component of precontact writing and alphabetic text reflected the oral component. The pictorial tradition in Yucatan, by
contrast, was far weaker, and the syllabic system more developed, so that
alphabetic writing in Maya took root in the 1550s, just a decade after the
conquest of the region.

In central Mexico, the Mixteca, and Yucatan, literacy passed from friars to
indigenous elites in municipal communities. In all three areas the indigenous
escribano (scribe or notary) was the primary practitioner of literacy. Most
documents in native languages can be defined as notarial, in that they were
written by the community notary, authored by local officials, and more or less
conformed to Spanish documentary genres. Unlike Spanish notarial material,
most indigenous documents were products of the native community or town
(the Nahua *altepetl*; the Mixtec *ñuu*; and the Maya *cah*). Like their Spanish
counterparts, native notaries were members of the local indigenous ruling
elite and enjoyed a social standing close to that of the highest political officers
in their communities. The highest municipal office for indigenous people
in colonial times was the male governor, who in many cases was the local
hereditary ruler – the Nahua *tlatoani* in central Mexico, the Mixtec *yya toniñe*
in Oaxaca, or the Maya *batab* in Yucatan.

The nature of corporate documentation, directed by male escribanos of the
all-male Spanish-style municipal council called the *cabildo*, tended to exclude
indigenous women from the act of writing. Although women are represented
in almost every documentary genre in all three areas, they were not trained
to write. There is no evidence that any Nahua or Maya women were literate before the twentieth century. Nor are there many extant examples of
nonnotaries writing notarial documents in Nahuatl or Maya. There are a few
documents written in Mixtec suggesting that some noblewomen and men of
lesser social status were literate, but they are exceptions to the rule.

Genres of Writing

Indigenous-language material might be organized into two categories: official notarial documentation, defined as legal cabildo-generated documents
fulfilling the requirements of the Spanish ecclesiastical or civil court system;

and unofficial, nonnotarial manuscripts. With respect to central Mexico, much of the unofficial material has been classified by scholars in the past as "Classical Nahuatl" and includes songs, speeches, and annals. There is also a fair amount of personal correspondence and records and a few census reports.

First we will consider the nonnotarial genres of writing. Church-sponsored materials created mainly under the auspices of the Franciscans, Dominicans, and Augustinians were often the first indigenous-language alphabetic texts to be produced and usually the only writing to be printed. Manuscripts and imprints cover a wide variety of genres: dictionaries and grammars; confessional manuals and *doctrinas* (catechisms); language instructional materials, speeches, songs, and plays; and ethnographic works such as the Florentine Codex, the largest and most impressive native-language work of the early period, consisting of twelve books written in Nahuatl and Spanish (see Chapters 3 and 9 for excerpts from these books). The vast majority of native-language manuscripts and imprints are in Nahuatl. The impression that friars often took sole responsibility for these works should not conceal the fact that indigenous aides and bilingual (and sometimes trilingual) speakers were at least contributing authors, usually produced the final version of texts, and often participated in every level of production and printing. It also appears that many of these ecclesiastical texts were intended for the use of literate indigenous laity as well as clerics. There are about one hundred extant examples of Nahuatl church-sponsored publications, but there are less than a dozen for each of the other major Mesoamerican languages.

Another nonnotarial Nahua genre of writing that survived the Conquest and was not sponsored by the church is the annals, which organizes entries into year units based on the Mesoamerican calendar (and in the post-Conquest period the Christian calendar, too). The content of Chimalpahin's *Diario*, excerpted in Chapter 6, exemplifies the genre's focus on noteworthy public events and prominent people of the time, including natural events such as earthquakes, solar eclipses, and comets. Authors tend to report everything from their own local point of view, centered on one altepetl or another. Often, the coverage is so local that authors include references to personal matters in their entries.

Mixtec and Nahuatl personal letters constitute another genre of writing that was not done under the auspices of the local indigenous cabildo. For Yucatan, unofficial writing includes the Books of Chilam Balam (compilations of fables, myth/history, calendrical and medicinal information; see Chapters 8 and 9) and the genre known as the *título primordial* (see Chapter 3). The primary function of the "primordial title" was to lay claim to lands on behalf of the community or one of its factions. Most titles contain versions of past events that legitimate present concerns and claims. Nahuatl and Mixtec primordial titles, like the Yucatec Maya titles, performed both official and unofficial roles and seemed to combine features of many genres at once. Naturally, the more these genres are studied in detail, the more simple categories become unhelpful. For example, much indigenous writing fulfilled functions in both the Spanish legal world and the local sphere of the native community – testaments are a prime example of this convergence. In highland Guatemala, primordial titles were written in both Spanish and Maya languages and vary greatly in length and content; the best known such text, which is parallel in some ways to the Chilam Balam literature of Yucatan, is the Popol Vuh of the Quiché Mayas.

The second type of writing, official notarial records, comprises the vast majority of extant documentation. At least half of all surviving native-language documents are last wills and testaments. The success of the testament can be explained by the fact that it represented a continuation of an indigenous oral tradition, and fulfilled both religious and secular require-ments of the Church and native communities. The existence of a model Nahuatl will in the 1569 edition of fray Alonso de Molina's *Confessionario Mayor*, and evidence of the inspection of Maya wills by eighteenth-century Yucatec bishops, helps demonstrate that the basic format of the native will was imposed by the Spaniards. Native-language wills resemble Spanish testa-ments in their formula and format. However, indigenous notaries varied this format according to community tradition and practice, ultimately reshaping it to suit their own needs (see Chapters 5 and 6). For indigenous communities, testaments allowed one to die in a state of grace, to provide for one's burial and purgatory mass, and to settle one's estate. Significantly, the testament also gave the community a written, legal record of property distribution and genealogical relationships. Thus, the role of indigenous testaments was far more expansive than that of the Spanish will. Many members of the native community served as witnesses to the testamentary ritual, validated by the presence and signatures of the cabildo officers.

After testaments, the best-represented genre is that of land transactions. Wills were in a sense also land documents, but legal transactions involving exchanges of land were more specific. The process of sale or donation of land under Spanish law entailed a number of stages, some of which were often not observed by either Spaniards or natives; furthermore, indigenous use of the relevant Spanish legal terms tended to be inconsistent.

Remaining genres are unevenly represented. For example, there are more surviving criminal records in Mixtec than in Nahuatl and Maya. Overall, how-ever, the greatest variety of documentation exists for the Nahuas of central Mexico. For example, the daily proceedings of the sixteenth-century *cabildo* of Tlaxcala are preserved in Nahuatl (see Chapters 4, 5, and 6), something not found in other Mesoamerican languages.

Distribution and Timing of Writing

Nahuatl-language writing evolved evenly throughout central Mexico, spreading rapidly from Spanish centers to most Nahua communities. By 1570, at the latest, every altepetl had its own notary. Texts written in Nahuatl first appear as early as the 1540s, reaching a peak in terms of variety and quality, and perhaps quantity, in the period 1580–1610. After 1770, writing in Spanish eclipsed Nahuatl-language script, partly as a result of official decrees that native languages cease to be used for notarial purposes, but mainly because many communities were now able to do so. Consequently, the number of surviving Nahuatl documents declines sharply and Nahuatl-language writing virtually disappears by the turn of the nineteenth century. We must remember that surviving documents represent a mere fraction of the hundreds of thousands of indigenous-language sources produced in New Spain. The total number of extant Nahuatl sources is difficult to estimate and continues to grow; in addition, the varied nature and length of texts makes it hard to define what is a single document and what is a corpus. Suffice it to say that in collections in Mexico, Guatemala, the United States, and Europe there are probably tens of thousands of manuscripts. The documents are complemented by material only now surfacing from other parts of Mesoamerica, where Nahuatl was written by both Nahua satellite communities and non-Nahua indigenous groups in lieu of their own spoken languages (such as Mazatec, Trique, Ixcatec, Cuicatec, Chatino, and Mixe), as far south as Guatemala and north to Saltillo.

Maya documents have likewise survived from the entire colonial Yucatec area, but their temporal distribution contrasts strongly with that of central Mexico. The sixteenth century is not well represented in Yucatan – a question, perhaps, of survival, as Maya writing skills appear fully developed within a generation of the founding of a provincial capital (Merida, 1542). Manuscript numbers increase steadily after 1640, climaxing in the very period of written Nahuatl's decline (1770–1820). The last Maya notarial documents date from the 1850s, a tribute to the perseverance of Maya-language writing in the relative absence of Spanish-language speakers. Variations in quality tend to be regional rather than temporal (a reflection of a general Yucatec pattern). Only very recently has an effort been made to uncover all Maya-language sources; so far, the total is some fifteen hundred, but this many again may surface in the coming decades. Collections exist in the United States and in archives in Seville, Mexico City, and the Yucatan peninsula.

Other Maya languages are less well represented, in part because they were spoken over a smaller area before and after the Conquest. The Chontal Maya primordial title excerpted in Chapter 3 is a rare example of that language written in the colonial period; Chontal Maya ceased to be written down sometime before the nineteenth century and today is a dead language. Sources in Cakchiquel and Quiché from the highlands of Guatemala are certainly more numerous than in Chontal, but the vast majority of those that probably exist remain undiscovered and unstudied; the impression given so far is that Spanish gradually replaces both Guatemalan tongues in the eighteenth century as the language of written record.

Mixtec-language documents were produced in the major centers of Dominican activity by the early 1570s, coinciding with the publication of a lengthy doctrina (printed in two variants of the language) in 1567 and 1568. By 1600, writing was practiced in all the larger Mixtec communities of the Mixteca Alta, the heartland of the Mixtec region. The peak period of quantity and quality was 1670–1720, when writing in central settlements such as Yanhuitlan and Teposcolula coincided with its practice in numerous smaller communities. In a collection of several hundred Mixtec-language documents, more than sixty ñuu (towns) are represented from the 1560s to 1807. The number of surviving documents declines steadily after 1770, however. Bilingual Mixtecs were speaking and writing Spanish as early as the late seventeenth century, so the decrease of Mixtec-language texts did not necessarily signal the end of Mixtec literacy. The search for Mixtec-language sources in local and national archives has only recently begun; the same may be said for two other languages of Oaxaca, Zapotec and Chocho.

By quality of documentation we are referring not only to the legibility, length, and condition of the papers – often ravaged by water, humidity, fungus, worms, ink acids, and maltreatment – but also to the ethnohistorical potential of the sources. By this definition, a testament that consists solely of religious formula is not as useful as one that provides details about one's estate and perhaps digresses with informal comments on the property and heirs in question. Similarly, a corpus of the same genre enables the reconstruction of social patterns, although the occasional single unique document can prove invaluable in revealing practices usually assumed and thus not recorded by the indigenous notary. Criminal records, for example, frequently diverge from a predictable, structured formula and reveal information on indigenous patterns of behavior that are otherwise difficult to find.

Multilingualism

The preeminence of written Nahuatl in the central area affected the development of writing in other indigenous languages, a result of both pre-Conquest Nahua dominance and the prominence given to the Nahuatl language and the Nahua area by the Spaniards. Whereas a province as relatively isolated as Yucatan reveals no written use of Nahuatl, this language was a lingua franca in much of the rest of New Spain (including coastal and to some extent highland Guatemala); in Oaxaca, Nahuatl served as a mediating language between Spaniards and relatively small indigenous groups, like the Chocho, Cuicatec, Mixe, Chatino, and Trique. Nahuatl-language documentation in the Mixteca Alta predates alphabetic Mixtec writing for a brief period but then is quickly supplanted in all but the most peripheral areas. The importance of Nahuatl is especially evident in the case of interpreters and notaries in sixteenth-century Oaxaca, who often were fluent in Nahuatl and one other language. For example, two interpreters often would be necessary for any translation assignment in the Mixteca Alta: one who knew Spanish and Nahuatl and another who spoke Nahuatl and Mixtec. Likewise, when Cakchiquel Mayas in the Guatemalan capital wished to petition the King of Spain in the 1570s, they hired a local *nahuatlato* to draw up the petitions in Nahuatl. The Nahuatl term "nahuatlato," literally "one who speaks clearly," became the accepted word for "interpreter" from the very beginning in New Spain.

Legal proceedings in New Spain tended to be bilingual or multilingual when more than one native language was used. Whenever indigenous communities were involved as plaintiffs or defendants, native-language testaments and land transaction records were placed in (or copied into) the case as evidence. The proceedings themselves, with the exception of the petitions that initiated the case, would be in Spanish. The further an indigenous-language document traveled (in original or copied form) from its originating native community toward the pinnacle of the Spanish court system (Mexico City, or even Seville), the greater the likelihood of its survival. Thus, native-language documents can be found in local, state, national, and international archives.

Implications of Indigenous Literacy

Native-language sources reveal how people referred to themselves in relation to others. The idea that Nahuas thought of themselves as members of a specific altepetl compares with the Maya view that focuses on the Yucatec equivalent, the cah. Cakchiquel and Quiché identities likewise appear to have been highly localized, focusing far more on the municipal community than on a broader concept of ethnicity. Chontal Maya identity seems to have had more of a linguistic-ethnic component, as the Chontal region was more or less unified under one ruling dynasty and was surrounded by communities of Nahuatl and non-Chontal Maya speakers, communities whose relations with the Chontals in pre-Conquest and early-colonial times were frequently hostile. Mixtec identity was clearly associated with the local ñuu but was complemented and transcended, at least in the Mixteca Alta, by a distinct linguistic and ethnic identity that originated in pre-Conquest times. In both notarial and church texts, people from this region consistently referred to themselves, their region, and their language with the term "ñudzahui," meaning "the place of rain" (or "the place of the rain deity," known as Dzahui).

One of the most visible expressions of community identity, autonomy, and empowerment was represented by the native-language notarial document. Indigenous writing originally was cultivated by the friars and encouraged by civil authorities in order to facilitate the evangelization and colonial administration of the "Indians." Indigenous communities took the alphabet and used it to keep their own records. Before long, it became a self-perpetuating tradition; literate native nobles trained other men within their social circles. Communities also gained access through the Spanish genres of notarial writing to the Spanish court system. When necessary, native plaintiffs and defendants used their own native-language records as evidence to advance or protect personal or corporate claims within the legal system, especially regarding land claims and political privileges – often confronting and sometimes prevailing over Spaniards. In these cases, their writings were appended to the legal dossier that the Spanish notaries produced as a record of the legal proceedings before other Spanish officials. These types of documents, if extant, can be found in municipal, state, and national archives. But it is likely that the vast majority of native-language writings never left the communities in which they were produced. The writings were kept in personal hands, in local archives, or simply perished. We believe that most native-language writings produced within Mesoamerican communities have not survived the test of time.

The strength of the indigenous community is evident in the fact that individual members could bring legal suit against each other without destroying the integrity of the community. This is not to say that indigenous litigants always gained justice; there was an inevitable bias toward Spaniards, despite the frequent provision of free attorneys to native communities. The inability of the system to cope with the volume of litigation could prolong cases for decades. Part of the reason for this volume was the readiness of indigenous communities to take advantage of their access to the system, especially the right to appeal their cases to the *Audiencia* – the high court of Spain. Yet most native lawsuits were against other natives, a fact resulting from the population distribution of New Spain (indigenous people were still an overwhelming majority of the population in Mexico and Guatemala by the end of the colonial period) and the sheer number of indigenous communities that continued to dominate the landscape outside of Spanish urban areas throughout much of the colonial period, even in central Mexico and especially in Oaxaca and Yucatan. Also, increased demand for native lands by the late seventeenth century, as the population of New Spain began a modest but steady recovery, increased competition among communities and at times exacerbated tensions among them.

The eventual transition from native-language writing to Spanish, almost complete by the end of the colonial period, did not spell the end of indigenous literacy and does not necessarily signify the disempowerment of native communities. In many of the more centrally located areas, writing in Spanish became more practical and widely recognized, much as alphabetic writing had been more pragmatic than pictorials some two to three centuries earlier. Indigenous communities adopted alphabetic writing to defend their own interests in response to Spanish demands.

By contrast, the loss of native-language writing corresponded to the steady decline of native languages in the face of the dominant language of

Mexico and Guatemala. Elites and local authorities within native communities became conversant with Spanish legal genres and authorities to the point that they no longer needed native languages to perform their daily tasks. The eventual use of Spanish reflects deep-seated changes within native communities as they came into increasing contact with a steadily growing *mestizo* (person of Spanish and indigenous descent) and Afro-mestizo population that spoke mainly Spanish, that resided in native communities or in nearby cities, or that lived in nearby communities or on haciendas. The pace of this process quickened by the time of independence in the 1820s.

Indigenous literacy ultimately facilitated the function of local self-government and daily business, recording the details of political office, land tenure, property exchange, the wishes of the dying, the complaints of the injured, and the collection, expenditure and payment of community funds and taxes. In summary, native-language sources contain a wealth of information on numerous topics and have greatly enriched our knowledge of life in colonial Mesoamerica.

PART TWO

3

VIEWS OF THE CONQUEST

Whereas Spaniards wrote many volumes about their conquest of Mexico, very few native writers had the opportunity to write down their own accounts of the wars that Spaniards waged against Mesoamericans in the early sixteenth century. Only a handful of native-language writings have survived. By far the best and most extensive of these posterior accounts focuses on the Spanish-led siege of Tenochtitlan, as it was recorded in Book XII of the Florentine Codex. This "codex" consists of twelve books written entirely in the Nahuatl language (accompanied by a Spanish translation), with several hundred illustrations, that was produced by a small group of Nahua noblemen from Tlatelolco, an altepetl that was located at the center of the Mexica empire (on the same island as Mexico-Tenochtitlan, in fact). The texts were written from the 1540s to the early 1570s, and were compiled under the supervision of the Franciscan scholar fray Bernardino de Sahagún. The original title of the work is *General History of the Things of New Spain* (*Historia universal de las cosas de la Nueva España*).

Here we provide ten of the forty-one chapters from Book XII of the Florentine Codex (document 3.1). We also include selections from a separate work, called the Annals of Tlatelolco (document 3.2), which present another Tlatelolcan view of the conquest. (Document 4.2, in the next chapter, a letter from Xochimilco to the King of Spain, provides yet another perspective on these events and their implications for the altepetl of Xochimilco.) We include no Mexica version because, with the exception of a brief, fragmented account called the Codex Aubin, none has survived. We also include a pair of late colonial accounts in Nahuatl and Mixtec from the Valley of Oaxaca (documents 3.4 and 3.5), as well as two Maya-language texts, written in Chontal and Yucatec (documents 3.6 and 3.7). Images from the Florentine Codex and the Lienzo of Tlaxcala (documents 3.3 a–d), a pictorial account of the conquest from the Tlaxcalan perspective, complement the alphabetic texts presented here.

As we shall see, all the accounts were written many years after the events and provide a highly localized perspective. There is no single indigenous version of the conquest because Mesoamericans neither shared a common sense

Some major Nahua altepetl in and around the Valley of Mexico.

of political identity nor experienced the Spanish invasion in the same way or at the same time. For central Mexico, past histories have overemphasized the strength and organization of the Aztec or Mexica empire, and have failed to recognize the strong traditions of autonomy and independence that each altepetl cherished and guarded, whether they paid tribute to Mexico-Tenochtitlan (and thus were part of the "empire") or not. For example, although Tlatelolco was Tenochtitlan's neighbor, it is clear from Tlatelolca accounts that they present a particular view of events, which highlight their heroic efforts while representing the Mexica *tlatoani*, Moteuczoma, as an indecisive and ineffective ruler and the Mexica warriors as cowards. No doubt, the fact that the Mexica had forcefully brought the Tlatelolca into the empire only a few decades before the arrival of the Spaniards tempered their view of the Mexica. At the same time, and in spite of these local accounts, the Tlatelolca made observations about the Spaniards and drew conclusions about the conquest that must have been shared by many Mesoamericans, and their narrative recounts many aspects of the oral tradition or social memory of the people of the region.

Whereas the Tlatelolca could not possibly deny their role in fighting the Spaniards, some altepetl strategically argued that they had never fought Cortés and his men but had provided them with invaluable assistance from the beginning. Members of the complex altepetl of Tlaxcala, the most recognized and rewarded indigenous ally of the Spaniards in Mesoamerica, actually portray themselves as the victorious conquerors of Tenochtitlan and many other places, from Michoacan to Guatemala (document 3.3). Indeed, after the fall of Tenochtitlan, the conquest spread quickly from the center, encountering prolonged resistance only to the far north and south of Mesoamerica. Spaniards used multiple native "allies" to continue the conquest, and then relied on them as settlers and intermediaries in many of their newly created cities.

This chapter also includes versions of the conquest that were written and presented to Spanish officials in the late colonial period, but were back-dated to the 1520s, in order to verify claims of possession to disputed lands (documents 3.4 and 3.5). The Mixtec and Nahuatl *títulos primordiales* or primordial titles from Oaxaca rely on a rich oral tradition that makes sense of the past in the light of present concerns, and include both fanciful and factual information. The Mixtec account is accompanied by a pre-Conquest-style painting that is based on the authors' impression of how images should appear in the 1520s.

The perspective of the Mayas of Yucatan, where the Spaniards established a colony in the 1540s, is likewise based on a localized sense of identity and loyalty. In the Yucatan peninsula in the early sixteenth century, small regions of towns were loosely organized into polities or kingdoms held together by the prominence of a ruling noble dynasty – such as the Pech (document 3.6) and the Paxbolon (document 3.7). In documents designed to promote dynastic legitimacy and consolidate territorial claims (like the primordial titles from Oaxaca), Pech and Paxbolon rulers present themselves as immediate allies of the first Spanish invaders, allies whose support made the conquest possible and turned the Maya lords themselves into prominent conquistadors. The Pech king, Ah Naum Pech, even adopts the name of the Spanish leader or *adelantado*, becoming baptized as don Francisco de Montejo Pech. Thus, what was in reality a complex process of resistance, accommodation, and negotiation is reduced for political and narrative purposes to a simple tale of inspired pragmatism on the part of Maya rulers.

Altogether, these documents reflect both the complexity of the Spanish Conquest in Mesoamerica – too often reduced to the dramatic battle between Spaniards and Aztecs over Tenochtitlan – and the diversity and sophistication of Mesoamerican perspectives on sixteenth-century events.

3.1. A Nahuatl Account of the Conquest of Mexico in Book XII of the Florentine Codex[1]

Nahua nobles from the nearby altepetl of Tlatelolco wrote this particular view of the war on Mexico-Tenochtitlan a few decades after the event. The account appears in the

1 Translated from Nahuatl by James Lockhart (1993), modified slightly for this volume, with Lockhart's permission; the commentary on the contents of Book XII (in italics) is by Terraciano.

twelfth and final book of the Florentine Codex, which is titled "How war was waged here in the altepetl of Mexico." Book XII consists of forty-one brief chapters, each with a separate title, and 158 illustrations. Fray Bernardino de Sahagún, the Franciscan friar who compiled the Nahuatl-language writings, must have determined the format of the work because it resembles Spanish narrative histories in its organization and style. Nahuas wrote the account in their own language, and Sahagún translated the Nahuatl into Spanish in a parallel column. It is unknown how much the Franciscan censored the content of the account. The portrayal of greedy Spaniards, the lack of references to Christianity, and the sad tone in the end, however, all suggest that Sahagún did not intervene directly in this version.

The narrative can be divided into two parts, before and after the Spaniards' arrival in Tenochtitlan. Information for the first part was presumably transmitted through the oral tradition and lacks the eyewitness quality of the second part; the vocabulary of the two parts is different, as well, suggesting that the first part was written at a later time. Part Two presents a specific Tlatelolcan view of events. In fact, the authors go out of their way to demonstrate how the Tlatelolca bravely resisted the Spaniards, whereas the Mexica or Tenochca of Tenochtitlan abandoned the fight in the end. The Tlatelolca authors go so far as to portray Moteuczoma, the Mexica tlatoani, as an indecisive and ineffectual leader. Clearly, the Mexica would have told a different story if they had written a comparable account (which they did not). The local bias of the second part reinforces the fact that people identified primarily with their altepetl, and not with the Mexica empire. This fact helps explain why the Spaniards were able to defeat the Mexica and their allies, with the assistance of many other altepetl.

Chapter 1 of Book XII presents eight bad omens that occurred before the arrival of the Spaniards. These omens, in retrospect, seem to have presaged defeat. In Chapter 2, Mexica emissaries go out in boats to greet the Spaniards, who are sailing in a ship along the coast. The ambassadors perform the "earth-eating gesture" and give gifts to the Spaniards, because "they thought it was Topiltzin Quetzalcoatl who had arrived." According to the narrative, they identified the Spaniards with a legendary Toltec deity who, it was said, would return one day from the east to conquer Mexico. It is unclear whether they thought the Spaniards were deities at first glance, or the authors used this legend to explain what had happened in the past. In any case, the ambassadors go directly to Tenochtitlan to report to Moteuczoma, who instructs them to be silent about what they have seen. In Chapter 3, Moteuczoma marvels at the glass beads that the Spaniards had given the Mexica ambassadors as gifts, and orders that the coast be watched for the strangers' return. When they are sighted again, he sends five lords to the coast to give them gifts. According to the narrative, Moteuczoma believed that it was Quetzalcoatl.

Chapter 4 describes the regalia and gifts that the Mexica lords brought to the Spaniards who were sighted along the coast. The gifts include four elaborate costumes of Mesoamerican deities, including Quetzalcoatl, Tlaloc, and Tezcatlipoca. Moteuczoma instructs five emissaries to present the gods' appurtenances to "our lord the god" by way of greeting. They travel to the coast and approach the Spaniards in their boats.

In Chapter 5, presented here, the lords greet the Spaniards on their ships and begin to dress up Hernando Cortés in one of the costumes. In return, Cortés intimidates the messengers and sets a bellicose tone by challenging them to combat and showing off his superior weaponry.

Fifth chapter, where it is said what happened when Moteuczoma's messengers went into don Hernando Cortés's boat

Then they [Moteuczoma's messengers] climbed up, carrying in their arms the goods. When they had climbed into the boat, each of them made the earth-eating gesture before the Captain [Cortés]. Then they addressed him, saying,

"May the god listen: his agent Moteuczoma, who is in charge in Mexico for him, says to him, 'The god is doubly welcome.'"

Then they dressed up the Captain. They put on him the turquoise serpent mask attached to the quetzal-feather head fan, from which hung the green-stone serpent earplugs. And they put the sleeveless jacket on him, and around his neck they put the plaited green-stone neckband with the golden disk in the middle. On his lower back they tied the back mirror, and also they tied behind him the cloak called a *tzitzilli*. And on his legs they placed the green-stone bands with the golden bells. And they gave him, placing it on his arm, the shield with gold and shells crossing, on whose edge were spread quetzal feathers, with a quetzal banner. And they laid the obsidian sandals before him.

And the other three outfits, the gods' appurtenances, they only arranged in rows before him.

When this had been done, the Captain said to them, "Is this everything you have as greeting and salutation?"

They answered, "That is all with which we have come, our lord."

Then the Captain ordered that they be tied up; they put irons on their feet and necks. When this had been done they shot off the cannon. And at this point the messengers fainted and swooned; one after another they swayed and fell, losing consciousness. And the Spaniards lifted them into a sitting position and gave them wine to drink. Then they gave them food, fed them, with which they regained strength and got their breath back.

When this had been done the Captain said to them, "Listen, I have found out and heard it said that these Mexica are very strong, great warriors, able to take others down. Where there is one of them he can chase, push aside, overcome, and turn back his enemies, even though there should be ten or twenty. Now I want to see it, I want to see how strong and manly you are." Then he gave them leather shields, iron swords, and iron lances. He said: "Well now, very early in the morning, as dawn is about to come, we will fight each other, we will challenge each other, we will find out who will fall down first."

They answered the Captain, saying, "May the lord listen, this is not at all what his agent Moteuczoma ordered us to do. All we came to do was to greet and salute you. We were not charged with what the lord wishes. If we should do that, won't Moteuczoma be very angry with us because of it, won't he destroy us for it?"

Then the Captain said, "No, it is just to be done. I want to see and behold it, for it is believed in Spain that you are very strong, great warriors. Eat while it is still before dawn, and I will eat then too. Outfit yourselves well."

The following four chapters recount the release of the messengers; the Spaniards humiliated and intimidated them but apparently did them little physical harm. They run back to Tenochtitlan to report on the Spaniards' appearance, weapons, food, horses, and dogs. Moteuczoma is shocked and terrified. He orders that captives be sacrificed, and that spells be cast on the Spaniards. As Moteuczoma and his circle of lords try to make sense of it all, lamenting and weeping and deeply troubled by the news, Cortés and his men make a landing and begin to march inland from the coast with the assistance of "a woman, one of us people here," in reference to the woman who would be called Malinche. On hearing that these people are coming to meet him, Moteuczoma struggles to control his emotions and prepares himself for the encounter.

In Chapter 10, the Spaniards are led by a person from Cempoallan, an altepetl near the coast. They reach the great Nahua altepetl of Tlaxcala and encounter some Otomí-speaking people. After seeing how the Spaniards easily defeated the Otomis, the Tlaxcalans decide to negotiate with the Spaniards rather then fight them, hoping to build an alliance with these powerful outsiders rather than risk a costly defeat at their hands. Although it is clear from the Spaniards' reports that Tlaxcala did initially resist them, the myth of an immediate alliance with the Spaniards that the Tlaxcalans carefully constructed and cultivated in their own conquest accounts prevails in this Tlatelolcan interpretation of events, as well.

In Chapters 11 and 12, presented here, the Spaniards accompany their new allies from Tlaxcala to the altepetl of a hated local rival, Cholula, which is allied with the Mexica. The Spaniards massacre the Cholulans and continue their march to Tenochtitlan. Moteuczoma's gifts only whet their appetites for more gold.

Eleventh chapter, where it is said how the Spaniards reached Tlaxcala

The Tlaxcalans guided, accompanied, and led them until they brought them to their palace(s) and housed them there. They showed them great honors, they gave them what they needed and attended to them, and then they gave them their daughters.

Then [the Spaniards] asked them, "Where is Mexico? What kind of place is it? Is it still far?"

They answered them, "It's not far now. Perhaps one can get there in three days. It is a very favored place, and the Mexica are very strong, great warriors, conquerors, who go about conquering everywhere."

Now before this there had been friction between the Tlaxcalans and the Cholulans. They viewed each other with anger, fury, hatred, and disgust;

they could come together on nothing. Because of this they [the Tlaxcalans] persuaded the Spaniards to kill them treacherously.

They said to them, "The Cholulans are very evil; they are our enemies. They are as strong as the Mexica, and they are the Mexica's allies."

When the Spaniards heard this, they went to Cholula. The Tlaxcalans and Cempoalans went with them, outfitted for war. When they arrived, there was a general summons and cry that all the noblemen, rulers, subordinate leaders, warriors, and commoners should come, and everyone assembled in the temple courtyard. When they all came together, [the Spaniards and their allies] blocked the entrances, all of the places where one entered. Then people were stabbed, struck, and killed. No such thing was on the minds of the Cholulans; they did not meet the Spaniards with weapons of war. It just seemed that they were stealthily and treacherously killed, because the Tlaxcalans persuaded the Spaniards to do it.

And a report of everything that was happening was given and relayed to Moteuczoma. Some of the messengers arrived as others were leaving; they just turned around and ran back. There was no time when they were not listening, when reports were not being given. And all the common people went about in a state of excitement; there were frequent disturbances, as if the earth moved, as if everything were spinning before one's eyes. People were frightened.

And after the dying in Cholula, the Spaniards set off on their way to Mexico, coming gathered and bunched, raising dust. Their iron lances and halberds seemed to sparkle, and their iron swords were curved like a stream of water. Their cuirasses and iron helmets seemed to make a clattering sound. Some of them came wearing iron all over, turned into iron beings, gleaming, so that they aroused great fear and were generally seen with great fear and dread. Their dogs came in front, coming ahead of them, keeping to the front, panting, with their spittle hanging down.

Twelfth chapter, where it is said how Moteuczoma sent a great nobleman along with many other noblemen to go to meet the Spaniards, and what their gifts of greeting were when they greeted the Captain between Iztactepetl and Popocatepetl

Thereupon Moteuczoma named and sent the noblemen and a great many other agents of his, with Tzihuacpopocatzin as their leader, to go meet Cortés between [the volcanoes] Popocatepetl and Iztactepetl, at Quauhtechcac. They gave the Spaniards golden banners, banners of precious feathers, and golden necklaces.

And when they had given the things to them, they seemed to smile, to rejoice and be very happy. Like monkeys they grabbed the gold. It was as though their hearts were put to rest, brightened, renewed. For gold was what they greatly thirsted for; they were gluttonous for it, starved for it, they piggishly wanted it. They came lifting up the golden banners, waving them from side to side, showing them to each other. They seemed to babble; they spoke to each other in a babbling tongue.

And when they saw Tzihuacpopocatzin, they said, "Is this one then Moteuczoma?" They said it to the Tlaxcalans and Cempoalans, their lookouts, who came among them, questioning them secretly. They said, "It is not that one, our lords. This is Tzihuacpopocatzin, who is representing Moteuczoma."

The Spaniards said to him, "Are you then Moteuczoma?" He said, "I am your agent Moteuczoma."

Then they told him, "Get out of here! Why do you lie to us? What do you take us for? You can't lie to us, you can't fool us, turn our heads, flatter us, make faces at us, trick us, blur our vision, distort things for us, blind us, dazzle us, throw mud in our eyes, put muddy hands on our faces. It is not you. Moteuczoma lives; he will not be able to hide from us, he will not be able to find refuge. Where will he go? Is he a bird? Will he fly? Or will he take an underground route? Will he go somewhere into a mountain that is hollow inside? We will see him, we will not fail to see his face and hear his words from his lips."

Thus they just scorned and disregarded him, and so another of their meetings and greetings came to naught. Then they went straight back, directly to Mexico.

In the next three chapters, Moteuczoma tries in vain to dissuade the Spaniards from coming to Tenochtitlan, including blocking some roads along the way. The prognosticators and priests see nothing but bad omens and ominous visions. By now, even the common people of Tenochtitlan feel a sense of dread. Moteuczoma was paralyzed with fear. Meanwhile, the Spaniards march from Iztapalapan to Mexico-Tenochtitlan. In Chapter 15, the authors pay much attention to the organization and appearance of the intruders: the horses and dogs, the standard bearer, the iron swords and lances, the wooden shields, the crossbows, the smoking arquebuses (guns), the indigenous warriors from many altepetl, and the carriers who dragged the cannons and transported all the provisions of this formidable army.

In Chapters 16 and 17, presented here, Cortés and Moteuczoma meet at last, and exchange polite speeches by way of Marina's (Malinche) translations. When the Spaniards are invited into the palace, Moteuczoma is immediately seized and held captive, along with the ruler of Tlatelolco. Chaos and discord follow as the Spaniards demand to be served and search frantically for riches.

Sixteenth chapter, where it is said how Moteuczoma went in peace and quiet to meet the Spaniards at Xoloco, where the house of Alvarado is now, or at the place they call Huitzillan

And when the Spaniards had come as far as Xoloco, when they had stopped there, Moteuczoma dressed and prepared himself for a meeting, along with other great rulers and high nobles, his rulers and nobles. Then they went to the meeting. On gourd bases they set out different precious flowers; in the midst of the shield flowers and heart flowers stood popcorn flowers, yellow tobacco flowers, cacao flowers, made into wreaths for the head, wreaths to be girded around. And they carried golden necklaces, necklaces with pendants, wide necklaces.

And when Moteuczoma went out to meet them at Huitzillan, he gave various things to the war leader, the commander of the warriors; he gave him flowers, he put necklaces on him, he put flower necklaces on him, he adorned him with flowers, he put flower wreaths on his head. Then he laid before him the golden necklaces, all the different things for greeting people. He ended by putting some of the necklaces on him.

Then Cortés said in reply to Moteuczoma, "Is it not you? Is it not you, then? Moteuczoma?"

Moteuczoma said, "Yes, it is me." Then he stood up straight, he stood up with their faces meeting. He bowed down deeply to him. He stretched as far as he could, standing stiffly. Addressing him, he said to him,

"O our lord, be doubly welcomed on your arrival in this land; you have come to satisfy your curiosity about your altepetl of Mexico, you have come to sit on your seat of authority, which I have kept a while for you, where I have been in charge for you, for your agents the rulers Itzcoatzin, the elder Moteuczoma, Axayacatl, Tiçocic, and Ahuitzotl have gone, who for a very short time came to be in charge for you, to govern the altepetl of Mexico. It is after them that your poor commoner [myself] came. Will they come back to the place of their absence? If only one of them could see and behold what has now happened in my time, what I now see after our lords are gone! For I am not just dreaming, not just sleepwalking, not just seeing it in my sleep. I am not just dreaming that I have seen you, have looked upon your face. For a time I have been concerned, looking toward the mysterious place from which you have come, among clouds and mist. It is so, that the rulers on departing said that you would come in order to acquaint yourself with your altepetl and sit upon your seat of authority. And now it has come true, you have come. Be doubly welcomed, enter the land, go to enjoy your palace; rest your body. May our lords arrive in the land."

And when the speech that Moteuczoma directed to the Marqués [Cortés] had concluded, Marina reported it to him, translating it for him. And when the Marqués had heard what Moteuczoma had said, he spoke to Marina in return, babbling back to them, replying in his babbling tongue,

"Let Moteuczoma be at ease, let him not be afraid, for we greatly esteem him. Now we are truly satisfied to see him in person and hear him, for until now we have greatly desired to see him, to look upon his face. Well, now we have seen him, we have come to his homeland of Mexico. Little by little he will hear what we have to say."

3.1a The meeting between Moteuczoma and Cortés, with Marina (Malinche) in the middle serving as translator. The volutes or "speech scrolls" represent the act of speaking. Courtesy of the Archivo General de la Nación. Facsimile edition Sahagún 1996, Book XII: f. 26.

Then the Spaniards took Moteuczoma by the hand. They came along with him, stroking his hair to show their good feeling. And the Spaniards looked at him, each of them giving him a close look. They would start along walking, then mount, then dismount again in order to see him.

And as to each of the rulers who went with him, they were: first, Cacamatzin, ruler of Tetzcoco; second, Tetlepanquetzatzin, ruler of

Tlacopan; third, the Tlacochcalcatl Itzquauhtzin, ruler of Tlatelolco; fourth, Topantemoctzin, Moteuczoma's storekeeper in Tlatelolco. These were the ones who went. And the other Tenochca noblemen were Atlixcatzin, the Tlacateccatl; Tepehuatzin, the Tlacochcalcatl; Quetzalaztatzin, the Ticocyahuacatl; Totomotzin; Ecatenpatiltzin; and Quappiaztzin. When Moteuczoma was taken prisoner, they not only hid themselves and took refuge, they abandoned him in anger.

Seventeenth chapter, where it is said how the Spaniards went with Moteuczoma to enter the great palace, and what happened there

And when they had reached the palace and gone in, immediately they seized Moteuczoma and kept close watch over him, not letting him out of their sight, and Itzquauhtzin (the ruler of Tlatelolco) along with him. But the others were just allowed to come back out.

And when this happened, the various guns were fired. It seemed that everything became confused; people went this way and that, scattering and running about. It was as though everyone's tongue were out, everyone were preoccupied, everyone had been eating [hallucinogenic] mushrooms, as though who knows what had been shown to everyone. Fear reigned, as though everyone had swallowed his heart. It was still that way at night; everyone was terrified, taken aback, thunderstruck, stunned.

And when it dawned, everything the Spaniards needed was proclaimed: white tortillas, roast turkeys, eggs, fresh water, wood, firewood, charcoal, earthen tubs, polished bowls, water jars, large clay pitchers, vessels for frying, all kinds of earthenware. Moteuczoma himself ordered it. But when he summoned the noblemen, they would no longer obey him, but grew angry. They no longer performed their duty to him, no longer went to him; no longer was he heeded. But he was not therefore forsaken; he was given all he needed to eat and drink, and water and deer fodder for the Spaniards.

And when the Spaniards were well settled, right away they interrogated Moteuczoma about all the stored treasure of the altepetl, the devices and shields. They greatly prodded him, they eagerly sought gold as a thing of esteem. And then Moteuczoma went along leading the Spaniards. They gathered around him; he went in their midst, leading the way. They went along taking hold of him, grasping him. And when they reached the storehouse, the place called Teocalco, then all the shining things were brought out: the quetzal-feather head fan, the devices, the shields, the golden disks, the necklaces of the devils, the golden nose crescents, the golden leg bands, the golden arm bands, the golden sheets for the forehead.

Thereupon the gold on the shields and on all the devices was taken off. And when all the gold had been detached, right away they set on fire, set fire to, ignited all the different precious things; they all burned. And the Spaniards made the gold into bricks. And they took as much of the jade as pleased them;

as to the rest of the jade, the Tlaxcalans just snatched it up. And the Spaniards went everywhere, scratching about in the hiding places, storehouses, places of storage all around. They took everything they saw that pleased them.

In the following two chapters, the Spaniards go to Moteuczoma's personal palace and loot it. When Marina instructs the Mexica to bring food and water for the Spaniards, people are too fearful to respond. Chapter 19 alludes to the fact that Cortés has left Tenochtitlan to confront a group of Spaniards, led by Pánfilo de Narváez, that were sent by the governor of Cuba to arrest Cortés and his party. In his absence, Pedro de Alvarado, second in command, witnesses a feast dedicated to the Mexica deity, Huitzilopochtli. The preparations for the feast and ritual ceremonies are described in considerable detail.

    In Chapter 20, presented here, Alvarado and the Spaniards fall on the celebrants of the feast and begin to massacre anybody and everybody in the temple courtyard. The Mexica warriors gather to confront the Spaniards, and war breaks out in the city.

Twentieth chapter, where it is said how the Spaniards killed and annihilated the Mexica who were celebrating the feast of Huitzilopochtli, at what they call the Teoithualco (Divine Courtyard, Courtyard of the Gods, temple courtyard)

When things were already going on, when the feast [of Huitzilopochtli] was being observed and there was dancing and singing, with voices raised in song, the singing was like the noise of waves breaking against the rocks.

    When it was time, when the moment had come for the Spaniards to do the killing, they came out equipped for battle. They came and closed off each of the places where people went in and out: Quauhquiahuac, Tecpantzinco, Acatliyacapan, and Tezcacoac. And when they had closed these exits, they stationed themselves in each, and no one could come out any more.

    When this had been done, they went into the temple courtyard to kill people. Those who were assigned to do the killing just went on foot, each with his metal sword and his leather shield, some of them iron-studded. Then they surrounded those who were dancing, going among the cylindrical drums. They struck a drummer's arms; both of his hands were severed. Then they struck his neck; his head landed far away. Then they stabbed everyone with iron lances and struck them with iron swords. They struck some in the stomach, and then their intestines came spilling out. They split open the heads of some, they cut their skulls to pieces; their skulls were cut up into little bits. They hit some on the shoulders; their bodies broke open and ripped. Some they hacked on the calves, some on the thighs, some on their stomachs, and then all their entrails would spill out. And if someone tried to run it was useless; he just dragged his intestines along. There was a stench that smelled like sulfur. Those who tried to escape could go nowhere. When someone tried to go out, they struck and stabbed him at the exits.

dela conquista mexicana *fo.29.*

in ie iuhq uj mon:ochi mu
ne chico in teucujtlatl. Njnia
ieic qujoalnotza, quioal
ne notzallanj injxqujchtin
inpipiltin in Malintzin; tla
panco oalmoqueth, atenan
ticpac: qujtoa. Mexica xioal
hujan caconca ie tlai hiovia
in Espanoles: xiqual cuja
in tlaqualli, in chipaoacaH,
yoan injxqujch moneqzj, ca
ie tlai hiovia, iequjcia vi, ie
qujhio via, iemociauvi, ie
mjhiovia: tleica in amo can
oallazze quj ~ ic neci caan
qualanj. Auh in Mexica ca
njma asonjo motlapaloa sia
in ma on vian, conca moma
uhtiaia, mauh ca conegujia
mjhicaviaia, conca ma viz
tli onoc, mavis tli mo teta ca
aoac tlaxtlapaloa, caiuhqj:
taguanj vncta, caiuh qujn
tlalli mjctoc: cel amoie mo
caoa, amoie netzotzonalo in
concaoa injxqujch in techmo
nequj, cam mauheac in con
caoaia, can momamauhtiti
vi, ca on momauh catlaloa

136

3.1b A page from the Florentine Codex depicting Cortés and Marina (Malinche) on the roof of the palace in Tenochtitlan (in the top frame). Marina communicates Cortés's demands for food and gold to the Mexica. The Mexica gather the goods reluctantly. Some of the gold pieces (bottom frame), such as the arm bracelets, are identified by the parts of the body on which they were worn. Courtesy of the Archivo General de la Nación. Facsimile edition Sahagún 1996, Book XII: f. 29.

But some climbed up the wall and were able to escape. Some went into the various calpulli temples and took refuge there. Some took refuge among those who had already died by pretending to be dead, and they were able to escape. But if someone took a breath and they saw him, they stabbed him. The blood of the warriors ran like water; the ground was almost slippery with blood, and the stench of it rose, and the intestines were lying all dragged out. And the Spaniards went everywhere searching in the calpulli temples, stabbing in the places where they searched in case someone was taking shelter there. They went everywhere, searching all the calpulli temples.

And when it became known what was happening, everyone cried out, "Mexica warriors, come running, get the shields and arrows. Hurry, come running, the warriors are dying; they are dead, they have been annihilated, Mexica warriors!" Then there were war cries, shouting, and the beating of hands against lips. The warriors quickly came outfitted, bunched together, carrying arrows and shields. Then the fighting began; they shot at them with barbed darts and spears, and they hurled darts with obsidian points at them. A cloud of yellow reeds (arrows) spread over the Spaniards.

In Chapter 21, the Spaniards barricade themselves and the Mexica tend to their many dead. Itzquauhtzin, the ruler of Tlatelolco, speaks on behalf of Moteuczoma and beseeches the Mexica and Tlatelolca warriors to make peace because the Spaniards are too powerful. This message is rejected by many angry warriors who want revenge. Instead, they besiege the Spaniards and forbid anyone to assist them or to give them food. In Chapter 22, Cortés returns and the fighting continues. Several days of close-hand-to-hand combat in the ceremonial precinct leaves many Mexica warriors dead.

In Chapter 23, presented here, Moteuczoma and Itzquauhtzin, the rulers of Tenochtitlan and Tlatelolco, are among the dead. The Spaniards are caught dumping their bodies unceremoniously in the lake. This account does not specify who killed the lords, a controversial topic even in the sixteenth century. The account of the different treatment of the two lords' corpses reflects yet another Tlatelolcan bias in Book XII of the Florentine Codex.

Twenty-third chapter, where it is said how Moteuczoma and a great nobleman of Tlatelolco died, and the Spaniards threw their bodies out at the entryway of the house where they were

Four days after people had been cast down from the temple, the Spaniards removed the bodies of Moteuczoma and Itzquauhtzin, who had died, to a place at the water's edge called Teoayoc (Place of the Divine Turtle), for an image of a turtle was there, carved in stone; the stone represented a turtle.

And when they were seen and recognized as Moteuczoma and Itzquauhtzin, they hastened to take Moteuczoma up in their arms and brought him to the place called Copolco. Then they placed him on a pile of wood and set fire to it. The fire crackled and roared, with many tongues of flame, tongues of flame rising up like tassels. And Moteuczoma's body lay sizzling, and it let off a stench as it burned.

And when it was burning, some people who were enraged and disheartened scolded him, saying, "This miserable man made the whole world fear him, in the whole world he was dreaded, in the whole world he inspired respect and fear. If someone offended him only in some small way, he immediately disposed of him. He punished many for imagined things, not true, but just fabricated tales." And there were many others who scolded him, moaning, lamenting, shaking their heads.

But Itzquauhtzin they put in a boat; they took his body in a boat until they got him here to Tlatelolco. They grieved greatly, their hearts were broken; the tears flowed down. Not a soul scolded him or cursed him. They said, "The lord Tlacochcalcatl Itzquauhtzin has suffered, for he suffered and was afflicted along with Moteuczoma. What tribulations he endured on our behalf in the past, during all of Moteuczoma's time!" Then they outfitted him, equipped him with the lordly banner and other items of paper, and they gave him provisions. Then they took him and burned him in the temple courtyard at the place called Quauhxicalco. His body was burned with great splendor.

After four days of fighting, the Spaniards were enclosed in the house for [another] seven days. But when the seven days were past, they came back out for a while to take a look, looking around here and there; they went as far as Maçatzintamalco. They gathered stalks of green maize that were only beginning to form ears. They just gathered the maize leaves as one does in war, going in great haste. They went only where they were going, then they quickly went back into the building. When they had come out the sun was already off to one side, about to set.

The following five chapters relate how the Spaniards retreat from Tenochtitlan by night, fighting their way from one place to the next. Mexica warriors and their allies pursue the Spaniards and attack them along the way; many lives are lost on both sides (including Moteuczoma's son). On the following day, the Mexica begin to retrieve all the corpses and search the canals for items that the Spaniards lost in their hasty retreat. Meanwhile, the Spaniards vent their rage on the people of Calacoayan and massacre them without cause. Finally, the Spaniards make it to the altepetl of Teocalhueyacan, where they find refuge and sustenance. The Spaniards regroup and go from one altepetl to another, pursued at a distance by groups of Mexica warriors who engage them sporadically in combat. As the Spaniards continue to retreat, the Mexica begin to think that they are gone for good, and celebrate a feast that commemorates the warriors that died in battle. But once again the Spaniards begin to return, fighting along the way and moving from one altepetl to the next.

Chapter 29, presented here, recounts the terrible diseases and hunger that had begun to afflict "the people here." The diseases were as relentless and deadly as the Spanish warriors, who continue to make their way to Tenochtitlan again.

Twenty-ninth chapter, where it is said how, at the time the Spaniards left Mexico, there came an illness of pustules of which many local people died; it was called "the great rash" [smallpox]

Before the Spaniards appeared to us, first an epidemic broke out, a sickness of pustules. It began in Tepeilhuitl. Large bumps spread on people; some were entirely covered. They spread everywhere, on the face, the head, the chest, etc. The disease brought great desolation; many people died of it. They could no longer walk about, but lay in their dwellings and sleeping places, no longer able to move or stir. They were unable to change position, to stretch out on their sides or face down, or raise their heads. And when they made a motion, they called out loudly. The pustules that covered people caused great desolation; very many people died of them, and many just starved to death; starvation reigned, and no one took care of others any longer.

On some people, the pustules appeared only far apart, and they did not suffer greatly, nor did many of them die of it. But many people's faces were spoiled by it, their faces and noses were made rough. Some lost an eye or were blinded.

This disease of pustules lasted a full sixty days; after sixty days it abated and ended. When people were recovering and reviving, the pustules disease began to move in the direction of Chalco. And many were disabled or paralyzed by it, but they were not disabled forever. It broke out in Teotleco, and it abated in Panquetzaliztli. The Mexica warriors were greatly weakened by it.

And when things were in this state, the Spaniards came, moving toward us from Tetzcoco. They appeared from the direction of Quauhtitlan and made a halt at Tlacopan. There they gave one another assignments and divided themselves into groups. Pedro de Alvarado was made responsible for the road coming to Tlatelolco. Cortés went and established himself in Coyoacan, which became his responsibility, along with the road coming from Acachinanco to Tenochtitlan, for Cortés considered the Tenochca (Mexica) great and valiant warriors.

The following five chapters describe how the Spaniards build boats at the edge of the lake in Tetzcoco, outfit them with guns, and renew their siege by water. The Spaniards attack by water and by land, causing panic and destruction wherever they go and leaving bodies in their wake. Meanwhile, the Spaniards' allies begin to fill up the canals in order to block the waterways. In Chapter 32, the people of Tenochtitlan begin to stream into Tlatelolco, but the Tlatelolcan warriors continue to go to Tenochtitlan to fight. The narrative testifies to the bravery of those warriors who fight heroically to defend their communities. They repel countless attacks and inflict many damages of their own. By this time, Quauhtemoc has emerged as the Mexica tlatoani, and he receives offers of support from other altepetl, including Xochimilco. However, the Xochimilca take advantage of the situation and begin to plunder Tenochtitlan, carrying away men and women as captives. The Mexica, angered and betrayed,

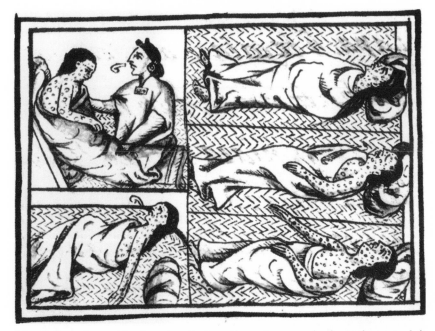

3.1c Victims of an epidemic outbreak of smallpox. A woman healer in the upper left frame tends to a patient. Courtesy of the Archivo General de la Nación. Facsimile edition Sahagún 1996, Book XII: f. 53v.

annihilate the Xochimilca and their accomplices. The Mexica also capture and execute many Spaniards, as they continue to engage in close hand-to-hand combat in many parts of the city.

Chapter 35, presented here, recounts the capture and sacrifice of Spaniards and their many allies. At the same time, starvation, disease, and warfare continue to take a heavy toll on the people, who suffer as never before.

Thirty-fifth chapter, where it is told how the Mexica took captives. According to the count of the Spaniards they captured, there were fifty-three, as well as many Tlaxcalans and people of Tetzcoco, Chalco, and Xochimilco, and how they killed all of them before their former gods

And at this point they let loose with all the warriors who had been crouching there; they came out and chased the Spaniards in the passageways, and when the Spaniards saw it they [the Mexica] seemed to be intoxicated. Then captives were taken. Many Tlaxcalans, and people of Acolhuacan, Chalco, Xochimilco, etc., were captured. A great number of people were captured and killed. They made the Spaniards and all the others go right into the water. And the road became very slippery; one could no longer walk on it, but would slip and slide.

And the captives were dragged off. This was where the banner was captured; that is where it was taken. It was the Tlatelolca who captured it, at the place now called San Martín. They thought nothing of it, they did not even take care of it. The other Spaniards escaped; the Mexica harassed them as far as Colhuacatonco, at the edge of the canal, where they regrouped.

Then they took the captives to Yacacolco, hurrying them along, going along herding their captives together. Some went weeping, some singing, some went shouting while hitting their hands against their mouths. When they got them to Yacacolco, they lined them all up. Each one went to the altar platform, where the sacrifice was performed. The Spaniards went first, going in the lead; the people of all the different altepetl followed, coming last. And when the sacrifice was over, they strung the Spaniards' heads on poles [on the skull rack]; they also strung up the horses' heads. They placed them below, and the Spaniards' heads were above them, strung up facing east. But they did not string up the heads of all the various [other] people from far away. There were fifty-three of the Spaniards they captured, along with four horses.

Nevertheless, watch was kept everywhere, and there was fighting. They did not stop keeping watch because of what had happened. The people of Xochimilco went about in boats surrounding us on all sides; there were deaths and captives taken on both sides.

And all the common people suffered greatly. There was famine; many died of hunger. They no longer drank good, pure water, but the water they drank was salty. Many people died of it, and because of it many got dysentery and died. Everything was eaten: lizards, swallows, maize straw, grass that grows on salt flats. And they chewed at colorín wood, glue flowers, plaster, leather, and deerskin, which they roasted, baked, and toasted so that they could eat them, and they ground up medicinal herbs and adobe bricks. There had never been so much suffering. The siege was frightening, and great numbers died of hunger. And eventually they pressed us back against the wall, herding us together.

In Chapters 36 through 39, the fighting has reached the marketplace in Tlatelolco, where Tlatelolcan warriors make a heroic stance. The temple is burned down. The destruction and killing continues. By now it is clear how many other indigenous altepetl have joined the Spaniards and are eager to profit from the fall of Tenochtitlan and Tlatelolco. The Spaniards build a catapult, which does not work very well. After numerous contested battles and heroic feats, Quauhtemoc, the new Mexica tlatoani, and all the remaining high rulers consult among themselves about the tribute that they would pay the Spaniards, and how to surrender. Sadly, Quauhtemoc sets out in a boat to give himself up.

Chapter 40, presented here, describes the surrender of Quauhtemoc and the other native lords, who appear ragged and dirty. The Spaniards take many slaves, branding them as a sign of possession. Disease and starvation have ravaged the population.

Fortieth chapter, where it is said how the Tlatelolca and Tenochca and their ruler submitted to the Spaniards, and what happened when they were among them

And when they had captured him [Quauhtemoc] there and put him on land, all the Spaniards were waiting. They came to take him; the Spaniards grasped him by the hand, took him up to the roof, and stood him before the Captain [Cortés], the war leader. When they stood him before him, he looked at Quauhtemoctzin (Quauhtemoc), took a good look at him, stroked his hair; then they seated him next to him. And they fired off the guns; they hit no one, but they aimed over the people, the shots just went over their heads. Then they took a cannon, put it in a boat, and took it to the home of Coyohuehuetzin. When they got there, they took it up on the roof. Then again they killed people; many died there. But the Mexica just fled, and the war came to an end.

Then everyone shouted, saying, "It's over! Let everyone leave! Go eat!" When they heard this, the people departed; they just went into the water. But when they went out on the highway, again they killed some people, which angered the Spaniards; a few of them were carrying their shields and war clubs. Those who lived in houses went straight to Amaxac, where the road forks. There the people divided, some going toward Tepeyacac, some toward Xoxohuiltitlan, some toward Nonoalco. But no one went toward Xoloco and Maçatzintamalco.

And all who lived in boats and on platforms in the water and those at Tolmayeccan just went into the water. The water came up to the stomachs of some, to the chests of others, to the necks of others, and some sank entirely into the deep water.

The little children were carried on people's backs. There was a general wail; but some went rejoicing and amusing themselves as they went along the road. Most of the owners of boats left at night, though some left by day. They seemed to knock against one another as they went.

And along every stretch of road the Spaniards took things from people by force. They were looking for gold; they cared nothing for green-stone, precious feathers, or turquoise. They looked everywhere with the women, at their bottoms, under their skirts. And they looked everywhere with the men, under their loincloths and in their mouths. And the Spaniards took, picked out the beautiful women, those with yellow bodies. And some women only got away by covering their faces with mud and putting on ragged blouses and skirts, clothing themselves all in rags. And some men were picked out, those who were strong and in the prime of life, and those who were barely youths, to run errands for them and be their errand boys, their assistants. Then they burned (branded) some of them on the mouth; some they branded on the cheeks, some on the mouth.

And when the weapons were laid down and we collapsed, the year count was Three House, and the day count was One Serpent.

And when Quauhtemoctzin went to give himself up, they took him to Acachinanco; it was already dark. And the next day, when there was a little sun, the Spaniards came again, a great many of them; they too had reached the end. They came equipped for battle, with iron cuirasses and iron helmets, but not with their iron swords and their shields. They all came pressing narrow white cloths to their noses because the dead made them sick, for they smelled bad and stunk. They all came on foot, holding Quauhtemoctzin, Coanacochtzin, and Tetlepanquetzatzin by their cloaks; only the three of them came in line. And the Cihuacoatl Tlacotzin, the Tlillancalqui Petlauhtzin, the Huitznahuatl Motelchiuhtzin mexicatl, the Achcauhtli Teuctlamacazqui [senior lordly priest] Coatzin, and the treasurer Tlaçolyaotl guarded all the gold.

Then they went straight to Atactzinco, where the home of the warrior, the Tlacochcalcatl Coyohuehuetzin, was located. The Spaniards were in a long line. And when they reached the home of Coyohuehuetzin, they went up on the roof to a platform. Then they sat down. They placed a canopy of cloth over Cortés; then he sat down, and Marina sat beside him.

And Quauhtemoctzin was next to the Captain [Cortés]. He had tied on a shining maguey fiber cloak, each half different, covered with hummingbird feathers, Ocuillan style. It was very dirty; it was all he had. Then Coanacochtzin, the ruler of Tetzcoco, was next. He had tied on only a plain maguey-fiber cloak with a flowered border, with a spreading design of flowers; it too was very dirty. Next was Tetlepanquetzatzin, the ruler of Tlacopan, who likewise had tied on a maguey cloak; it too was dirty, very dirty . . .

The final chapter recounts how the frustrated victors are concerned with only one thing: they interrogate Quauhtemoc and the other lords about the location of more gold. The lords are at a loss to respond; they point out that the Spaniards had already taken all the gold from the palace. Nonetheless, Cortés demands two hundred pieces of gold – Tenochtitlan's first forced tribute payment. The destroyed city is impoverished. The final chapter of Book XII of the Florentine Codex ends on a somber note, as represented in the following excerpt:

When Moteuczoma was still alive, when there was a conquest somewhere, the Mexica, the Tlatelolca, the Tepaneca, and the Acolhuaque all went together. All of us, some Tepaneca, some Acolhuaque, and some people of the chinampas, moved together when we went to conquer, but when the altepetl [of Mexico Tenochtitlan] fell, then everyone came back, each one heading for his own altepetl.

3.2. Excerpt from the Nahuatl Annals of Tlatelolco[2]

The Annals of Tlatelolco *were first set down on paper in Nahuatl around the 1540s, at least two decades after the events that are described in its pages. It is thus*

2   Translated from Nahuatl by Lockhart (1993), modified slightly for this volume by Terraciano, with Lockhart's permission.

comparable to the Florentine Codex, which also was created by nobles from the altepetl of Tlatelolco. This excerpt confirms and extends the general Tlatelolcan perspective on the fall of Tenochtitlan and their own altepetl to the Spaniards, which was presented in the Florentine Codex. But this account is condensed and even more local in its patriotic portrayal of self. In brief, the Tlatelolca fought bravely, whereas the Tenochca (Mexica) ran and hid themselves. Almost needless to say, the Mexica would not have shared this view of the past. The obvious rivalry and bitterness between neighbors indicates that, despite being a part of the Mexica empire, the Tlatelolca did not identify themselves with the Mexica. In any case, this account suggests a sad ending for all.

The Spaniards established themselves permanently and began fighting us. After they had fought us for ten days, their boats appeared. For twenty days, the fighting was exclusively at Nonoalco, and second, at Maçatzintamalco. When their boats appeared, they appeared at Iztaccalco; at that time the people of Iztaccalco submitted; from there they came ahead this way, then they stationed the boats at Acachinanco. Then also the Huexotzinca and Tlaxcalans set up temporary huts for themselves there on both sides of the road.

Then the Tlatelolcan boats dispersed. The Nonoalca fought on the road, and there also was fighting at Maçatzintamalco, but at Xoxohuiltitlan and Tepeyacac no one fought. Only we Tlatelolca held the road when their boats arrived. The next day, they abandoned Xoloco. There was fighting for two days at Huitzillan.

At this time the Tenochca fought among themselves. They said to one another, "Where are our children? Are they going to use them in the war? Will they ever live to grow up?"

They quickly seized four people and began killing them. The first they killed was Quauhnochtli, leader at the Tlacatecco [temple of Huitzilopochtli]; then Quapan, leader at Huitznahuac [temple of Tezcatlipoca], and incense-offering priests; the priest at Amantlan; and the priest at Tlalocan. These are the ones who lost their lives the second time the Tenochca fought among themselves.

The Spaniards came and set up a gun in the middle of the road at Tecaman. They aimed it along the road in this direction; when they fired the gun, the shot landed at Quauhquiahuac.

Then all the Tenochca decamped. They took Huitzilopochtli in their arms and brought him into Tlatelolco, establishing him at the *telpochcalli* (youths' house) in Amaxac. And they set up their ruler Quauhtemoctzin (Quauhtemoc) at Yacacolco, and at that time all the common people left their former altepetl at Tenochtitlan; on coming into Tlatelolco they stopped among our houses; then they settled down everywhere against the walls of our houses and on our roofs.

And during all this time, while we were being attacked, the Tenochca appeared nowhere on all the roads here in Yacacolco, Atizaapan, Coatlan, Nonoalco, Xoxohuiltitlan and Tepeyacac. They became the responsibility of the Tlatelolca alone, and likewise the canals all became our exclusive responsibility.

And the Tenochca who were war captains cut off their hair to avoid recognition, and all the subordinate leaders cut their hair, and the scraped-heads and the Otomis wrapped up their heads. Nowhere did they show their faces during the time when we were being attacked; only all the Tlatelolca surrounded their leader.

And all their women also shamed and scolded the Tenochca, saying to them, "You are just lying there doing nothing, you have no shame. A woman will never decorate herself to be next to you." Their women went about weeping and begging the Tlatelolca; and seeing this, the people of the altepetl sent word, but nowhere did the Tenochca appear. They hid their faces.

But the Tlatelolca scraped-heads and the Otomis, the war leaders, were dying from the guns and iron bolts.

At this time we Tlatelolca set up skull racks; the skull racks were in three places. One was in the temple courtyard at Tlillan, where the heads of our lords [the Spaniards] were strung; the second place was in Yacacolco, where the heads of our lords were strung, along with the heads of two horses; the third place was in Cacatla, facing the Cihuateocalli [literally, "Woman Temple"]. It was the exclusive accomplishment of the Tlatelolca.

After this the Spaniards drove us from there and reached the marketplace. That was when the great Tlatelolca warriors were entirely vanquished. With that the fighting stopped once and for all.

That was when the Tlatelolca women all let loose, fighting, striking people, taking captives. They put on warriors' devices, all raising their skirts so that they could give pursuit. The fighting in the marketplace lasted ten days.

And all this is what happened to us and what we saw and beheld. What we suffered is cause for tears and sorrow. The water we drank was salt. Adobe bricks dipped in a well were a prized possession, guarded under a shield. If someone tried to toast something, it had to be guarded with a shield. We ate colorín wood, grass from the salt flats, adobe, lizards, mice, things full of dust. We fought over eating worms when they put them on the fire and their flesh began to cook; they picked them out of the fire and ate them.

And we had a price [as slaves]. There was a price for a youth, a priest, a maiden, or a little child. The price for any ordinary person was just two handfuls of shelled maize. Ten cakes of water flies or twenty of grass from the salt flats was our price. Gold, jade, tribute cloth, plumes, and all the precious things were considered as nothing and just spilled on the ground.

3.3. Images from the Lienzo of Tlaxcala[3]

The Lienzo of Tlaxcala images presented here were copies of an earlier sixteenth-century lienzo (painting on cloth) that is now lost. Native artists attempted to copy

---

3   From Torre, García Quintana, and Martínez Marín, eds. (1983). Commentary on images by Terraciano.

ycmoquayateq que tlatoque

3.3a The four Nahua *tlatoque* or lords of Tlaxcala receive the sacrament of communion. The four lords represent the four parts or constituent altepetl of the complex altepetl of Tlaxcala. Cortés and Malinche attend the ceremony, before images of Christ and the Virgin Mary. Courtesy of the Instituto Nacional de Antropología e Historia. Facsimile edition Torre, García, and Martínez 1983, p. 70.

Tlaxcallan.

3.3b Through Malinche, the translator, Cortés and a *tlatoani* of Tlaxcala negotiate an alliance in which the Spaniards receive gifts of food. Most of the lienzo is designed to document this historic alliance in the Conquest period. Courtesy of the Instituto Nacional de Antropología e Historia. Facsimile edition Torre, García, and Martínez 1983, p. 92.

3.3c The siege of Tepotzotlan. This battle is depicted as a joint conquest by Tlaxcalan warriors and Spaniards. In Nahuatl, the word *tepozotl* refers to a dwarf; hence, the depiction of a dwarf inside the palace. Malinche is armed with a sword and shield. Courtesy of the Instituto Nacional de Antropología e Historia. Facsimile edition Torre, García, and Martínez 1983, p. 85.

3.3d The siege of Quetzaltenanco. As the Conquest spread from central Mexico, the battle scenes in the Lienzo of Tlaxcala tend to contain more Tlaxcalan warriors and fewer Spaniards. Quetzaltenanco is located in present-day Guatemala. Courtesy of the Instituto Nacional de Antropología e Historia. Facsimile edition Torre, García, and Martínez 1983, p. 161.

the essentials of the original work. In any case, the intent of the paintings is clear: they wanted to portray themselves as faithful and indispensable allies of the Spaniards, and good Christians. They neglect to mention their own battles against the Spaniards but, rather, focus on how they went everywhere with Cortés and Malinche and other conquistadores to carry out the conquest of New Spain. The following scenes include a peace established between Tlaxcala and Cortés, in which Tlaxcala offers the Spaniards food and other items. The four representatives of the four altepetl of Tlaxcala offer Cortés an honorary Tlaxcalan headband when he and Malinche are seated as the new rulers of Tenochtitlan. Men and women dutifully and willingly receive baptism. Finally, Tlaxcalan warriors (identified by their red-and-white headbands) lead the attack of a given community. A variation of the last scene occurs repeatedly in the Lienzo, representing a different conquest of yet another altepetl. Thus, according to the Lienzo of Tlaxcala, the Tlaxcalans were conquistadores in their own right.

3.4. The Nahuatl Title of Mexicapan, Oaxaca[4]

Two communities in the Valley of Oaxaca attempted to lay claim to disputed territory by presenting competing titles, ostensibly written in the 1520s, to Spanish authorities in the 1690s. The titles present each community's account of the Spanish Conquest of Oaxaca and subsequent colonial events. This genre of indigenous writing, called the "primordial title," arose in response to late-colonial land verification programs, in which communities were required to furnish proof of possession in the form of official land titles, which were granted by the Spanish legal system. Having none, some communities manufactured titles, providing information that they thought a title should contain, including a discussion of how they came to occupy the land in question. Thus, primordial titles often draw on existing written records and local oral traditions to recover and represent the past, and tend to treat the conquest as a major event in the history of their communities.

This first Nahuatl-language title from Mexicapan (literally, place of the Mexica) recounts how four Nahua warriors, all named after legendary heroes from central Mexico, responded to a call for help from the great "Noblewoman of the Zapotec" in distant Oaxaca. She complained that the Mixtecs threatened her people and had cannibalized members of a previous rescue party. The warriors appeared before Hernando Cortés, the "Ruler of the Children of the Sun," and sought to convince him by staging a mock battle that they could succeed where others had failed. Impressed by this show of force, Cortés sent them into battle. They fought their way through the mountainous Mixteca and descended into the Valley of Oaxaca, where they defeated the Mixtecs with the help of a windstorm and an earthquake. In victory, they were given a place for their descendants to settle. But when Cortés came to Oaxaca, the alliance disintegrated and the Spaniards and Nahuas prepared for war. As the fighting

---

4   Translated from Nahuatl by Sousa and Terraciano. The original document is in AGN-Tierras 236, 6. See Sousa and Terraciano (2003) for a transcription and translation of the document, an analysis of its contents, and a discussion of the titles genre.

began, the Nahuas frightened and confounded the Spaniards by unleashing a flood of water from underground. After the Spaniards sued for peace, the Nahuas proudly proclaimed that they had defeated everyone and had even captured a few African slaves. These "famous Mexicans" called their victory the "original conquest."

This version of the conquest tries to explain how Mexicapan came to possess its land, without admitting defeat to anyone at anytime. Mexicapan was a satellite community whose ancestors apparently accompanied the Spaniards during the Conquest of Oaxaca and were given some land to settle as a reward. They argue that they defeated the Mixtecs on their own, however, even before Cortés came to Oaxaca, by helping out the Zapotecs. And then they took on the Spaniards and taught them a lesson, too. Incidentally, we do know of a Zapotec-Mexica marriage alliance in the decades before the Spaniards arrived. As in most titles, legend and history are intertwined in Mexicapan's version of the distant past. And as with many indigenous versions of the Conquest, defeat is never admitted. Written nearly two centuries after the arrival of the Spaniards, the following two titles offer a fascinating glimpse into the social memory of a community.

I, the Noblewoman of the Zapotec, went to ask the Great Ruler of the Children of the Sun named Cortés about the people who hate me, make war on me and all my children, and want to steal my land and property. It is true that I went before our Great Ruler of the Children of the Sun named Cortés, and asked him to assist me by sending his people against the Mixtec people. When our Great Ruler of the Children of the Sun named Cortés heard [our request], he sent seven of his children, who perished. The second time he sent four more, who helped me. It is true that the Mexican people, likewise, will know of my story. It is true that I gave them and their children a place to settle, so that no one would make war on their children. It will be their property. Thus, I advised the Mexican people to write on paper exactly how it was given to them, because they won it. The Mixtec people who waged war on me surrendered because they [the Mexican people] defeated them. It is true that they surrendered, for the Mexican people will tell you in stories how they were given a place for their children to settle. It is true that when these people helped us, we asked if they would settle next to us. None of the Mixtecs wanted to accept them [the Mexican people], so they gave them a portion of their land, called Acatepetl, to settle. It is true that we left them with that, and now they have their property. Thus they won it and have settled it. As to how they won it, the Children of the Sun know how they came bearing log drums, shields, obsidian-blade clubs, and arrows. It was done joyously through war, as they wished. They were recognized as the truly famous Mexicans. It is true that it happened, because I requested it of our Great Ruler of the Children of the Sun. It is true that they [the Mixtecs] killed my children and ate them. Likewise, my children who encountered these Mixtec cannibals were beheaded. Therefore, I went to the Children of the Sun and asked them to help me. It is truly my land and no one is to steal it. What I requested from our Great Ruler of the Children of the Sun was done.

Thus, the Mexican people know it and will tell others in stories what happened to us.

First, the leaders requested it. I, Tlacahuepantzin, along with my brother, Tonalyeyecatzin, and my two cousins, Chimalpopoca and Axayacatzin, conferred as to how we would go to ask our Great Ruler of the Children of the Sun, and how the Noblewoman of the Zapotec came to request that he send his children to help her. He sent seven, of which three were eaten and four others perished. Therefore, we went before the [Ruler of the] Children of the Sun Cortés and all four of us requested that he send us, for we dared to wage war on the Mixtec people. The [Ruler of the] Children of the Sun responded: "How will it be possible [to wage war] with just four when seven have perished?" We answered him that we four would win it through war. The [Ruler of the] Children of the Sun asked us [to demonstrate] how we would be able to do it. We joyously consented to stage [a mock battle] in the presence of the [Ruler of the] Children of the Sun. He ordered us: "Enter the fortress and wage war." We entered with log drums, wielding shields, obsidian-blade clubs, and arrows, and wearing stone sandals. We went in and sought the approval of our Great Ruler of the Children of the Sun. He responded that perhaps what we assembled was good enough, perhaps it would be enough to engage them [in battle]. We responded: "Good." Then he said to us: "If you do it joyfully, perhaps you will truly win land for your children." Then we staged [the mock battle] and advised the [Ruler of the] Children of the Sun not to be frightened by our actions. He said: "I will not be frightened." And then we started to play with shields, obsidian-blade clubs, and arrows. The [Ruler of the] Children of the Sun said: "That's enough, it is true that they will win the land." He truly believed it, so he sent us.

First, the four of us left and arrived in the Mixteca, where we won a little land for our children. Then we four emerged and went to war. We and the Noblewoman of the Zapotec enriched ourselves. We reached Totoltepetl, where our log drums sounded. The Mixtec people heard it. They asked: "What's that sound?" They were told that the Mexican people had arrived. They [the Mixtecs] asked: "What are they looking for? Let's go see." So they came to ask us [the Mexican people] why we came and what we sought. We responded that we came to see our land next to the Zapotec, and to see who is fighting with them and wants to steal our land. Then they replied: "We are the Mixtecs. What do you want, war?" We responded: "War it will be." Then they instructed us where and which day to meet them, so that we could play. They would advise their children which day to do battle, as they informed us. We flew to the hill near the place called Mexicatepelyan, on the right hand-side, where we beat the log drums. They heard the war song and assembled. Then, on both sides, the war leaders summoned the women and children. When they came to where we were, we started the battle. The wind blew and the earth moved, and they were killed. We withdrew only when the Mixtec people said: "Let it be, for you are truly the famous Mexican people.

We give you a place where your children can settle." Then they gave us our land, up to where it [now] ends. They gave it to us. We responded how we and the Zapotec people would settle once and for all. Then the Mixtec people said: "It will not be possible. Let the Zapotec stay next to us and we will give you another place to settle." It is true that we said that we would settle next to our children, so that none of them would be killed, and that we would regard it as our property. Then they replied to us: "It will be all right after all." We left and consulted with the Ruler of the Mixtec people in order to live as brothers, so that we would not kill each other. Then we said: "Let it be done. Let them also give us a place to wait for our children to be brought to settle. We will not turn back. we will await our children. Never again will there be war." Then they gave us a place to settle called Acatepetl, where the four of us went and waited for our children to come.

It is true that we went to rest near the hill called Huaxacatzin; also, they [the Spaniards] sat down and rested. It was there that they first sought to fight us. We climbed up Acatepec, where we met those who had won the land. He [Cortés] rebuked us: "Who would kill us and who wants to make us slaves?" At that very moment we raised the water through a reed from below the ground. Cortés saw how nobody dared to kill us. Then he told us: "Let there be no more war. Let us live as brothers. We shall settle willingly beside the Mexicans, as brothers." When they saw the water [still] ascending, the Spaniards were angry that we raised the water over the hill. They began to battle with great strength and fought us until we, the Mexican people, defeated the Children of the Sun. Then they said: "That is enough, let it be." He [Cortés] declared: "You are truly the famous Mexican people." We believe in the true ruler God.

Just like the Spaniards we died in battle and we sought war.
We captured two blacks.
Also, like the Spaniards, we won it with war and gunpowder.

We three rulers decreed it: first, the Ruler of the Marquésado, don Fabián de Cervantes; the Ruler of San Martín Mexicapan, don Francisco de los Ángeles Vásquez; and the Ruler of Xochimilco, don Marcos de los Ángeles. It is true that once and for all we decreed as God commanded, along with the King, as to how an alguacil mayor and an alguacil [would] be responsible for three places: Xochimilco, San Martín and the Marquésado. It is his duty to patrol, and to punish and jail those who are bad each Thursday. It will be his duty to respect us, to serve us food, and to provide us with drink on every single Thursday. In this manner we established our cabildo. It is true that the way in which it is done must never stop. It will always be the alguacil mayor alone who will keep a record of all borders marked with crosses, and with his account he will shed light on the painting. Then he will serve food and provide people with drink, and the people of San Pedro and San Jacinto will notify him as to what he should bring. They will bring a little honey, as is necessary. Thus, it will be done as obligated.

These are all the orders that we three have set forth for our children and grandchildren to keep forever. This original conquest will be in their hands. We three provide our signatures in this altepetl cabecera. We three witnessed our written document. I am the tlatoani of this altepetl of San Martín. [In] the year of 1525.

> don Fabián de Cervantes y Velásquez
> don Francisco de los Ángeles Vásquez
> don Marcos de los Ángeles

3.5. The Mixtec Title of Chapultepec, Oaxaca[5]

The Mixtec community of Chapultepec submitted this document, accompanied by a painting, to refute Mexicapan's claim to conquest. They rejected the Nahua version and offered their own account of these events. They claimed to have welcomed and honored Cortés when he came to Oaxaca; they even gave him and his men some land to settle. All was well until Cortés returned with a group of Nahuas from central Mexico, with whom they began to fight. The Spaniards intervened only after the Mixtecs had forced the Nahuas to surrender. The Mixtec ruler cooperated with Cortés and accommodated everyone's interests. Thereafter, Mixtecs, Nahuas, Zapotecs, and Spaniards coexisted peacefully in the Valley of Oaxaca. In contrast to Mexicapan's version, the Mixtecs were already in the Valley of Oaxaca, and did not need to claim that they came from anywhere.

The protagonist of the title is don Diego Cortés Dzahui Yuchi, the lord of this community at the time of the Conquest, who adopted the name of the Spanish conqueror while retaining his own Mixtec name, Dzahui Yuchi (Rain Flint). Don Diego portrays himself as a faithful Spanish ally and the brave defender of his community against the bellicose Nahuas who, in the end, were forced to make an agreement with him. The pictorial portion of the title shows don Diego protecting himself with a coat of arms; the painting evokes some of the iconographic conventions and motifs of a pre-Conquest–style or early colonial painting, such as the seated male and female couples and the use of place glyphs. But the resulting hybrid composition, which combines European style and relies on alphabetic text, is undoubtedly a late-colonial work. The "place of guaxe trees" referred to in the text was called Ñunduhua in Mixtec, Huaxyacac in Nahuatl, and Oaxaca in Spanish (based on the Nahuatl).

Title of don Diego Cortés of the *ñuu* (local state or community) of San Juan Yuchayta and the barrio of Santa Ana. When our lord [Hernando] Cortés first

---

5   Translated from Mixtec by Terraciano. The original document is in AGN-Tierras 236, 6. See Sousa and Terraciano (2003) for a transcription and translation of the document and an analysis of its contents and the accompanying map.

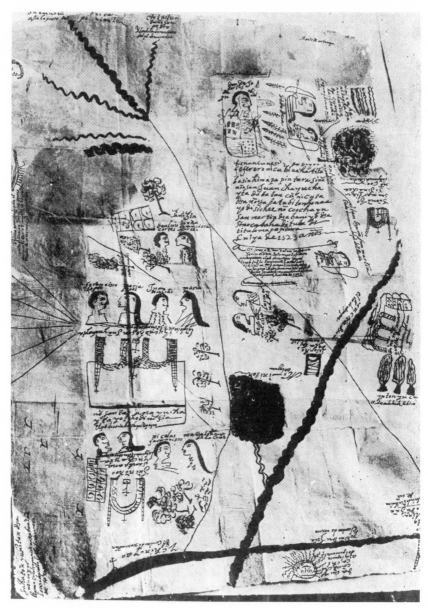

3.5 The Mixtec Map of Chapultepec, drawn c. 1690 but dated 1523. Courtesy of the Archivo General de la Nación. AGN-Tierras 236, 6.

arrived with a crowd of white people, he came to our *ñuu tayu* (*tayu* is short for *yuhuitayu*, a complex community). Then he came out to meet us and to name us. He received and named our *yya* (lord) don Diego Cortés Dzahui Yuchi.

The yya don Diego Cortés was baptized and, second, all the nobles were baptized and, third, all the commoners were baptized.... Then, at first, he founded a city at the place called Ñocuisi, because there was no water where the Spaniards lived, those who made war at the place of the guaxe trees.

And then don Diego Cortés responded in a noble manner before all the great ones: "I, lord don Diego Cortés, shall give you a gift." Then we lived together in peace with the white people, the great ones, and we gave them a place to build the big church.

The second time that our lord [Hernando] Cortés came he brought many Mexicans from the head palace of Mexico City, all in the company of our lord Cortés. When they arrived in our ñuu, we went to fight with the Mexicans at the hill called Saminoo (Mixtec term for Mexica). We were defended by arrows from Yuchaticaha (Cuilapan), and Noyoo (Xoxocotlan) also supported us when we encountered the Mexicans.

And then the Spaniards arrived. They stopped our fighting when we defeated the Mexicans. Only because of the will of our lord [Hernando] Cortés, the Marqués, we gave the Mexicans some land to settle. The Ñudzahui (Mixtecs) of the ñuu of San Juan Yuchayta (Chapultepec), the barrio of Santa Ana, and the barrio of Yucucuii, were the three barrios belonging to me, don Diego de Cortés Dzahui Yuchi. Half of the commoners will settle there in the *cabecera* of Yuchaticaha the old (Cuilapan), and the other half will settle there at the entrance of the ñuu of Ñuyoo (Xoxocotlan), the large ñuu which borders with the yuhuitayu of San Juan Yuchayta (Chapultepec).

I, don Diego de Cortés, have given half of the lands belonging to us to the Mexican nobles of the tayu ñuu of San Martín. It is a large ñuu with seven barrios, which is one of the four parts or cabeceras belonging to our lord the Marqués [Hernando Cortés]. Today, I mark the borders before all the nobles and elders of San Juan Yuchayta. I, don Diego de Cortés, will-fully give my lands on which my grandchildren and great-grandchildren will live.

Thus, today, I guard the title that belongs to me, don Diego Cortés, and my map, which I entrust to the hands of all the nobles of my ñuu, San Juan Yuchayta. Let them acquire the tribute in gold for our lord Marqués, and for my grandchildren and great-grandchildren to keep and guard, to record and recount what pertains to the lordly title. He who attempts to interfere with our lord Marqués will be fined three hundred pesos, for the title belongs to the ñuu. It is said and done.

Diego Cortés, before me don Luis de Salazar, notary.

Today, Tuesday, the eighth day of the month of February, 1523.

[Mixtec-language text on the map from Chapultepec]

Today, Monday, the eighth day of the month of February, the title and painted map belonging to the ñuu and tayu of San Juan Yuchayta were made, concerning all the borders † agreed upon and recognized by the Mexican people of the tayu of San Martín [Mexicapan]. Thus we conclude our title and painted map in the year of 1523.

3.6. The Title of Motul, a Pech Maya Account of the Conquest[6]

Like the Conquest accounts from Oaxaca (documents 3.4 and 3.5), the following narrative of the Spanish invasion of Yucatan was written down as a result of a dispute over land. The surviving Maya-language text was written in the eighteenth century, supposedly from a sixteenth-century original, although the text may have gone through several generations of copies in the centuries between. The narrative views the conquest from the perspective of the Maya cah (town, community) of Motul and of the Maya dynasty named Pech. Motul was one of the prominent settlements in the northwestern corner of the Yucatan peninsula that had been ruled by the Pech dynasty before the conquest. After Spaniards established a colony that included the Pech kingdom, Pech nobles continued to dominate the region through control over cah governorships, even though most of the tribute they received from their subjects was passed on to Spanish colonial administrators in the nearby provincial capital of Merida.

The purpose of the Title of Motul is to promote the continued legitimacy of the Pech dynasty by presenting the region's ruler or king as not only receptive to the Spanish invasion but also as some kind of prophet who anticipated the coming of Christianity. The Pech perspective thus omits the fierce resistance that Spaniards met in their failed invasions of the 1520s and 1530s, emphasizing instead the Spanish-Pech alliance of 1541 that permitted the Spaniards to found Merida in 1542. This alliance also allowed Pech nobles to lead Maya warriors against other Maya groups to the east and south, campaigns to which the Title of Motul alludes. The rival dynasties of Xiu and Cocom, whose kingdoms lay to the south of the Pech and who resisted Spanish incursion longer than did the Pech, are portrayed here as less cooperative and reliable than the Pech.

The year 1541.

This is the declaration of how the Spaniards came here to this land, through the will of our lord, the ruler God, here in this province. It is also

---

6   Translated from Yucatec Maya by Restall. This text forms a part of the larger pair of manuscripts, the Pech histories dubbed by Restall the Titles of Chicxulub and Yaxkukul. The Title of Motul is included in the Chicxulub manuscript in TLH and TULAL (photostat copies, Regíl manuscript): pp. 12–15, and in the 1769 Yaxkukul manuscript in TULAL: ff. 7r–8r. An earlier version of this translation appeared in Restall (1998: 121–25). The original text is untitled; the heading "the Title of Motul" is Restall's (Martínez Hernández 1926: 25 titles it "Chronicle of Ah Naum Pech, named don Francisco de Montejo Pech, Cacique [i.e., governor] of Motul").

the statement of our lord *señor* don Juan de Montejo, and don Francisco de Montejo, who were the first to come here to this land and also to order the building of churches in the head-town and cahob [towns] of every district, a *cah* home [town hall], and a temple for our lord, the great ruler, and also a town guesthouse, a home for travelers.

It is likewise the account of our great lord, Ah Naum Pech, don Francisco de Montejo Pech, and don Juan Pech, as were their names when they were baptized by the padres. And the *adelantado*, the first captain of those who came here to this land of Yucal Peten – given the name of Yucatan by the first lord Spaniards – and our lord Spaniards likewise declare that this indeed is what was done. When they said that we are to live eternally with God, the Maya people, as they were called, heard them.

Naum Pech then spoke to his subjects of every district: "Know that one deity is coming to the town, to the province; the true God; by the sign of the true God will you live! Welcome him! Do not wage war against him! Offer up your food or drink – maize, chickens, turkeys, honey, and beans to eat – so that Christianity may enter the town and that we may be servants of God." They then agreed that nobody would wage war but that they would commit themselves to going and helping the Spaniards in their conquests and to travelling together with the foreigners.

Likewise Nachi Cocom, of the town that headed the district of Sotuta in the province that was called Chichen Itza, and Ah Cohuoh Cocom, assisted the word of God and our great ruler, raising up the standards and banners of our great ruler and of the conquest. And so the adelantado [Montejo] and our lords the padres, the clergy assigned to the towns, also did not make war, but refrained from evil, and laid out a temple and homes for their town subjects.

Nadzi Mabun Chan also established in his district the understanding of how eternal life was coming to the town, and wished that truly would be delivered to God the Catzin and Chul people of the district of Mani, as well as the Tutul Xiu, and here to the east those of Lakin Chel and Cupul, and Nadzaycab Canul in Campeche. Thus was this province here redeemed by its service to God.

Here on the mound, the home, of Sacmutixtun of Sacuholpatal, here in this town, Tunal Pech of Motul settled. And here Ah Naum Pech called the young men and said to them: "Know that One Imix is the name of the day when, at dawn, there will come from the eastern districts bearded men carrying the sign of one deity to the province! Go and receive them with your white pendants! Do not make war on them! Go and receive them with true joy!" Therefore they went and journeyed beneath the trees, beneath the branches, until they arrived at the patio of Nadzaycab Canul in Campeche. Then they told him: "Your guests are coming very soon, Ah Nadzaycab Canul; receive them promptly, O lord!" That is what they said. When the ships appeared at the entrance to the port of Campeche, and when they saw the waving of the banners and white pendants, they knelt down before the adelantado.

Then they were asked by the Christians and the adelantado, in the Castilian language, "Where do you live?" As they did not understand the language, they could only reply, "We do not understand what you are saying." Because of these words, they said that this land here of the wild turkey, this land of the deer, was Yucatan.

Therefore the captains and our lord the adelantado don Francisco de Montejo went on; and they made much cloth and thread to cut into clothing for the horses, as they wished to go to the town of Mani, where Ah Tutul Xiu was. When they reached Yiba, they confered in Yiba; leaving Becal, they arrived at Nohcacab; thus the Spaniards passed through and arrived at Mani, where Tutul Xiu was. And he then appointed Officer Ikeb, Officer Caixicum, and Officer Chuc to go and invite Ah Cuat Cocom. As a result, they were put in a cave by his subordinates and their eyes were put out beneath a large sapote tree. Then they took one of them whose eyes had not been put out at the sapote, and in Weasel Cave they put out his eyes. Then they set them on the road to go groping to where the adelantado was in Mani; thus returned those who were thrown out of the town of Ah Cuat Cocom. Then Ah Naum Pech left with two of them and went to bring Ah Cuat Cocom. When they arrived, he said to Ah Naum Pech that he had neither seen nor heard of the incident; he said he had gone to Chichen Itza. Straight away he was brought by the Pech and arrived at Mani to give up the prisoners; Ah Cocom quickly said that he had not seen what had happened in his town and that he had given authorization for those who had committed the crime to be seized.

Then Ah Pech came to the towns in order to see his subject people; there he had come when the foreigners also came, because it happened that a foreigner had been killed by his subordinates. Then they passed on and went to where Ah Batun Pech and Cay Chel were; having seen them, they went to Maxtunil, where Nachi May and Ah Macan Pech were. They then returned to their lands in their jurisdiction of Yaxkukul, so as not to abandon the deputies. In Tixkumcheil they did not give up building a palisade around the town because they did not want foreigners in the town. Therefore Ah Naum Pech stayed put in Yaxkukul, for he was not envious of them; those of the town at Tixkumcheil had always been treated like dogs; their end was shown by the will of God in the towns.

3.7. A Chontal Maya Account of the Conquest, Excerpted from the Title of Acalan-Tixchel, 1612[7]

Although the Spaniards under the Montejos did not establish a permanent colony in Yucatan until the 1540s, they attempted a series of invasions beginning in 1527, while

7   Translated from Chontal Maya by Restall. An earlier version of this translation appeared in Restall (1998: 62–68); the excerpt is, in the original document, AGI-Mexico 138 (reproduced in facsimile in Scholes and Roys 1948: between 366 and 367): ff. 71v–75r. The passage recounting the events leading to the death of Quauhtemoc is also reproduced and discussed in Restall (2003: 147–56).

a large Spanish-Nahua expedition under Cortés passed along the base of the peninsula in 1525 (the narrative here erroneously gives Cortés his son's name and misdates the expedition). Cortés's purpose was not to conquer the Chontal Maya kingdom but to resupply his expedition before continuing on across northern Guatemala into Honduras. The visit of 1525 was the Chontal Mayas' first encounter with the Spanish empire, and its events set the tone for how the Chontal kings of the Paxbolon dynasty would accommodate Spanish colonial demands while preserving local autonomy as much as possible.

The key moment in 1525 is the decision by the Chontal king, Paxbolonacha, not to join Quauhtemoc, the captive Mexica emperor, in an uprising against the Spaniards, but instead to betray the Aztec lord to Cortés. Spanish and Nahua accounts of Quauhtemoc's death omit any mention of a Maya role in the story, so it is not clear how crucial a part Paxbolonacha really played. Still, as tempting as it may be to condemn Paxbolonacha for his decision, it is clear that he acted in the best interests of his people. The narrative that follows, the sole surviving copy of which was written down in 1612 in Chontal Maya (a language very similar to Yucatec), details how the region became gradually incorporated into the colony of Yucatan without any apparent invasion or settlement of Spaniards. Indeed, the Chontal Mayas are portrayed as taking the initiative in becoming Christian converts, whereas the text emphasizes their cooperative response to the demands of the early encomenderos of the region.

The Castilian men arrived in the year 1527. Their captain was named don Martín Cortés. They entered near Tenosique and passed by Tachix, emerging at the border of the lands of Çacchutte, and stopping for a while in the cah of Tuxakha. While staying there with their followers, they called for the summoning of Paxbolonacha, the aforementioned ruler. He assembled all his officers and rulers of his lands – the ruler of Tadzunum, the ruler of Atapan, and the ruler of Taçacto – because nothing could be done without informing these rulers of the aforementioned four subject communities. Thus they listened to what he began to tell them, to the statement by their principal ruler; he discussed with them what would be best for them under his rule, considering that he had been summoned by the Capitán del Valle [Cortés], the Castilian man, who was in the town of Tuxakha. They said it was not appropriate for their ruler to go, as they did not know what the Castilian man wanted. Then one of the rulers, one named Ruler Palocem, stood [and said], "Stay in your realm and in your town!"

Then he went before the Captain [Cortés] with some principal men named Patzinchiciua, Tamalbinyan, Paxuanapuk, and Paxhochacchan, companions of the ruler Palocem. When they appeared before the Castilian man, the Capitán del Valle, some of the Castilian men would not accept them, for someone must have told the Castilian men that the ruler was not there. Therefore the Captain said to them, "Let the ruler come, for I wish to see him. I do not come to make war; I wish only to go and see the whole country. I will be good to him if he receives me well." This he said to the men who had come on behalf of their ruler, who returned to tell their ruler Paxbolonacha, who was in the cah of Itzamkanac. All the rulers of the province's towns were thus gathered together – this was for the second time – and he said to them, "Fine! I shall go and see and hear what he wants, the Castilian man who has come."

And so the ruler Paxbolonacha went. And the Capitán del Valle went out to meet him with many gifts – honey, turkeys, maize, copal, and a great quantity of fruit. Then he said to Ruler Paxbolon, "I have come here to your lands, for I am sent by the lord of the earth, the emperor seated on his throne in Castile; he sends me to see the land and those who live in it, not for the purpose of wars. I wish only to ask for the way to Ulua, to the land where gold and plumage and cacao come from, as I have heard." Then he [Paxbolonacha] replied that it would be good if he left, but that he should come first to his land, to his home, to his town, where they would discuss what would be best. "Let us rest first," the Capitán del Valle then told him; therefore they rested for twenty days.

The ruler Quauhtemoc was there, having come with him [Cortés] from Mexico. And it happened that he said to the aforementioned ruler Paxbolonacha, "My lord ruler, these Castilian men will one day give you much misery and kill your people. In my opinion we should kill them, for I bring many officers and you also are many." This is what Quauhtemoc said to Paxbolonacha, ruler of the people of Tamactun, who, upon hearing this speech of Quauhtemoc's, replied that he would first think about what he wished to do about his speech. And, in considering his speech fully, he observed that the Castilian men behaved well, that they neither killed a single man nor beat a single man, and that they wished only to be given honey, turkey hens, maize, and various fruits, day after day. Thus he concluded, "I cannot therefore display two faces, two hearts, to the Castilian men." But Quauhtemoc, the aforementioned ruler from Mexico, continued to press him about it, for he wished to kill the Castilian men. Because of this, the ruler Paxbolonacha told the Capitán del Valle, "My lord Capitán del Valle, this ruler Quauhtemoc who is with you, observe him so that he does not revolt and betray you, for three or four times he talked to me about killing you." Upon hearing these words the Capitán del Valle seized him [Quauhtemoc] and had him bound in chains. He was in chains for three days. Then they baptized him. It is not known what his baptismal name was; some say he was named don Juan and some say he was named don Hernando. After being named, his head was cut off, and it was impaled on a ceiba tree in front of the pagan temple at Yaxdzan.

Then the Capitán del Valle [Cortés] came with the ruler Paxbolonacha and all the Castilian men and all the indigenous men, and they arrived at the city of Itzamkanac. While they were there they determined where a bridge could be made in order to cross our river, which was one league wide. And thus they filled up the swamp land in order to cross the river. It was finished in four days because they were very many men. They also cleared the way as far as Cehach, and two officers – named Çelutapech and Macuaaua – were sent to organize things. Çelutapech died – he was killed by the Cehach men – but Macuaaua, his aforementioned companion, escaped and returned to the town of Itzamkanac. For this reason, the Castilian men went on with trepidation in their hearts, but as they killed five or six of the [Cehach] soldiers upon arriving in Cehach, it was Cehach men who cleared the way through to Tah Itza. Thus the Castilian men reached the entrance to the island, but when they saw that they could not cross [the lake], they came back and took the route that emerged at Champoton.

A year after the Castilian man, the Capitán del Valle, passed through here, the ruler Paxbolonacha went to a certain town named Tachakam, where he died. Having died, he was placed in a canoe by his people, who brought him to their city of Itzamkanac, where they buried him. This ruler had been dead three years when other Castilian men came, passing through the same way the Capitán del Valle had passed through, entering at Tachiix and emerging at the town of Çacchutte. It was not known which of those who came was their captain, but Francisco Gil, Lorenzo Godoy, and Julián Doncel were the principals and leaders of the Castilian men. When they reached the town, they asked for the ruler; they were told, "he is dead." So they asked for his sons, who were brought before them. The oldest of the sons was named Pachimalahix, the second, Alamatazel, and the youngest, Paxtun. They placed the eldest of the aforementioned sons in prison for two days and told him that he should give them tribute. And thus turkeys and maize, honey, copal, beans, squash seeds, and many other things, countless things, were given to them. Then they crossed the bridge, just as the Captain [Cortés] had crossed the river.

The adelantado [Montejo] did not pass through Acalan, through Tamactun; only his deputy arrived and went on to Champoton, where they [the Chontal Mayas of Acalan] went to see them [the Spaniards], and they stayed there a long time. They brought tribute and many times returned to assist them there at the aforementioned Champoton. Then they [the Spaniards] went to Yucatan to conquer its lands. Then Pachimalahix died, at which time the rulership went to Alamatazel. During the period of his governorship the padres fray Luis de Villalpando, fray Juan de la Puerta, and fray Lorenzo de Bienvenida arrived. These padres came at a time when they [the Mayas] had not yet destroyed and finished with listening to the words of their own priests. The Castilian men came with the padres to conquer the land; they came to bring the truly true god and his word. They taught the people that already our gods were destroyed and the day had already come when their worship would be ended: "You will never again see them worshipped, and he who does worship them lives a life of deceit; anyone who does worship them will be really punished. For they have had their time. Therefore nobody shall deceive the people, for that time has now passed."

All the principal men and the ruler and all the towns under their jurisdiction heard what those priests said.

Then the ruler Alamatazel died, but only after he had assembled all the principal men together and declared to them that he was dying with sorrow in his heart, for he had not seen the singular faith of Christianity. As my life is ending, I entreat you to serve one god. I have seen and heard the word of the priests; it will not be destroyed and ended. The truth and goodness of their statements is becoming realized. Therefore you should seek and bring the preaching padres to preach to you and teach you." After making this speech the ruler Alamatazel died.

Then the rulership went to Paxtun, his younger brother and the son of Paxbolonacha. He heard the news of the teaching and the baptizing by the padres. And having discussed it with all his rulers, he gathered the town officers to go look for the padre in Campeche; and so the ruler Paxtun went with his lieutenants to seek the padre who was in Campeche. God wished it that the day after they reached Chinil, padre fray Diego de Béjar arrived from Tabasco. They met him there and declared to him, "My lord and father, we have come here to seek you for the sake of all our children; we have come, leaving behind our home, our land of Acalan – whose second name is Tamactun – to fetch you so that you will come and explain to our ears and teach us of the word of that god Dios, for we have already heard news that men are being baptized by you padres. We wish this too and thus we have come to seek you." Thus spoke the ruler Paxtun and his companions.

Having heard what these men said, the padre fray Diego de Béjar replied, "My sons, it gives me much pleasure that you wish to take your souls out of the hands of the devils and that you wish to hear and understand the word of God, for such a duty and burden is mine and that of us padres. But I cannot come with you right away, as I have my duties with my fellow padres. Therefore you would be well advised to return, for I will soon come back, either to Campeche or to Champoton, where I will meet whomever you may send for me." This was what the padre said. Therefore they went back to their lands at Acalan Tamactun.

When one month had come to pass, which was the time designated for the fetching of the padre by canoe, they reached Campeche, to the pleasure of the other padres. Thus fray Diego de Béjar came, arriving at Tamactun Acalan on the 20th of April of the year 1550; and his arrival brought great pleasure to all the people. Immediately all the principal men were gathered together – Kintencab, Çelutholcan, Buluchatzi, Caltzin, Catanatz, Papcan – the principal men were called together by the padre, [who said], "My sons, I am aware that in order to seek me and bring me you went a long way, a journey of ten or fifteen days. I am pleased to be with you, although I have endured the miseries of the road and the canoe. First of all I must tell you that you cannot worship two lords, two fathers; only one father is to be loved. I have come to tell you, to explain, that the one single God is three in one person – God the Father, God the Son, God the Holy Spirit – who created the invisible heaven." And he told them other things about the word of God. "I wish you all to come and show me your devils." Having heard what the padre told them, they began to bring and display their devils, including the devil of the ruler Cukulchan, also the devil of Tadzunum, the devil of Tachabtte, the devil of Atapan, Taçacto, and the other devils, all of which were brought before fray Diego de Béjar – who burned them. Then he began to teach them to recite and sing the Paternoster, the Ave Maria, the Credo, the Salve, and the articles of the faith.

Then they were given their names. The ruler was named don Pedro Paxtun; Kintencab [the priest Tencab] was named don Mateo; and Caltzin was named don Francisco. And thus they became Christians.

The devils which had been buried in secret places by the people – such as a devil called Ek Chuah, another called Tabay, also the devil Ix Chel, and Cabtanilcabtan, and many other devils in these places – were sought out in all the towns of the jurisdiction. The guardians of the devils went to fetch them to be burned, for those men who kept them were imprisoned and beaten before the eyes of all the people. In this way the devils disappeared. Some willingly caused them to disappear; others caused them to disappear out of fear.

As already written in the document, beginning with the second time the Castilian men passed through Acalan Tamactun – when Francisco Gil, Lorenzo Godoy, and Julián Doncel passed through – from then on tribute was taken and paid in Tabasco every six months. Also every two months there was another which was not a fixed assessment, but still they took as tribute canoes and paddles, honey, copal, hens, cotton blankets, beans, maize, squash seeds, chiles, cotton, calabashes. Whatever else they wanted to be given, of both food and drink, they took as tribute to Tabasco – to him, Palma. Then the town was placed in the hands of Diego de Aranda. We do not know who placed the town in the jurisdiction of Campeche, but Diego de Aranda ordered us to send the tribute there to Campeche. When Diego de Aranda died, Francisca de Velasco [his widow] married Antón García; Antón García ordered us to take and pay tribute at Chilapa.

4

POLITICAL LIFE

Throughout the colonial period, native peoples greatly outnumbered Spaniards in Mesoamerica. How were the colonists therefore able to rule these indigenous subjects? This question can in large part be answered by the existence of a single institution: the native *cabildo* or municipal council. The native council consisted of many of the eligible male nobles who had performed similar tasks before the Conquest. They served as intermediaries between their communities and Spanish officials, especially the Spanish *alcalde mayor*, who acted as a resident first-instance judge and tax collector in a given jurisdiction. With his supporting staff of deputies, notaries, and translators, he interacted regularly with members of the native cabildo. Spaniards asserted a monopoly on regional politics, creating a network of colonial political jurisdictions across New Spain; but by and large they left the business of day-to-day politics and government at the local level to the old native ruling classes. This fact served to strengthen the centrality of the semiautonomous Mesoamerican community – called the *altepetl* in Nahuatl, the *ñuu* in Mixtec, the *cah* in Yucatec Maya, and so on. It also limited the nature of relations among the various communities, however.

The adoption of the Spanish-style municipal council by the hereditary nobility of New Spain meant that, despite the destruction of the Mexica imperial capital of Tenochtitlan in 1521, and the construction of Mexico City upon its ruins, a Mexica altepetl of Tenochtitlan (also called Mexico) continued to exist within the new city – complete with its own ruling council, divided into four parts along traditional lines. Members of the native cabildo were elected annually from a limited pool of eligible male nobles (who represented about 5–10 percent of the population). The highest offices were rotated among the most prestigious nobles in a *cabecera* (head community) and its various *sujetos* (subject settlements), based on the Spanish sociopolitical reorganization.

As document 4.1 shows, the town council included members of the old Mexica royalty, the Moteuczoma family. Yet the integrity and authority of native cabildos did not go unchallenged. In document 4.1, the Mexica town councillors are forced to petition to retain control over local municipal government, whereas in documents 4.3 and 4.7 Nahua and Maya cabildos seek to retain control over the process whereby their town governor is chosen. In both cases, political factionalism within the towns easily can be read between the lines of the petitions. Community authorities are forced to contend with both internal and external challenges.

Document 4.2 from Xochimilco reveals the full range of challenges that nobles at the center of New Spain faced as they competed directly with Spaniards for access to resources, especially labor, tribute, and good land. In this case, the nobles confronted none other than the Marqués (Cortés) himself; they feared that he was about to add another conquest to his name by manipulating the legal system to his advantage. The Xochimilca are well aware of the dangers that aggressive Spaniards pose, and they are certainly not standing by and letting things happen. Yet it was clear to them, as it is to us, that they are at a decided disadvantage in the new system. Hence, they are writing this rather desperate letter to the king. Both documents 4.1 and 4.2 take a tactful approach to complaining, blaming royal agents rather than the king himself. Both letters also implore the king to enforce a law that prohibits nonindigenous people from entering native communities.

Defending the community from colonial demands and burdens was serious business. In document 4.4, from Tlaxcala, and a pair of petitions from two Yucatec towns (documents 4.5 and 4.6), we can see that Spanish policies such as *congregación* (congregation – the wholesale relocation of entire communities into a central location) and the unrestricted abuse of native labor were potentially very useful to colonial interests but equally devastating to native community prosperity. As a result, Mesoamerican cabildos fought hard in the colonial courts to limit the impact of such policies and practices, using all the petitionary ploys at their disposal. The documents here are thus a testimony as much to the vitality of native politics and the Mesoamerican cabildo as they are to the exploitative nature of colonial rule.

Document 4.8 from the Mixteca reveals another face of community politics that was even more rooted in preconquest traditions than the cabildo. Hereditary rulers, in this case both male and female, continued to exert considerable authority within their communities. This document from 1569 presents one excerpt of a palace possession ceremony in Teposcolula, on precisely the ground where part of the original palace stands today. Today, the palace is called *la casa de la cacica*, "the house of the female ruler." As we shall see, it is aptly named.

The final document in this chapter provides a glimpse into the daily expenditures of a Mixtec community in the middle of the sixteenth century, showing how the all-male cabildo came to eclipse the authority of female rulers in the Mixteca.

4.1. Letter from the Nahua Cabildo of Tenochtitlan to the King of Spain, 1554[1]

As with the letter from Xochimilco that follows, the cabildo of Tenochtitlan wrote directly to the King of Spain, complaining about the way that they are being treated. Whereas the nobles from Xochimilco appealed to the crown on the grounds that they had served the Spaniards from the beginning, the cabildo of Tenochtitlan obviously could not take that approach and, instead, politely pointed out the contradictions between Spanish theory and practice and enumerated the ways in which the king's decrees and laws were not being carried out. This was standard colonial discourse that many Spaniards employed, too, for who would dare to accuse the crown itself of wrongdoing? Even translated into English, one can sense that the writers employed a noble, reverential language in their petition. Their reference to being saved from aggressive Spaniards by the friars reveals something of the rivalry between Spaniards and friars over the control of native resources, and how the cabildo members tried to use this competition to their advantage. Also, the cabildo makes a typical appeal to keep nonindigenous peoples from entering the altepetl, according to the law. As we can sense from this petition, however, law and reality were two different things in colonial Mexico.

Our much revered ruler:

We Mexica and Tenochca bow down to you and kiss your precious hands and feet, you our ruler and prince who guards things for our lord Jesus Christ there in old Spain and here in New Spain. We place before you our weeping, tears, and great concern, because we know very well that you greatly love us, we who are your humble commoners, we who are residents here in New Spain, as it is called.

Your benevolence appears in the very good orders with which you and your precious father our great emperor have defended us. If your orders for us had been carried out, we would have had no concern and would have lived in great happiness. We think that it is because of our failings that your orders have been futile, which greatly increases our concern, so that it is not in vain that we place before you our weeping, tears, and concerns.

Please listen, our much revered ruler and prince: although you have sent a great many orders here to benefit us your humble commoners, those who serve you and guard your rule here in New Spain do not carry them out for us, which causes us great suffering and loss of many possessions and much property. This has been happening for some time now. And although it is

1 Translated from Nahuatl by Lockhart, and modified by Sousa and Terraciano, based on a transcription of the original Nahuatl-language document by Günter Zimmermann (1970: 15–16). We are grateful for Lockhart's original, unpublished translation of this document in his UCLA History 165C reader, and his reference to the transcription of the original document in the Zimmermann volume.

very sad and distressing, we merely set our weeping and tears before our god and ruler God our Lord so that he will remedy it when he wishes.

There is another great affliction of ours that now newly concerns us, with which we cry out to you, our precious prince, for now in the year of 1554 the rule and governorship that our fathers and grandfathers bequeathed us was going to be taken from us and given to the Spaniards. And this, O ruler, would have been carried out if our fathers the friars of San Francisco (Franciscans) had not supported us; they would have made us all their slaves. And those who wish to do this are making every effort to carry it out; we think they will really impose their will on us if you and your precious father do not defend us. Two *alcaldes mayores* (Spanish officials) were appointed, one to serve in Mexico City and the second to serve in Tlatelolco, and they were to be in charge of governance, administration, and justice.

When we heard of the order we brought complaint before your representative don Luis de Velasco the viceroy, and the friars of San Francisco also spoke to him on our behalf. Then he gave orders that the two should not be called alcaldes mayors, that they only be called protectors, and he instructed them that their only duty would be to save us from any Spaniard, mestizo, black, or mulatto afflicting us in the marketplace, on the roads, in the canals, or in our homes; he instructed them to be on the watch day and night so that no one afflict us. We greatly approve this order of your viceroy, for we need it very much, and we beg you to order them to take great care with their task, for the Spaniards, mestizos, blacks, and mulattos do greatly harm us. We also implore you that no one take our government and jurisdiction from us. If it is thought that we do not know how to rule, govern, and do true justice, let such laws be made for us as are necessary so that we can perform our duties properly, and if we do not observe them let us be punished. Let the right to rule, which belongs to those who will follow us, not be taken from them.

And if it is thought that we do not love our ruler and king of Castile, we hereby take an oath as rulers in order to put your mind to rest, all of us who govern your altepetl of Mexico. We who write this letter swear and take oath as rulers before God and St. Mary and all the saints and before you our ruler that we will always love, obey, and revere the ruler and king of Castile until the end of the world. And we want this oath to hold for those who are born after us, and so that this, our statement and our rulers' oath, will be valid we set down here our names and signatures.

Done here in Mexico City on December 19, 1554.

Your humble commoners who kiss your precious hands and feet.

Don Esteban de Guzmán, judges, don Pedro de Moteucçoma, don Diego de Mendoza, alcalde. Francisco de San Pablo, alcalde, don Pedro de la Cruz, regidor, don Luis de Paz, regidor, Bartolomé de San Juan, regidor, don Baltasar Tlillancalqui, regidor, Diego Tezcacoacatl, regidor, Martín Cano, regidor, Martín Coçotecatl, regidor, Francisco Jiménez, regidor,

Martín Tlamacicatl, regidor. Thoribio Tlacochcalcatl, regidor. Melchor
Díaz, regidor; Martín Pauper, escribano publico.

4.2. Letter from the Nahua Nobles of Xochimilco to the King of Spain, 1563[2]

*Nobles of the altepetl of Xochimilco sent this letter, written in Spanish, to the King of
Spain. Because it was written in Spanish, the letter uses the Spanish term "indio,"
which was rarely used by Nahuatl-language writers; nonetheless, this document has
so much in common with other native-language letters to the King. The representatives of Xochimilco respectfully request justice, the granting of certain privileges, a
reduction in tribute and labor, and various other favors. They base their appeal on
good behavior. In particular, they claim to have helped the Spaniards in their siege
of Tenochtitlan, just as the Tlaxcalans had done. But whereas the Tlaxcalans have
received certain advantages for their services to the crown, these men from Xochimilco feel that they have received nothing and that things are only getting worse. Their
claim to never having resisted the Spaniards contradicts Spanish accounts; Bernal
Díaz del Castillo, for example, wrote that Xochimilca warriors put up a fierce resistance. To be fair, Tlaxcalan accounts also make no mention of fighting the Spaniards,
even though we know that they did fight them for several days before suing for peace.
At this time, as in our own, present concerns and needs shape one's views of the past.*

*Most important, this letter speaks directly to the challenges and dangers encoun-
tered by many altepetl in the Valley of Mexico, which came into direct competition
with Spaniards over valuable resources. The Marqués, don Hernando Cortés, is very
much involved in this competition, and these nobles from Xochimilco obviously do
not trust him – or any other Spaniards, for that matter. They are fully aware of the
consequences of these post-Conquest changes for their community. Unfortunately,
even though this letter was written in Spanish and not Nahuatl, one has to wonder
whether such a detailed list of grievances from a particular altepetl had any impact
in Spain.*

Sacred Catholic Royal Majesty

We the *caciques* (lords) and Indians who are natives of the city of
Xochimilco, which is a part of the royal crown and is five leagues from Mexico
City in New Spain, humbly implore your majesty and your royal council of
the Indies to be informed that we did not make war against nor resist the
Marqués del Valle [Cortés] and the Christian army. Rather we aided and
favored them then and in the time since in whatever has presented itself. So
that the said Marqués could take Mexico City, we gave him two thousand

2   Translated from Spanish by Terraciano, based on Lockhart's original, unpublished translation
    of this document in his UCLA History 165C reader. Again, we are grateful to Lockhart for
    referring us to this letter. The letter is reproduced in CDI, vol. 13: pp. 293–301.

canoes in the lake, loaded with provisions, with twelve thousand fighting men, with which they were aided and with who they won Mexico City. As for the Tlaxcalans, since they came from a distant land, fatigued and without supplies, they were aided also. And the true help, after God's, was what Xochimilco gave.

In addition to this, we served your majesty in the conquest of Honduras and Guatemala with Adelantado Alvarado, our *encomendero*. We gave him twenty-five hundred fighting men for the voyage and all the provisions and other things necessary. As a result those jurisdictions were won and put under the royal crown, because the Spaniards were few and poorly supplied and were going through lands where they would not have known the way if we had not shown them; a thousand times we saved them from death.

In addition, when the said Marqués and the said Adelantado Alvarado went to conquer the province of Pánuco, where there were as many men as leaves of grass, we helped them with many provisions and munitions and with five hundred fighting men who went with them. Along with those who went to Honduras and Guatemala, none returned, because all died of the cruel, hard labor.

Likewise, we served your majesty in the conquest of Jalisco with Nuño de Guzmán, and we gave him six hundred fighting men with many supplies and munitions, and they served the Spaniards, your majesty's soldiers; with this aid the said kingdom was won, and not an Indian returned home. And since we have done your majesty so many services and we are poor and have been dispossessed of many lands and jurisdictions that the Marqués and other judges who have governed took away from us, confident that we know little of litigation and cannot defend ourselves (which towns and lands will be declared below), and aside from the prejudice and loss suffered by the said city, the damage pertains to the royal crown whose vassals we are. For all of these reasons we implore – without long lawsuits but immediately on the establishment of the truth – that restitution be made, since all of it is almost at the walls of Mexico City, from where the Spanish citizens are sustained and supplied. And since your majesty gave great boons and privileges to Tlaxcala, it is only fair that your majesty should show the same favors to us, who have served no less. The towns and lands of which we have been dispossessed are the following:

The town and settlement of San Agustín, which has two thousand men and many lands, jurisdictions, and forests, and is between Xochimilco and Coyoacan on the road to Mexico City, is one of the most notable assets of this realm and very important for the sustenance and supply of Mexico City. About thirty-eight years ago the Marqués and the people of Coyoacan dispossessed us of it; afterwards we regained possession, but about fifteen years ago they dispossessed us again and now improperly hold it, and so we have brought suit against the said Marqués and his town of Coyoacan and certain individuals. We have a sentence in our favor, and the suit is concluded pending appeal, but the party of the Marqués and his lawyers are delaying it, saying that it is included in his privileges and that he is sending to apply for a new grant and that our suit and recourse should be silenced. We implore your majesty to take notice of this; and since San Agustín and Xochimilco belong to the royal crown and are such important assets, the Marqués should be denied in this case. Rather, it should be decreed and ordered that the matter be decided promptly, and that restitution be made to your majesty and to the said city.

Furthermore, we say that the said city was dispossessed of the Indian towns, lands, and districts of Totollan, Quauhmilpan, Chalchiuhtepec, Cuentepec, Atonco, Metepec, Nepopohualco, and Ahuatlan; and granting that your majesty possesses them, many caciques and noblemen of the said city of Xochimilco had and have there their lands, *macehuales* (commoners, based on Nahuatl word, *macehualli*), and other interests. We implore your majesty that they be restored and that the lordship of Xochimilco be recognized, and that everything be assessed together, that they bring their tributes to the said city as their *cabecera*, and that each natural lord and nobleman be given that which is his and of which he has been dispossessed.

Furthermore, we implore your majesty that because from time immemorial, when the Spaniards came and before, the caciques and noblemen of the said city of Xochimilco by way of patrimony and lordship used the services of all the craftsmen – carpenters, masons, woodcutters, metalworkers, fishermen, feather-workers, sandalmakers, and other craftsmen and people of the market – and other natives served them by taking care of their fields and held them in high recognition, giving them tokens of respect and presents, but now it is done no longer and they are dispossessed, and since it pertains to their patrimony and lordship, we implore your majesty to order the abovementioned restored to us.

In addition, we advise your majesty that at the time when the Spaniards came and since, assessments were made of what the macehuales were to give their caciques and natural lords for their sustenance and by virtue of their lordship; now the said macehuales, aided by some Spanish lawyers and attorneys, have evaded it and do not want to pay or recognize their caciques, who are the caciques of Tecpan, Tepetenchi, and Ollac, who are dying of hunger. In pagan times they were great lords and the said Indians and macehuales served in their houses, building adobe walls and performing other personal services, but now the caciques are as beaten down as the macehuales, and all are equal. We implore your majesty to decree and order that our lordship and patrimony be honored and our assessments be fulfilled, and that the macehuales not be permitted to rise up against us nor involve us in lawsuits, and that upon our verifying the above-said we be restored in our rights and sustained.

Item: whereas the said city of Xochimilco from time immemorial has had and possessed the outlying districts and lands of Santa Marta, San Gerónimo,

San Agustín, San Benito, San Antón, San Pedro and other subject districts, which are attempting to free themselves and be independent in such a way that they do not obey the governor, alcaldes, or caciques and always go about agitating, for which reason the Audiencia has exiled and punished them. And since they are not noblemen, but macehuales and subjects of the said city, we implore your majesty to order that they recognize it and not withdraw, and upon establishment of the truth with witnesses and documents which we are ready to present we be confirmed in our possession and lordship, and in everything the honors, faculties, privileges, and freedoms which are customarily observed for other cities of your majesty's be observed for us as well, privileges which we as natural lords and caciques should have and enjoy.

Furthermore, we announce to your majesty that presently and continually the said city of Xochimilco, as its regular service to Mexico City for buildings, cultivation, and personal services to the Spaniards, has given and gives three hundred workmen regularly, which is a great hardship because they spend their lives in the said services and are very badly treated by the Spaniards. And since the lands they work and the farms with which they maintain themselves are the Indians' themselves, they should content themselves with that, without our being obliged to serve them and make them rich with our own physical labor and patrimonies. And since the natives of the said city are diminishing rather than increasing, and of the thirty thousand men that there were when we gave dominion to your majesty, at present there are no more than about six or seven thousand men, and we are a city and your vassals who pay tribute. We implore your majesty to order a royal decree sent to the effect that in view of our services and diminution we not be obliged to give the said service, and that the Spaniards and city council let us freely sell the things we grow and raise, because they order and compel us to give them for less than what others sell them for, and that an ordinance be passed that Spaniards not live or take up citizenship in the said city nor be given lands or lots, because they oppress us and carry on illicit dealings with us and want everything for themselves, and they come in at little expense and later end up the masters of everything.

Item: We implore your majesty and advise that the natives of the said city, when they have some lawsuit, do not bring it in the first instance before the governor and alcaldes, but come to Mexico City and hire lawyers and attorneys who rob them, especially a Francisco de Escobar, attorney in the Audiencia, who for his individual advantage induces them to initiate and carry on the said lawsuits before the judges of the Audiencia in the first instance no matter of how small consequence they should be, and the said noblemen and natives are summoned and removed from home and disturbed by the said suits in very insignificant cases and on the basis of false reports, all because of not recognizing the said city and its justices. We implore your majesty that all cases come in the first instance before the governor and judges of the said city and go to the Audiencia only on appeal and that in this matter what was decreed by the viceroy of New Spain be observed, being the same thing that we request in this paragraph.

Furthermore we say that since in all the area surrounding Mexico City your majesty granted the title of city to Tenochtitlan, Tetzcoco, and Xochimilco, ordering that the lords and governors of these three cities enjoy the privileges that according to law they should enjoy, we implore your majesty to order and decree that the said natural lords be preferred over the other towns of the surroundings of Mexico City, and that if the viceroy and Audiencia judges should be considering matters having to do with Indians they should be present at the said meetings, which otherwise should not be held, since it is the most important matter in all the realm and what sustains and supplies it all.

Item: We say that in the said city there are about four hundred natives who are gentlemen, cavaliers, and free nobles of well-known houses who with their forebears from time immemorial have been exempt from paying duties, tributes, services, or taxes either royal or local, and even when Moteuczoma tyrannized this land he observed their noble privileges; but about ten years ago they imposed certain tributes on them for expenses of the community and local government, of which your majesty receives nothing. We humbly implore that their ancient privileges and nobility be ordered observed, that a verified list be made of the noble Indians, and that they be relieved of the said tribute.

Furthermore, we implore your majesty to order that the Indians who serve in the churches of the said city, who are singers and masters of the choir and of book-writing, and the musicians who play flutes, chirimías, and trumpets, and other officials of the said churches in service of divine worship, be relieved of tribute while they are occupied with the above duties, because they do not cultivate, dig, or plow, nor do they have patrimonies from which to pay taxes; they are most necessary for the honor of God and your majesty, and there are only about thirty of them in all.

Furthermore, we say and advise your majesty, for the good government of the said city, that there are installed each year a governor in addition to the three caciques and natural lords, three alcaldes, seven regidores, two high constables, six notaries, a jailor, and an interpreter for Spanish, who are always chosen from the lineage of nobles, cavaliers, and gentlemen. They receive no fees or benefits whatsoever from these offices, nor has it ever been the custom [to receive benefits for their services]. Viceroy don Luis de Velasco assigned the salary which they are to receive by virtue of their offices, which is very little and is paid from excess tributes, and thus they suffer necessity and there is no one who wants the offices. We implore your majesty to order that the said salary be increased somewhat beyond the viceroy's assessment so that they can receive a moderate sustenance and do what they should and are obliged to do in their offices.

And may our Lord guard and raise up your sacred Catholic royal majesty as your royal heart desires. From Mexico City, May 20, 1563. And since Diego Díaz del Castillo is going as our representative in these matters and others, we implore your majesty to have him heard and attended to according to your pleasure, considering our great services and loyalty and that we are poor, mute, and defenseless Indians.

Your sacred Catholic royal majesty's least and most humble servants who kiss your royal hands and feet. Don Pedro de Santiago, governor. Don Alonso de Guzmán, alcalde, don Joaquín de Santa María, don Bartolomé de San Lorenzo, Domingo de Alameda, Marcos Rodrigo, Pedro de San Francisco, Francisco Juárez, Francisco de Luna.

4.3. Debate Over the Removal of the Governor from the Nahua Cabildo of Tlaxcala, 1556[3]

The most famous indigenous cabildo in all of New Spain was that of Tlaxcala, if for no other reason than its surviving cabildo minutes, written entirely in Nahuatl. The surviving records of its proceedings, covering primarily the years from 1547 to 1567, reveal so much about the four-part altepetl of Tlaxcala, its hundreds of nobles who sat on the council, and the issues with which they grappled in the sixteenth century. The following document addresses one of those many issues: the election of a governor. In the new cabildo, the old tlatoani or cacique usually held the highest cabildo office – the governorship. The most important male of the community usually was called "cacique and governor." He continued to exercise many of his old powers. The Spaniards manipulated the early governors, deposing those unsatisfactory to them, but those whom they named as replacements were always other local candidates for the rulership. The tlatoani would normally be governor from the time he was named for the rest of his life. But the Spaniards forced the cabildo members to elect new officials annually (or every two years) so that the governor would not always be the tlatoani of an altepetl; native electors (all noblemen) responded to this law by rotating the office of governor among tlatoque (pl. of tlatoani) or lords from various parts of the altepetl.

In this case, Tlaxcala elected a governor every two years, and simply rotated the position among the highest ranking members of each of the four altepetl that made up Tlaxcala: Tizatla, Quiahuiztlan, Tepeticpac, and Ocotelulco. In fact, it relied on the principle of rotation among its four parts for many activities and events. But in 1556, the Spanish viceroy of New Spain ordered the cabildo to choose a new governor before the present governor from Quiahuiztlan had served out his turn, presumably because he had been denounced by someone from Tlaxcala. The order caused a debate in the cabildo. As it turns out, all the representatives of the altepetl of Tepeticpac, led

---

3   Translated from Nahuatl by Sousa and Terraciano, based on the transcription and translation in Lockhart, Berdan, and Anderson (1986: 97–103).

by a high noble named don Juan Martín (who ended up becoming the new governor when the order was carried out), support the order and accuse the present governor of wrongdoing, hinting at their possible role in the viceroy's order and revealing some of the tensions among the four constituent altepetl of Tlaxcala. The altepetl of Ocotelulco also favors the order. The discussion shows a tradition of spirited debate among the various lords of Tlaxcala but also reveals how the various parts could disagree and, when push came to shove, how some factions were willing to involve Spanish authorities to advance their own interests. Once again, some of the names of the cabildo members, such as Maxixcatzin, show them to be the descendants of pre-Conquest lords.

In the loyal city of Tlaxcala on the 18th day of the month of December, year of our lord Jesus Christ 1556, the magnificent lord Francisco Verdugo, corregidor and chief justice here in the city and province of Tlaxcala for his majesty, entered the cabildo here. In the presence of the cabildo members, here in the city and province of Tlaxcala, he presented to them the statement of the most illustrious lord viceroy about another governor being chosen. He informed them that he [the viceroy] wants a governor to be appointed, and he informed the cabildo members about the lord viceroy's letter. "I [said Verdugo, the corregidor] will report what they [the cabildo members] reply to the lord viceroy." A person named Diego Guerrero interpreted for the lord corregidor. Then each of the cabildo members expressed his opinions separately; here it is below. It was done before us, the escribanos of the cabildo, Diego de Soto and Julián de Silva.

Then first the alcalde Blas Osorio (from Tizatla) spoke; he said: "Concerning what we have heard about how the lord viceroy orders us that another person is to be chosen as governor: is perhaps someone here to be blamed for going to tell things to the lord viceroy? Why is this being done? Do the people of Quiahuiztlan not belong to the altepetl? Does someone wish their ruin? Let there be discussion of what is required. And from what we have heard in the viceroy's statement, it appears that someone here is giving false testimony concerning the governor."

Then don Juan Xicotencatl (ruler from Tizatla) spoke and he said: "We who are here in the cabildo have heard the statement of our ruler the lord viceroy that he wishes another to be chosen governor. Look at this carefully or else we shall be injured. The ruler Santillán came to put things in order and to remedy things because there was quarreling here in Tlaxcala; he thereby resolved all the disputes over land, the altepetl's fields. And it is known that every two years the governorship is changed among all of our four altepetl. Has someone given false testimony against us? Then let it also be very visible; let us not be destroyed by intrigue. Since we are subjects of the emperor and our ruler the viceroy governs us, if it is really he himself who wants this, perhaps it is not bad. But if someone is speaking to him and agitating him, let us ask him about it. Look into it well, you regidores."

Then Lucas García, alcalde (from Tepeticpac), said: "As to the governor don Martín's leaving his office, even if it is not his personal shame and fault, does it not become the altepetl's shame? It is known that the governorship goes along being changed every two years. But perhaps it is only of his own accord that the lord viceroy writes that another governor should be chosen. Let us consider well what may be required in our altepetl, our home. Should we go elsewhere?"

Then don Julián Motolinía (ruler from Quiahuiztlan) rose and said: "When the lord Santillán came to put us in order at the order of the Royal Audiencia in Mexico City, he left behind ordinances that he established about how things are to be in Tlaxcala, and we observe them so that there are not disputes. The governorship is alternated among each of our four altepetl every two years. And he halted all the disputes over our land that were plaguing us. But now begins the changing of governors after only one year. Consider that we might quarrel and argue over it. If some person from here went to complain to the lord viceroy, can he remedy it for us? If disputes and anger should begin, who will remedy it?"

Then don Francisco de Mendoza (ruler from Tepeticpac) said: "By the governor's leaving office, will not thereby our altepetl be injured? If our governor has done wrong, let it first be seen what his wrongs were. Let it be shown how much he stole or how many lands and fields he took from people. And let it be shown what the person who went to complain to the lord viceroy wants, and if it is necessary. Was it not at the order of the cabildo that another person be chosen as governor? For it is already known that the governor is changed every two years, according to the ordinances that the ruler Santillán left behind in order to put things in order. And will there be quarreling again, and are we to return to our respective homes, where the homes of our ancestors were? And will the fields of the altepetl be in various places, so that we four altepetl will fight over them? And will our corregidor or our guardian [priest, specifically a Franciscan] always live here in some part and will they be served as they have been accustomed to live? And as for us, where will we go? Are we to flee? First, let us just ask the lord viceroy who went to complain to him."

Then Hernando de Salazár, alcalde (from Quiahuiztlan), said: "What is happening to us in Quiahuiztlan is that now the ordinances of the ruler Santillán, the ones with which he came to remedy things here in Tlaxcala when there was quarreling, are being corrupted. Look carefully at it for us, we leave ourselves to you of Ocotelulco, Tizatla, and Tepeticpac, because this was the custom, when the Spaniards had not yet arrived. Are we not entirely equal in the four altepetl known as Tlaxcala? Does one leave the others out? And now that another is to be chosen as governor, who went to complain to the ruler viceroy? The ordinances of Santillán are destroyed; are there to be disputes again? And you know well that one time we had gone back to our home in Quiahuiztlan, and the Dominican friars had settled there. Will the same happen again? Look into it well."

Then don Julián de la Rosa, regidor (from Ocotelulco), said: "It appears that the governor alone did wrong; perhaps not all of us in the four altepetl have done wrong. If the governor alone leaves office through his own doing, then we will not be giving false testimony against him, since he has already done wrong."

Feliciano Ceynos, regidor (from Ocotelulco), said: "When the lord viceroy's message came, is it not thus what our lord God wishes to do to us? And does it not appear to our ruler the viceroy that we fail to do what he wishes? Who went to complain to the lord viceroy that the governor should be changed and another should be chosen? Were they the words of one of us? It must be that in truth we have done harm. And let us take an oath whether or not it was one of us who went to tell the viceroy. And as to that discord that has been mentioned, it appears that the quarreling is already being taken care of. Let us just wait for what God and the lord viceroy will want, and that will be done."

Don Alonso Maldonado, regidor (from Quiahuiztlan), said: "We who speak before the lord corregidor are very satisfied with this suggestion; truly, let us take an oath. Often we are accused of misunderstanding what is said. And let it be shown what the governor did wrong. It affects our home Quiahuiztlan, where the governorship is. In truth, there are the ordinances which Santillán came to establish, by which he put things in order in Tlaxcala. Just let the lord viceroy be asked who went to complain to him; let us hear it from him. We simply leave it in the hands of the lord viceroy; what he should wish we will obey, since he is the representative of our ruler the emperor."

Antonio Téllez, regidor (from Quiahuiztlan), said: "Our lord God wishes that it happen to us, that the governor be changed and another chosen. Perhaps he alone did wrong, not all of us. And is it not to be done as the lord viceroy wishes? We will obey him, since the altepetl of Tlaxcala is in his charge and he loves and honors it. Let what the lord viceroy wishes be done."

Don Juan Martín (regidor from Tepeticpac) said: "What the lord viceroy wants for us is very good; is it not done by order of our lord God? It will be good that another governor be chosen. The present governor never performs any of his duties; he does not know what he is to do. The alcaldes have to tell him in order to be able to perform the duties of their offices. As to the land that has been so much discussed, are we talking about land? Look to it well. In truth the lord viceroy loves the altepetl of Tlaxcala and does not shame it, but advises and befriends us in this."

Pedro de la Cadena, regidor (from Tizatla), said: "Let our hearts not be so fearful, let it be shown what the governor has done wrong. Let us leave it to the lord corregidor to write to the lord viceroy. Let us know about it; if someone is giving false testimony about us, let it be shown. Just let the governor complete a year in office. And the lord viceroy will decide what he wishes."

Antonio Flores, regidor (from Tepeticpac), said: "We leave it to our ruler the lord viceroy. It will be good that our governor leaves his office and that another is chosen. He does not mean to shame the altepetl of Tlaxcala. If the governor did something wrong, let another be appointed who will be our governor. The lord viceroy has befriended us."

Feliciano de Santiago, regidor (from Tepeticpac), said: "It is very good what the lord viceroy wants for us, that our governor be changed and another chosen and newly appointed. He truly befriends us, because the lords, noblemen, and commoners appreciate him. And our ruler the lord viceroy esteems the altepetl of Tlaxcala in return and does not wish to shame it. May our lord God grant us that another governor be put in office."

Those in whose absence the cabildo was held are: don Juan Maxixcatzin, don Antonio Calmecahua, Domingo Marmolejo, and don Julián Quapiltzintli, who are sick; don Domigo de Angulo, alcalde, was sent on assignment to Tepeyacac because an account is being made of the tithes by order of the lord viceroy; and the lord corregidor sent Alonso Delgado, regidor, to go look in the forest for a black man who killed someone.

4.4. Complaints Against Congregation from the Nahua Cabildo of Tlaxcala, 1560[4]

Although the many communities of central Mexico were densely populated and probably more concentrated than settlements of native peoples in any other part of the Americas, the altepetl was still more dispersed than the typical Mediterranean city-state in this period. With the notable exception of Tenochtitlan and Tlatelolco, which were located on an island, most settlements spread out rather evenly across the land. People tended to live next to the plots of land that they cultivated. Population loss in the sixteenth century must have contributed to the general appearance of dispersal. Spaniards intended to create more manageable and compact administrative and ecclesiastical units by moving some of the outlying settlements of a community to the center, relocating settlements from hilltops and slopes down to level valleys and plains, and recreating the semblance of a Mediterranean city with its central plaza and rural hamlets. These activities were called congregación. *In general, congregation did lead to increased concentration but not to the extent that Spanish officials had planned. And as we can see in this document, the indigenous response to this policy was invariably negative. People were not willing to leave their ancestral homes and fields, and often returned to them after they had been relocated. Here the famous cabildo of Tlaxcala considers the impact of such a plan on its people and devises a strategy.*

In the loyal city of Tlaxcala, on the 12th day of the month of January, year of our lord Jesus Christ 1560, there assembled in the cabildo the very noble lords don Domingo de Angulo, governor; and the alcaldes, Juan Jiménez,

---

4 Translated from Nahuatl by Sousa and Terraciano, based on the transcription and translation in Lockhart, Berdan, and Anderson (1986: 103–6).

Pablo de Galicia, don Domingo Marmolejo, and Antonio Flores; and the four rulers of divisions [the four sub-altepetls], don Juan Maxixcatzin, don Julián Motolinia, don Juan Xicotencatl, and don Francisco de Mendoza; and the regidores, Buenaventura Oñate, Feliciano Ceynos, Juan de Avalos, don Martín de Valencia, don Alonso Maldonado, Juan de Paz, don Julián Atempan, Baltasar Cortés, don Juan Maldonado asked permission to be absent, don Juan Martín, and Feliciano de Santiago; Juan de la Torre asked permission [to be absent]; before us, Diego de Soto and Sancho de Rosas, notaries of the cabildo.

They discussed how there is to be congregation of people, how the commoners are to be brought together at Topoyanco, Atlihuetzyan, Hueyotlipan, Atzompan, San Felipe, Santa Ana, etc. The rulers consider what is to be done very difficult; a great deal of suffering and affliction will occur, there are so many things. Namely, who will come to build houses for the commoners? They will leave behind their houses and all that they take care of: their fruit cactus, their cochineal-bearing cactus, their cherry trees, their maguey, their fruits, sweet potatoes, sapotas, chayotes, and quinces, peaches, etc. And then also their household fields which they clear and cultivate, and their dogs and their turkeys that they raise, some raise pigs, and their maize, the grainbins. Who will transport all the humble belongings of each person? When he comes to settle, will there be a house already there for him? And whoever settles on his land, will he not also appropriate for himself the fields? Where will he work land if they are entirely lost to him? And if he thus leaves behind his maize, chia, or cactus fruit, and his burial grounds, who will guard them for him? Will he not lose whatever he leaves behind? And the shepherds are causing great fear; they wander about the grasslands all over Tlaxcala. And even though the commoners are there now, sometimes the shepherds beat them and take their children from them; sometimes they take their daughters away, and they take their turkeys, mats, etc., from them.

And if they should have come to be gathered together, those who had been at the fields of lords or nobles, would his fields not then go to grass? Who would cultivate them? Because of this the cabildo says that there will be much affliction. And Tlaxcala here cannot be called a city until the nobles and rulers build their houses; we are as if on conquered land, as though everything had been destroyed by war. But cannot these noblemen who still have some commoners also build houses for themselves? Are the commoners alone to build houses for them? How are they to provide houses for themselves?

Because of this the lords of the cabildo said, "Let the established noblemen be the ones who are be assembled, since they are somewhat well-to-do and prosperous, so that they can make their houses and enclosures." And then the cabildo members said, "Let us request it of our great ruler the lord viceroy, don Luis de Velasco, who presides in Mexico City here in New Spain. We appoint Juan Jiménez, alcalde, Buenaventura Oñate, regidor, and [blank space], to go to implore the lord viceroy that at first only the established nobles be congregated and then the commoners only gradually; our ruler will consider how to help us. We await now what the lord viceroy responds."

Those who know how make their signatures on this paper.

Juan Jiménez, Pablo de Galicia, don Julián Motolinia, don Francisco de Mendoza, Buenaventura Oñate, Feliciano Ceynos, Antonio Flores, don Martín de Valencia, don Juan Martín.

Before us, notaries of the cabildo: Diego de Soto, notary of Tlaxcala.

4.5–4.6. Petitions from the Maya Cabildos of Tahnab and Dzaptun to Alleviate Colonial Burdens, 1605[5]

Whereas documents 4.1 and 4.2 were addressed simply to the King of Spain, the Maya petitioners below simultaneously direct their petitions at an array of the empire's most senior Spanish officials. These consist of, first, the Viceroy (called halach ahau, *literally "true lord," a title reserved for the highest-ranking rulers) in the great cah or city of Mexico, and second, the King (given the title of* ah tepale, *or supreme ruler) – with king and viceroy possibly conflated in the minds of the petitioners. The third addressee is the provincial governor of Yucatan (referred to in the Tahnab petition both with the Maya title of* halach uinic, *or chief ruler, and as Señor Gobernador), although both petitions make implicit criticism of the governor and seek to go over his head. The fourth addressee, most obviously in the second petition, is the* oidor, *a senior Spanish judge empowered to alter tribute arrangements (among other things), as these Maya town councillors seem well aware. They may have confused king and viceroy, but they nevertheless show an impressive understanding of colonial politics – as well as a firm grasp on petitionary style and on their obligations as the political representatives of their neighbors.*

It is unlikely that these petitions made it to the King in Spain, but as they are archived in Mexico City, they may well have made it to the Viceroy's office. Nor is it clear whether Tahnab and Dzaptun received any immediate relief from colonial burdens as a result of these complaints. But either way, in the long run the townspeople of these cahob *(plural of* cah*) were destined to bear the brunt of certain kinds of demands from the colonists. As the Tahnab cabildo officers state, "we reside here in the heart of the road," meaning that their cah lay midway along the royal highway or* camino real *between the two main Spanish settlements in Yucatan – the provincial capital of Merida and the port-town of Campeche, the gateway to the colony. Dzaptun was located further south than Tahnab, close enough to Campeche to be a source of firewood and house beams – and the laborers who were required to carry the wood into the Spanish town. In this way, geography, as well as history, condemned these Mayas to centuries of exploitation.*

---

5 Translated from Yucatec Maya by Restall, from the original documents in the AGN-Civil 2013, 1. Earlier versions of these translations appeared in Restall (1997: 324) and (1998: 173–75).

4.5. Petition from Tahnab

For the Viceroy, who is in the city of Mexico.

I who am don Alonso Puc, the governor, along with Simon Piste and Francisco Antonio Canul, the alcaldes, Juan Ucan, Gonzalo Poot, Gaspar Ku and Pedro Dzul, the regidores, we the cabildo have assembled ourselves in the name of God Almighty and also in the name of our redeemer, Jesus Christ. We now lower our heads before you, kneeling in great adoration in your presence, in honor of God, beneath your feet and your hands, you our great lord the King, supreme ruler, in order that you hear our statement of petition, so that you will hear, our lord, what it is that we recount and explain in our said petition. O lord, we reside here in the heart of the road to the cah of San Francisco Campeche. O lord, here is the poverty that is upon us, that we are going through. Here at the heart of the road, O lord, day and night, we carry burdens, take horses, carry letters, and also take turns in serving in the guest house and at the well. Here at the road's heart, O lord, it is really many leagues to the town of Campeche. Our porters, letter-carriers, and horse-takers go ten leagues as far as our cah, day and night. Nor are our people very great in number. The tribute that we give, O lord, is sixty cotton blankets. The tally of our tribute adds up to sixty, O lord, because they add us, the alcaldes, and all the widows too. That is why we are relating our miseries for you to hear, O lord. Here is our misery. When the lord governor marshal came he gave us very many forced labor rotations, seventeen of them, though our labor rotations had been abolished by our lord the Oidor Doctor Palacio because of the excessive misery we experience here on the road. Our misery is also known by our lords the past provincial governors, and our lords the padres (Spanish priests) also know it, O lord. Every day there are not enough of us to do so much work, and being few, neither can we manage our fields nor sustain our children. In particular, we are unable to manage the tribute burden that is upon us. Within each year we give a tribute of two cotton blankets, two measures of maize, one turkey and one hen. This is what we give, O lord, and we really cannot manage it, because of the great work load that we have. Thus our people run away into the forest. The number of our people who have fled, O lord, who have left their homes, is fifty, because we are burdened with so much work. O lord, this is why we humbly place ourselves before you, our great lord ruler, the King, in honor of our redeemer Jesus Christ, we kiss your feet and hands, we the worst of your children. We want there to be an end to the labor obligations under which we serve, with which we are burdened. Because our fathers, many of them principal men, along with our porters, letter-carriers and horse-takers, serve day and night. We want to look after you, our lord, and greatly wish that you will be compassionate and turn your attention to us. We have neither fathers nor mothers. We are really poor here in our town at the heart of the road, O lord; nobody helps us. Three times we have carried our petition before you, our lord the Señor Governor, but you did not hear our words, O lord. Nor do we have any money in order that we may petition before you; our town is poor. Here, O lord, is the reason why our people flee, because it is known that in the forest, through the use [sale] of beeswax, one is given money on credit by our lord Francisco de Magaña. It really is the provincial governor's money that is given to people. This is our petition in your presence, lord, our great ruler, the king, made here in the town of Tahnab, today the ninth day of the month of July in the year 1605 years. Truly we give our names at the end.

Don Alonso Puc, governor; Pedro Ku, notary; Francisco Antonio Canul, alcalde; Simón Piste, alcalde; Juan Ucan, Gonzalo Poot, regidoresob; Gaspar Ku, regidor.

4.6. Petition from Dzaptun

Here in the cah of San Juan Bautista Dzaptun, today on the 20th day of July of the year 1605. The following words of ours are true, that we are forced to undergo hardship by the governor marshal. O father, great king, we are petitioning to you for the sake of our father, God; we kiss your hands and feet; hear our words! We are made to suffer hardship and a great deal of work, and also we cut wood for them but they do not give us our rightful payment. For this reason, they sent a judge who came here to our town. We are made to suffer hardship. You our father, you the king, know of the troubles of your cahob! They have no fields to feed them, and many of their children will die from lack of food. This is why we make a petition in your presence, so that you protect us and take pity, for the sake of you, our father, you, our great lord, you, the Viceroy, so our misery and poverty be seen by you, for God's sake. You, our father, take pity on us, alleviate our misery. There are many deaths among us, your children, because the provincial governor causes troubles, because of the fatigue of the people, because they carry planks of wood two or three leagues and raise up beams, and because we carry hay and firewood. All these miseries he gives to us. May you, our father, O lord, and also you, our father, the Oidor, know the miseries of us, your children, and intercede for us before the lord Viceroy! This is our statement and the petition of us, your children. For God's sake you are to do good to us and take pity. It is for the sake of our father, God, that you should help us. Our father, the padre, also knows our suffering and poverty. This is the reason that we make a petition to you, our father, you, our lord, and why we are telling you of our suffering, we, the local people of the jurisdiction of, we of the province of, Campeche. O father, our statement is over. May the blessing of our lord God be upon you.

Lorenzo Chi, *procurador*; Diego Chuc, regidor; Juan Cante, regidor; Gaspar May, regidor; Luis Na, alcalde; Juan Pol, alcalde; Juan Pot, alcalde; also in the presence of me, Antonio Kuil, notary; Francisco To; Gaspar Pol.

4.7. Petition from the Maya Cabildo of Xcupilcacab to Replace their Town Governor, 1812[6]

As we saw in document 4.3, the relationship between colonial Mesoamerican cabildos and town governors was always a complex one. In theory, the governor was not a member of the cabildo, and in the early colonial period tended to be a hereditary lord or cacique. By the late colonial period, however, the governorship was more often treated as the senior cabildo post. This was certainly true in Yucatan, where the batab *(as Mayas called the town governor) was typically not only a nobleman but had also held other cabildo posts earlier in his career – such as lieutenant, alcalde, or notary. As in document 4.3, the petition here illustrates how the eligibility and legitimacy of a town governor was tied up in the issues of individual careers, hereditary status, political factionalism, and the loose relationship between Spanish requirements and local native practices and traditions.*

The apparent simplicity of the situation presented here is probably deceptive. Note that the current batab, *who allegedly wishes to retire, does not appear as a signator to the petition, whereas the four candidates for his replacement are described in such a way as to heavily favor the first, Rafael Tzin. As was common in colonial Mesoamerican towns, a veneer of compliance with colonial procedures covers the real machinations of local politics and traditional practices.*

We the lieutenant, magistrates, regidores, and notary are from here, the cah of San Antonio Xcupilcacab, where we are appearing before our lord God and before his great honor our lord the Defensor, through whose good services, and in the name of our lord God, our petition is presented to his great honor our lord Governor of Yucatan. Wherefore, a great misery has befallen us: We have nobody to represent us, because our lord batab has grown very old and has lost the heart to rule. He is weak of mind and no longer desires to represent us. We request as a favor before our lord God and his great honor our lord the governor of the province that there be a change of the lord batab that governs us in this town and teaches us the commandments of our lord God. The four regidores and other principal men in this town request the favor that our lord Rafael Tzin govern us in this town, because he is of sound mind and has served as *alcalde mesón* (councillor in charge of the town guesthouse), chief regidor, and also as lieutenant. It is understood and remembered how very well he protects the town. Secondly, lord Felipe Tzab also served as chief regidor. It is understood and remembered how very well he protects the town also. Thirdly, there is Benito Puc. He too is known as a good man and an intelligent one. This completes and ends the statement made before our lord God and his great honor our lord the Defensor and his great honor

6   Translated from Yucatec Maya by Restall, from the original document in TULAL, Rare Manuscript Collection 1, 25: f. 2. A brief excerpt from the document was published in transcription and translation in Restall (1997: 80), where the document is also briefly analyzed and contextualized.

our lord the governor of Yucatan. This is the truth. We sign below on this day, the 15th of February, 1812.

Francisco Balam, lieutenant; Baltesar Tun, Antonio Pech, alcaldes; Martín Naal, Juan Jose May, Juan May, Toribio Ek, regidores; Damaso Baaz, notary.

4.8. Mixtec Palace Possession Ceremony, Teposcolula, 1569[7]

In the Mixteca, yya toniñe or rulers of yuhuitayu lived in royal residences or palaces called aniñe. Archaeological and documentary evidence suggests that the structural characteristics of palaces in the Mixteca were similar to those in central Mexico. In general, single-story stone and adobe structures, each with its separate entrance, were arranged around sunken patios. One of the best, earliest accounts of an aniñe comes from Yucundaa (Teposcolula). Documentation from the 1560s describes the aniñe of Yucundaa as a structure which stood "fronting the monastery," precisely on the site where a building called "la Casa de la Cacica" stands today. The decorative disc motif on the upper part of the outer walls conforms with motifs on palace structures in the Codex Nuttall, the Codex Yanhuitlan, and other writings from the Mixteca and central Mexico (for example, the Florentine Codex and the Codex Mendoza).

In the case of Teposcolula, doña Catalina de Peralta, an heiress to the rulership of Yucundaa, lay claim to the palace that belonged to her deceased uncle, don Felipe de Austria (not without dissent from another faction within Teposcolula). In 1569, she presented ancient paintings and colonial testaments as evidence of her claim. The palace consisted of separate dwelling places or rooms within a compound, divided by patios and separate entrances. The following excerpt describes an early colonial palace possession ceremony in which doña Catalina and her husband, a lord from another community in the Mixteca, walked through the palace and took possession of its various rooms in front of native nobles and Spanish officials. The ceremony personified a familiar image in the codices – ruling figures seated on reed mats, usually inside or in front of a palace. The image represented a Mixtec construction of male and female political rule known as the yuhuitayu. The royal palace was the site of a reed mat throne, the seat of power where the lords lived and ruled. The palace was built around the same time as the nearby church and its impressive outdoor open chapel. Just as the native palace combined Mixtec and European architectural features (such as hinged doors and arches), the ceremony itself is a hybrid series of gestures and postures: the ritual of slamming doors and throwing stones resembles typical Spanish ceremonial acts of possession in New Spain, whereas the seating ceremony on mats is reminiscent of the ancient codices. The act was part of a legal proceeding that generated a written record and title, presided over by Spanish officials. If native

7   Translated from Spanish by Terraciano and Sousa. The original document is in AGN-Tierras 24, 6: ff. 37–40. For a full discussion of this ceremony, see Terraciano (2001: 160–64).

ritual remained at the core of the ceremony in the 1560s, it faded from view in the later period. Only this early version of the ceremony records the seating of male and female lords on reed mats, representing and enacting the symbol of the yuhuitayu before the community. Later colonial descriptions of the ceremony focus on formal Spanish acts, crowned by the transfer of keys to the palace from the alcalde mayor to the male cacique.

Possession of the houses of the cabecera.

On the said day, the eighth of November of the said year of 1569, the said lord Juan Sarmiento, judge of the petition of the said doña Catalina de Peralta and don Diego de Mendoza, her husband, in compliance with the said royal order, went to the principal houses of the said don Felipe de Austria, that they say belonged to the said cacicazgo that are in the said pueblo, fronting the (Dominican) monastery of the pueblo. And being in the locked doorway to the houses, the lord judge ordered certain Indians who appeared inside to open the doors. But they did not want to open them, so the lord Francisco Montalegre ordered that they open them, and then they opened the said doors. When the said lord Francisco Montalegre and the lord judge Juan Sarmiento entered the patio of the said houses certain native men and women raised their voices. They wanted to enter the said house but the said lord Francisco Montalegre defended the door from them, and then the said lord judge ordered certain Indians who were in the said house to give him the keys of the chambers that were locked; they did not want to give him the keys.

Then the said lord judge ordered opened the main upper chambers of the said house, and he took the said doña Catalina Peralta and don Diego de Mendoza, her husband, by the hands and he led them inside the said chamber and then into another more interior chamber and then into another chamber, and in each one of the said rooms the said doña Catalina and don Diego passed through and closed and opened the windows of the house as a sign of possession and they went along throwing out certain people who were inside as a sign of possession, and after closing the doors they remained there inside and then the said lord judge, as a sign of the said possession, led them by the hands, the said doña Catalina and don Diego, into all the lower chambers of the house. And in one of those rooms where there were some *petates* (mats, from the Nahuatl *petlatl*) placed on the floor and *yquipales* (seats, from the Nahuatl *icpatl*), the said doña Catalina and don Diego seated themselves on them. And then they walked along and passed through the patio of the said house, all which they said they used to do and did as a sign that they took and seized true possession of the said houses, and they requested and required that the said lord judge order thrown out and ejected from [the houses] all the things and clothing that were there, that they [the houses] be made vacant and cleared and that possession be granted to them, whereupon the said lord judge ordered the alcaldes of the said pueblo who were present to clear it out and to leave them to enjoy their possession freely, the said doña Catalina and don Diego, which he granted them in the name of his majesty, and after having passed through it, the said don Diego and doña Catalina threw everyone who was there out of the said house; remaining inside they closed the doors to the street and placed in charge of keeping the houses don Diego de Mendoza, governor of the pueblo of Coyotepec; the father of the said don Diego de Mendoza remained inside the houses.

And they requested the testimony (official verification) of all that was said and declared through the tongue of the said Francisco Martín, interpreter. And I, the scribe, swear to all the acts of possession that they performed since entering through the doors to the street of the said houses until the last that occurred. Baltasar de Rivera disputed it in the name of the said pueblo, saying that he contradicted the said possession in the name of his faction and he requested testimony, and the said lord judge ordered that it [testimony] be required of all those present, who were witnesses: Juan de Valdevieso, Bartolomé de Laguna, Gaspar Peláez, Hernando de Ávila, and other lord nobles.

Juan Sarmiento. Francisco Martín. Alonso de Olivares.

And after the abovementioned, in the said day, month, and year, the said judge went to other houses that bordered the said houses on one side of the royal street, in the middle, they stood at the doorway of them, the said lord Francisco de Montalegre, the said lord Juan Sarmiento, judge, took the hands of the said doña Catalina Peralta and don Diego, her husband, and led them inside the said houses. And being inside of them, as a sign of possession, the said doña Catalina Peralta and don Diego de Mendoza told certain Indians who were present to leave the said houses, and they cleared them. And when they left the said doña Catalina and don Diego de Mendoza entered all the rooms of the said house and in one of them they sat down on some petates and yquipales seats that were there. And they asked for the key to one of the rooms that was locked, which was given to them, and the said don Diego opened it with his own hand and the said lord judge led him into the said room, with the said doña Catalina, his wife, and having passed through it they turned to leave and the said don Diego locked the said room and he gave and handed over the key to Francisco Pérez, alcalde of the said pueblo, in order to guard it, he who received it in the name of the said don Diego and doña Catalina, who then threw out of the said houses everyone who was present and, remaining inside of the said house they closed the main doors to the street, all which they said they used to do and did as a sign of possession. And they asked the lord judge to protect and defend them and they requested testimony, and thus the said interpreter declared it to all who were present. And the said Baltasar de Rivera, who spoke in the name of the said pueblo of Teposcolula, contradicted the said possession and requested testimony, and the said lord judge in the name of his majesty said that he granted and grants to the said don Diego and the said doña Catalina de Peralta, his wife, the possession of the said houses, and he ordered that nobody disturb them, and he required the testimony of the witnesses who were present: Juan de Valdevieso, Gaspar Peláez, Hernando de Ávila, and other Spaniards.

Juan Sarmiento. Francisco Martín. Alonso de Olivares.

And after the abovementioned, in the said pueblo of Teposcolula, on the said day of the eighth of November of the said year, the said lord judge, continuing with the said possession, went to other houses which are next to the abovementioned houses that are said to be part of the said cacicazgo. At the door the said lord Francisco de Montalegre, the judge, and the said Juan Sarmiento took doña Catalina de Peralta and don Diego de Mendoza by the hands and led them into the said houses as a sign of possession and the abovementioned, being inside, entered all the other rooms of the said houses and passed through them and sat on some mats and Indian seats that were there and ordered to open a room that was locked with a key, which was opened, and the said doña Catalina and don Diego entered the said room and closed it from within and the said don Diego locked it with his own hand, and he handed it over to the said Francisco Pérez, alcalde, who was to guard the keys in his name; and after it was verified the abovementioned don Diego and doña Catalina threw everyone who was present out of the said houses and closed the doors from the inside. All by means of the said interpreter, they said that they used to do and did it as a sign of possession and they asked the said judge to protect and defend them; and he requested the testimony of all those who were present. The said Baltasar de Rivera, in the name of his said faction, contradicted the said possession and requested testimony. And the said judge stated that in the name of his majesty he granted the said don Diego de Mendoza and doña Catalina, his wife, possession of the said houses and ordered to give testimony to the said factions, the witnesses being the said Juan de Valdivieso, Gaspar Peláez, Bartolomé de Laguna, Hernando de Ávila, and other Spaniards.

Juan Sarmiento. Francisco Martín. Escribano Alonso Olivares.

And later, the said don Diego and doña Catalina, his wife, as a sign of possession passed through their large patio that is in front of the said houses on the street, that they say is attached to them, and they threw stones from one part to the other and the said Baltasar de Rivera made the same contradiction

4.8a The "Casa de la Cacica" in Teposcolula, Oaxaca. The photo, taken by Terraciano in 2003, shows part of the complex described in the ceremony of 1569.

4.8b Image of the Mixtec yuhuitayu from the pre-Conquest–style Codex Becker II, p. 4. Courtesy of the Museum Für Völkerkunde, Wien. Facsimile edition by Akademische Druck u. Verlagsanstalt, Graz/Austria 1961.

and requested the testimony of all who were present. And the said lord judge ordered all who were present to give the abovementioned.

Juan Sarmiento. Francisco Martín. Escribano Alonso Olivares.

Later in the said month and year the said don Diego and doña Catalina, his wife, through the interpreter, said before the lord judge that, in front of and close to the main houses of which they were given possession, there are some rooms that at the present time are the lodgings of the said lord Francisco Montalegre, judge in residence, and a kitchen which belongs to the said houses for the receiving of nobles who come to them [the houses]. They request and require of the said lord judge to order to give them possession of the said rooms and kitchen and the said lord judge then took the said doña Catalina de Peralta and don Diego de Mendoza by the hands and he led them into all of the rooms where the said don Francisco Montalegre lodges, which are in the abovementioned place, and the said don Diego and doña Catalina passed through them and closed and opened the doors and, at the same time, they entered the said kitchen room and passed through it and its large patio, which is in front of the said rooms, throwing stones from one part to the next, all which they say that they used to do and did as a sign of possession and property. And they asked the lord judge for his protection, to defend them, and for the testimony of all those who were present. And the said Baltasar de Rivera, in the name of the said pueblo, contradicted the possession and requested testimony. And the said lord judge ordered it from the witnesses, the said Juan de Valdevieso, Gaspar de Peláez, Bartolomé de Laguna, and Hernando de Ávila.

Juan Sarmiento. Francisco Martín. Escribano Alonso Olivares.

4.9. Excerpt from the Mixtec Codex Sierra, or the Community Accounts of Santa Catalina Texupa, 1550–1564[8]

Written from 1550 to 1564, this "codex" is actually a book of accounts from Santa Catalina Texupa with parallel pictographic and alphabetic components. The pictorial portion is arranged on the left side of the page, with separate space for alphabetic commentary in the middle column, and numerical accounts on the far right. The alphabetic text is written in Nahuatl, but the manuscript comes from Texupa, a Mixtec-Chocho community in the Mixteca Alta. There are many indications that the text was written by Mixtecs who were fluent in the Nahuatl language before Mixtec-language alphabetic writing was fully developed in this area.

8 Translated from Nahuatl by Terraciano and Sousa, using a transcription of the original text in León (1933). See Terraciano (2000b) for a discussion of the Codex Sierra.

The account book reveals how this community spent its money during this period, but it does not tell us how it made the money. This part of the Mixteca Alta enjoyed a booming silk trade in the sixteenth century, and the Dominicans played an active role in promoting the new enterprise. This boom would turn to bust by the end of the century, as the indigenous population of the region continued to decline precipitously, and as tons of silk from the so-called China Trade (mainly from the Philippines) entered New Spain through the port of Acapulco. In any case, it is clear that the community of Texupa spent a substantial sum on church activities and religious objects during this period, including feasts for saints, food for priests, and much more. On behalf of the church, the community bought everything from trumpets and chalices to fancy vestments of taffeta and velvet. At least half of Texupa's monetary expenses from 1550 to 1564 were related to religious feasts, goods for the church, and food and wine for priests.

The local Spanish-style municipal council, the cabildo, is a prominent group in the manuscript. Although it is true that the new cabildo consisted of the same hereditary group of native nobles who ruled in pre-Conquest times, it was a Spanish institution that excluded women. In Mixtec society, women participated in political affairs by virtue of their position as hereditary rulers of the yuhuitayu. After the conquest, women continued to exercise important decision-making responsibilities within their communities, but they were ineligible for a seat on the officially sanctioned and salaried cabildo. The Codex Sierra suggests how female rulers (called cacicas in Spanish and yya dzehe toniñe in Mixtec) were marginalized by the all-male cabildo. In the earliest years of the document, the cacica doña Catalina is portrayed as a very prestigious person. Doña Catalina can be seen as early as 1551, when she is seated in the palace in front of the unnamed governor. It is likely that this anonymous governor was her spouse, who derived his position from her authority in the community. Doña Catalina appears several times with the governor and other nobles as representatives of the community. Each year, she is seated in front of all the nobles, receiving quantities of food and drink. One of the entries indicates that she is no longer responsible for the assessment of tribute, and hence the Spanish priest (vicar) receives more money for food and drink from the community than she and the other nobles do. She is last seen in 1554. In 1559, a full cabildo appears for the first time, and now the governor is seated in front of a body of nobles who occupy the various offices of the cabildo. Two years later, they appear in profile next to the caja de comunidad (community chest); they receive an annual salary for their positions on the cabildo.

Below are excerpts from the years 1551 and 1561.

1551

Today, in the year 1551 (the year is spelled out in Nahuatl, according to the vigesimal numbering system) the year (written in Mixtec, according to the Mixtec version of the Mesoamerican calendar) nuhuiyo (6 Reed), the vicar settled here. He is Alonso Maldonado, a secular priest. When it happened here in the altepetl, eight metal trumpets were purchased along with food for the Mexica who made them. All together it cost 120 pesos.

Twenty-nine pesos is the cost of all the iron that was needed for the chests and for the chest of the holy sacrament.

Sixty-one pesos were given for a blue velvet canopy to be hung in front of the holy sacrament; a yellow vase that is used for flowers and one gold cloth that hangs from the altar.

A white damask sacred vestment and a priestly cloak were purchased for fifty-seven pesos; it was all needed, it was purchased for Santa María.

Sixty-two pesos were needed when it was Easter of the Resurrection and church candles were needed for Holy Week and wine, cacao, turkeys, and food during Easter.

Forty pesos were given for one black taffeta altar covering and red altar coverings for the church there.

Two things: tall candlestick holders were made. The Mexica made them very well on a turning wheel; they gilded them. Because it was gilded forty-eight pesos were given. And another thing was purchased in Mexico [City] for fifteen pesos, which all together cost sixty-three pesos.

Sixty-two pesos were needed for the feast day of Santa Catalina, [for] the cacao, wine, turkeys, and fruit. Thus it was purchased along with some other things.

Thirty-two pesos were needed for the purchase of wine and food for [the feast of] Christmas.

Sixty-nine pesos a year for food for Alonso Maldonado, vicar here in the altepetl.

Five pesos for the orders of the *alcaldes* and *alguaciles* this year.

The food of the noblewoman doña Catalina when it was no longer her assessment (using the Spanish loan word *tasacion*), and the governor and the lords of the altepetl, forty-two pesos a year, that is all, forty-two pesos.

The alguaciles and the others who served the altepetl divided among themselves twenty pesos that were left from the silk [sales]. Twenty pesos, that is all.

1561

Today, [in] the year 1561 (the year is spelled out in Nahuatl) the year (written in Mixtec) *gamao* (3 House), for the first time money was taken out of the caxa (Spanish loan word for community treasury chest). The governor, alcaldes, regidores, mayordomos, fiscal, and alguaciles who serve [on the cabildo] were given 130 pesos.

[Some] large paper and blue, red, and black ink were bought for fifteen pesos; they are all Spanish items for the church books that are to be made. They are needed by the church for songs.

Nineteen pesos and four tomines were spent on twelve cotton cloaks that are needed by the hospital; one peso and five tomines were given for each one. That is all that was said.

One load of cacao (chocolate) was purchased for the lords of the palace; thirty pesos were given [for it].

Four arrobas (weight or liquid measure) of wax that the church needs were bought for one hundred pesos, and one arroba was measured for the Easter candle.

Fifteen pesos is its price – the Castilian copal incense, the Castilian *estoraques* (type of tree, the bark of which was used for incense), and some paper from here that was needed for the altar.

Woven [reed or palm] mats that the church needs now were bought for six pesos.

Fish, large shrimp, and eggs for Lent were bought for twenty-five pesos. They were needed for the lord vicar and [the people of] the palace to eat.

Six pesos were given for one load of large shrimp.

Two arrobas of wine were bought for sixteen pesos. They were given to the lord vicar for the masses that will be said.

Forty pesos were needed [for food] during Easter that was eaten by [the people of] the palace and the other rulers who came.

It cost 281 pesos for a white damask cloak, with dark blue and red velvet all along its border and one cloth that is adorned with red taffeta for the lord bishop. This cloth was made by Tomás de las Cuevas there in Oaxaca.

216 pesos were given to the lord Juan de Villafane because eight pounds of silk seeds (cocoons) were bought from him. It was done for twenty-seven pesos per pound.

Twenty-three pesos were given for one pound of tithe silk seeds (cocoons).

Forty-two pesos [were given] for the food of the Spaniard who cultivates the silk here, because we agreed to it this way.

Fifteen cloaks were purchased for forty-five pesos because the silk seeds (cocoons) will sprout from them; there are three pieces of cloth for each cloak.

Ten pesos for the two saddles that were made.

Eight pesos were given to two nobles because they went to Mexico [City] on behalf of the altepetl in order to take gold and silk.

Forty pesos were needed for the feast of the Holy Spirit, for things that were purchased by the palace.

Forty pesos were needed for the feast day of San Pedro and San Pablo.

Thirty pesos were given to Juan Frayle, Spaniard [and] mason; he will make repairs here in the hospital of the altepetl.

Sugar that the hospital needed was purchased for ten pesos.

Wine and raisins needed for the hospital were purchased for twenty pesos.

Fifty pesos were given to those who cure people, the curers there in the hospital and the medicinal herbs and all the commoners who work there.

Forty pesos were needed when it was Corpus Christi; there was a decree to purchase things.

Twenty-six pesos were needed for the feast of the lord Santiago; many rulers came here.

Fifty pesos were given to those whose property is the tithe; it was purchased with cotton.

Paint was purchased for twenty-three pesos and the cost of a painter who painted in the church.

Two wooden, golden images were made for forty-four pesos.

4.9a Page from the Codex Sierra depicting doña Catalina, the Mixtec *cacica* or hereditary ruler of Santa Catalina Texupa. Seated in the palace, in front of other lords, she
receives food from the community. From León 1933, p. 4.

Six blankets were purchased; they were needed for the priests who have been
in charge here. Twenty-four pesos were given.

Forty *varas* (measure of length) of Spanish cloth for mattresses were purchased for twenty-five pesos; it was needed by the hospital.

Twenty *fanegas* (measure of dry weight) of Castilian maize (wheat) were purchased for forty pesos; it was needed by the vicar and the community.

One hundred fanegas of maize were purchased for one hundred pesos here
in the altepetl; it was needed by the community and to feed the vicar.

Two *arrobas* of oil were purchased for five pesos; it was needed by the hospital.

Ten pesos were given to the nobles who went to Mexico [City] to pick up the
decrees for the alcaldes, alguaciles, and regidores and others.

Iron for the silk spinning wheel and other things were purchased for sixty-two
pesos and four tomines.

Forty pesos were given to the church people (native church attendants), as is
done every year for those who serve [the church].

Four cotton loads were purchased for thirty-two pesos in order to make
cloaks; it was needed for the feast day of Santa Catalina.

Forty-four pesos were given to four people who will take care of the sheep
house.

Wood that is needed there for the silk house was purchased for 162 pesos; it
was all done.

4.9b Page from the Codex Sierra depicting the all-male cabildo of Santa Catalina Texupa in 1561 (top frame), from León 1933, p. 35.

Reeds from Tuctlan were purchased for twenty-two pesos; it was all needed for the silk house.

Five hundred pesos were given for the tribute that was sent to Mexico [City].

130 pesos were given to the governor and all those who work here in the altepetl.

Fifty-six pesos and four tomines were needed for those who take care of the sheep house.

Fifteen pesos were given to a person from Tlaxiaco because every year he stays at the *estancia*.

Twenty handfuls of paper were purchased [because] it is needed for the church; eight pesos were given.

A golden ring with a jade stone inside was purchased [because] it is needed by the church; thirteen pesos were given for it.

Thirty-two pesos were given for a book of organ music.

Wood that was needed for an altar was purchased for twenty-two pesos, and to pay the carpenter who made it.

One arroba of candles was purchased because it was needed by the church; twenty-five pesos were given.

Seven bunches of quetzal feathers and other things were purchased for seventy-five pesos to decorate the *altepetl* properties.

Twelve *varas* of red velvet were purchased for 132 pesos to make sacred vestments; it will be needed for the church here.

Forty-one pesos and four tomines were needed for the silk to be brought to Mexico [City]. In order to do it, rope, mats, packframes, and palm baskets were purchased, and food for all those who carried it; all for forty-one pesos and four tomines.

One hundred pesos were given to the people who take care of the silk, ten pesos for each person.

5

HOUSEHOLD AND LAND

This chapter and the following one are closely related, as the documents in both provide insight into the topics of household and land, as well as society and gender. Both chapters also contain several examples of the most common genre of native-language writing, the last will and testament. Our focus in this chapter, however, is on how wills and other documents reveal the ways in which Mesoamericans constituted their homes, families, and neighborhoods and conceived of land use and ownership.

Indigenous landholding was communal only in a qualified sense. A household worked its own lands individually; the different members of the household divided multiple, scattered plots among them to work. A household could keep all its land through inheritance as long as there were members to work each of the plots. This was true of both nobles and commoners, and among both, holdings varied a great deal, some people having much more land than others, and some commoners having no land of their own. The community intervened, often immediately, to reallocate any land that was left uncultivated. Thus, native landholding did not easily divide into public and private categories, like the European system. Everything from the lord's land to that of an ordinary household shared both aspects. Everyone paid taxes to the community based on the extent of their landholdings and other forms of household wealth.

Land tenure categories were as complex as the social relations that governed the distribution of wealth and resources within Mesoamerican communities. In general, a complex terminology existed to specify whether the lands had been granted by the community or had been purchased, or whether they belonged to the palace or were inherited from family members. Other terms designated the type and quality of land.

After the Conquest, the whole system of household structure, land tenure, and organization, including all the categories, survived. As a result of the Conquest and with continuing depopulation, Spaniards took land for themselves, especially as their cities grew and they began to demand more land. But in most parts of Mesoamerica native people retained substantial amounts of land throughout the colonial period. The indigenous system underwent gradual but significant modification. Native pictorial and oral methods of recording land gave way to or converged with the last will and testament, which became an important register of lands and a *de facto* legal title to land in indigenous communities and in Spanish courts. This is one reason why they were so important in this period, and why so many have survived in the archival record. Another reason is that priests promoted the writing of testaments for obvious reasons: to account for one's body and soul, to settle matters of debt and inheritance, and to leave something for the church. In addition to being important sources of information on landholding, last wills and testaments also tell us much about kinship structure, inheritance patterns, houses, and material culture. The acquisition of European goods is notable, too.

The dictation of a dying person's last will and testament was a less private and more public ritual in Mesoamerican communities than it was in the Spanish world. A Spaniard's will normally was witnessed by three men, whereas a Mesoamerican will was a speech to a group of relatives and friends that was often recorded before some members of the *cabildo* or town council, who even put their names to the document, and any other men and women who were available. Although native wills were supposed to follow certain formulas established by the Church, in reality they exhibit considerable variety. Most do indeed open with a native-language version of the religious preamble used in Spanish wills, but even that preamble could be very long (document 5.6), or highly truncated (document 5.10), or very formulaic, varying little from year to year and testator to testator in any given town (documents 5.7 and 5.8). The declaration usually affirms the testator's belief in basic Christian principles, especially the Ten Commandments and Articles of Faith; often, requests are made for the intercession of the Virgin Mary and other saints on behalf of the soul and one's entry into Heaven. Alms are given to various saints and religious confraternities. These statements reflect only an impression of one's faith, but they do reveal how indigenous men and women actually talked about fundamental Christian concepts. After these religious parts, wills turn to earthly matters by enumerating the lands, possessions, debts, and credits of the sick one and by naming executors to ensure that the testator's will is carried out. Some wills amounted to no more than a few opening lines of religious formula, reflecting the poverty of the testator; others (but not many) are lengthy documents cataloguing the vast possessions of a powerful native lord. And one of the wills here is not technically a will at all; document 5.9 resulted from a Maya man dying intestate, obliging his cabildo to settle his estate for him.

The importance of native wills lies in the wealth of information they can provide historians – about, for example, patterns of inheritance, or ways of recording (or, in document 5.12, falsifying) land ownership in order to prevent or resolve disputes. Document 5.12, which is the legal record of a land dispute that embodies within it an old testament, is a good illustration of the intersection between wills and other types of documents. That intersection is further suggested by the other genres represented here, specifically an unusually detailed census document (5.1), and three different kinds of records (translated from Nahuatl, Zapotec, and Yucatec) of the transfer of plots of land from one Mesoamerican to another (documents 5.2, 5.4, and 5.9). These land records show the persistence of rich native rituals of possession and description, as well as the continual struggle to control access to land and prevent outsiders – be they Spaniards (documents 5.3, 5.4, and 5.5) or natives from a neighboring town (document 5.11) – from acquiring community lands.

5.1. Portion of a Nahuatl Census from the Cuernavaca Region, c. 1540[1]

This census of a calpulli, *a subdistrict of an* altepetl, *represents one of the earliest examples of native-language records, written about two decades after the conquest. Consequently, it has great relevance for understanding pre-Conquest customs and practices. For example, one can see immediately that the lord Martín Molotecatl has been baptized, but that his extended household includes five wives, one who has still not been baptized by the time the document was written. The practice of polygyny, reserved mainly for nobles, was condemned and prohibited by the friars. He pays tribute four times a year, based on the amount of land that he possesses, and he is obligated to feed people from time to time. Note the types of labor that men and women perform. Obviously, Martín has many houses and properties in this calpulli; he is able to provide for his immediate relatives as well as people from other parts who are looking for a place to live and work. These dependents make their living working Martín's land and providing other services and types of labor. Finally, the number of adults and children who have died suggest that the epidemics are taking a heavy toll on the population.*

Here are the members of a calpulli; they are divided into nine parts. It begins at the place called Molotlan.

1. Here one named Martín Molotecatl teuctli is in charge. Here are his five wives; four are baptized and one is not. The first is named María Teyacapan. Here is his second wife, named Isabel Tlaco. Here is his third wife, named Magdalena Xocoyotl. Here is his fourth wife, named Angelina Necahual. Here is his fifth wife, not baptized; her native name is Tlaco.

Here are his five children. One is named Francisco Tlohui; he was born last year. Here is the second, named Catalina Teiuc; she is now three years

---

1   Translated from Nahuatl by Sousa, based on an earlier unpublished translation by Lockhart. A transcription of this document is in Hinz, Hartau, and Heimann-Koenen (1983, I: 1–9).

old. Here is the third, named Luis Xochitototl; he is now four years old. Here is the fourth of his children, baptized, named Magdalena . . . ; she is . . . years old. Each of these has a separate mother. And here is the fifth of his children, Mateo Tocuiltecatl, who is married; his mother died fifteen years ago. He has two wives. The first is named Magdalena Papan; she has no children. Here is his second wife, named María Xocoyotl; she has a child named Magdalena Teyacapan, who was born last year.

Here is Molotecatl's older sister, Cencihuatl, a little old woman who has not been baptized. Her husband died fifteen years ago; her children are no longer alive.

There are fifteen who live together in this household. His fields are four hundred *brazas* of irrigated field and two hundred of hill maize, on the basis of which his tribute is assembled every eighty days: five Cuernavaca-style blankets, an embroidered skirt, and an embroidered blouse. Each year he delivers twenty Cuernavaca-style blankets and four outfits with embroidered skirts. And every twenty days he feeds people; he gives three tribute blankets, two towels, 140 cacao beans, a turkey, and ten eggs, so that in a year it makes forty tribute blankets, twenty-six towels, thirteen turkeys, 1,800 cacao beans, and 130 eggs. Four times he gives tribute each year, and it is also his duty to feed people thirteen times.

2. The second house is that of Molotecatl's older brother, who does not pay tribute separately. His name is Juan Acolnahuacatl; his wife is named María Teiuc. His three children are baptized. The first is named Pedro Xolotl; he is twenty years old and is not married. The second is Pedro Tlacatlatol, ten years old. The third is named Domingo Tecocol, eight years old.

Here are his fields: forty brazas of irrigated field that Molotecatl gave him, for which he lives next to him and cultivates Molotecatl's fields for him, and he contributes two-fourths of a blanket to the tribute, but Molotecatl gives him the cotton.

Here is Molotecatl's sister-in-law. She is only a little old woman who lives with his older brother. She is not baptized; her name is Teiuc. Her husband died twenty years ago. A son of hers is alive, named Francisco Nauhyotl. His wife is named Magdalena Xocoyotl; his child is named Tomás Tlilton, born last year.

Here are their fields: twenty brazas that Molotecatl gave them. They contribute one-fourth of a blanket to the tribute and Molotecatl also sends them on errands.

Here is a little old woman, Molotecatl's great-aunt; she also accompanies Molotecatl's older brother. She is not baptized; her name is Teyacapan. Twenty years ago (her husband died). She has a daughter named Ana Teiuc; her husband died three years ago; she has no children. The old woman also has a grandchild named P . . . ahua, twenty years old, not married; he was orphaned fifteen years ago.

Here is their land: twenty brazas of irrigated field that Molotecatl gave them. They give a fourth of a blanket for the tribute. Martín Molotecatl says: "the women do hired work, since I always give them the cotton, and the men cultivate the land."

Here is a woman who lives here, from Tepoztlan. Her name is Ichpochton; she is not baptized and is not married. Twenty years ago she was left an orphan. She helps with grinding the maize with the metate.

There are thirteen people together in this house.

3. At the third house is the aunt of Molotecatl. She is a little old woman named Magdalena Teiuc; her husband died fifteen years ago and none of her children are alive. She has a grandchild named María Teyacapan whose husband is named Pedro Tonehuatl; they have no children. Here is Pedro Tonehuatl's aunt, an old woman named Magdalena Cencihuatl; her husband died twenty-five years ago, and she has no live children.

Here is his field: twenty brazas of irrigated field that Molotecatl gave him. He too contributes a fourth of a blanket as tribute, which he gives to Molotecatl, and that is all.

Here is another person who is a dependent of Martín Molotecatl, from Ecatepec, called Ohuatl, not baptized; he lives together with Pedro Tonehuatl. Forty days ago his wife died; he has a child called Ana, and her native name is Ilamaton, who was born last year. Here is another dependent who lives here, a woman from Mexico City; her name is Ana, and her native name is Xoco; they came fifteen years ago. The woman has no husband.

Here is his field: twenty brazas that he works, that Martín Molotecatl gave him. All he does for it is go on errands, and also the woman helps with spinning cotton.

Six people live together in the three houses that share one patio.

Here is the third [sic] house, which also belongs to Martín Molotecatl. Here is a person named Xochitl, unbaptized; he has a wife named Teyacapan, unbaptized. They have no children. Here is the sister-in-law of Xochitl's wife, called Tecapan, not baptized; her husband died last year. A daughter of hers is married elsewhere. Here is Xochitl's niece, named Isabel; her native name is Teiuc. She is fifteen years old and not yet married.

Here is his field: twenty brazas of hill maize is all he works. All he does [in the way of tribute] is cultivate the fields of Martín Molotecatl, and his wife helps with the yarn. There are four people who live together in this house.

4. Here is another house that belongs to Martín. The head of the fourth household is named Tomás, and his native name is Xochtonal; his wife is called Magdalena Teiuc. They have two children, the first named Ana Tlacoton, three years old, and the second named Josef Tlamacaton, born last year. They

are not married in the church. Here are Tomás's niece and nephew. One is named Domingo Tlacocolilton, seven years old, and the other is named María Tlaco. Her husband is named Juan Ecatl; they have no children yet, and are not married in the church. Here is Tomás's older sister, called María Mocel; her husband is named Francisco Pilhua. They are not married in the church. They have a child named Quauhton, unbaptized, who was born sixty days ago. Here is Francisco's stepchild, named Juan Cihuatlato, eight years old. Here is a nephew of Tomás, named Mateo Xelli. His wife is called Magdalena Papan; they have no children yet. Here is a dependent of Tomás who came from Tepoztlan, named Magdalena Tecapan; she is fifteen years old, and was orphaned ten years ago.

Here is his field: forty brazas of irrigated field that Martín Molotecatl teuctli gave him. He makes no contribution to the tribute; all he does as his duty is cultivate the fields of Martín Molotecatl. Martín says: "I give them cotton, they spin it, and when it is spun they bring the yarn; that is all."

There are fourteen people who live together in this house.

5. Here is another house that belongs to Martín. At the fifth house is a person named Catalina Xocoyotl whose husband died this past year. She has two children, the first named Tomás Mimich, two hundred days old, and the second not baptized, named Coacihuatl, also two hundred days old. Here are Catalina's stepchildren, whom her husband had with someone else. There are two; the first is named Domingo Matlal, twenty years old and not yet married, and the second is named Magdalena Techuicho, fifteen years old and not yet married. Here is their aunt named Isabel Tlaco, not yet married, twenty years old.

Here is her field: five brazas of irrigated field, for which she helps with making yarn from the cotton Martín Molotecatl delivers and cultivates Martín's fields.

Here is another person, named Martín Itzcuin, from Mexicatzinco. His wife is named Ana Teiuc; their children are no longer alive. They came fifteen years ago. They live together with Catalina. All they did was try to make a living. He says: "Let us be given a field on which we will pay tribute; we will not go back to our hometown, since we came [here] a long time ago."

His field is three brazas of irrigated field that they granted him; he does nothing for it.

There are eight people who live together in this house.

6. Here is another house that belongs to Martín. At the sixth house is a person named Juan Chalchiuh; his wife is named Magdalena Tlaco. They have two children, the first named Juan Tlilhua, twenty years old and not yet married, the second named María Tecapan; she has a husband named Tomás Ixquet-zaloc and a child named Tlohui, unbaptized. Here is Juan's nephew called Xolotl; he is not baptized, and he is fifteen years old. Here is Juan Chalchiuh's

brother-in-law, named Francisco Quauhtli; his wife is named Ana Teiuc. They have no children; they just accompany Juan Chalchiuh.

Here is his field: forty brazas of irrigated field that Molotecatl gave him; for it he contributed two-fourths of a blanket to the tribute, which he gives to Martín Molotecatl, and that is all that he delivers every eighty days, and also he cultivates.

There are nine people who live together in this house.

5.2. Nahuatl Grant of a House Site in San Miguel Tocuillan, 1583[2]

This unusual document, recorded as part narrative and part dialogue, was generated by the native cabildo to document an internal land transfer. The land transfer process is very typical, however, in that individuals approach the local authorities to inquire whether they may take possession of some unused land. In this case, Ana's brother brings four representatives from the cabildo to consider the issue. Ana not only politely serves them tortillas and pulque, a fermented alcoholic beverage, but she also does all the talking on behalf of her little family. Note how they speak of the land as if it belongs to San Miguel, the patron saint of their community, and the other Christian references that they make, even though there are no Spaniards present. The deal ends with tears of happiness and promises of devotion.

Ana spoke and said to her older brother Juan Miguel, "My dear older brother, let us stay under your roof for a few days, only a few days. I don't have many children, only my little Juan, the only child. There are only three of us with your brother-in-law Juan."

Then her older brother said, "Very well, my younger sister. Move what you have, let all your things be brought up."

Then the woman answered and said, "Thank you very much, my dear older brother, I appreciate your generosity. Even if I should get drunk, I say that I will never act badly in your house; rather, I will behave respectfully, and as to my husband Juan here, if he should ever lose respect, well, you are all there, I leave it in your hands as long as you hold the king's staff (are members of the local cabildo)."

Then Juan Miguel spoke and said to his younger sister Ana, "My younger sister, am I going to pick arguments with my brother-in-law, if he goes along behaving himself?"

Now it is far into October, the 20th of the month, and they have spent a whole month here now.

Then Ana said, "Don't let us give you so much trouble; let us take a bit of the precious land of our precious father the saint San Miguel, and there

---

2 Based on Lockhart (1991: 70–74), with modifications by Sousa, with Lockhart's consent.

we will build a little house. When the water has gone down and things have dried out, we'll move down."

Then her older brother said, "Let me tell Juan Francisco, and Juan Miguel of Pelaxtitlan, and also Francisco Baltasar, and also Anton Miguel of Teopanquiahuac. Don't worry, younger sister, they will not want. . . . Let me go get them right away, and you be making a tortilla or two. There's nothing for you to worry about; there's pulque for them to drink when they come."

Then he went to get them.

Then he said to his younger sister, "We're already back, younger sister; come greet us."

Then the four men said, "May God keep you, and how have you been today? Here we are."

Then Ana said, "Come in."

Then they all came in and sat down.

Then Ana spoke and said to her older brother, "Give them some tortillas, let them enjoy them."

Then the elders answered, "Let us enjoy your hospitality. And is there something that concerns you, noblewoman?"

Then Ana said, "In a moment you will hear what it is that concerns us." And when they had eaten, Ana came in and addressed herself to them, saying to them, "It is really for no reason that he summoned you. Here is what we beg, that we might request a bit of the land of our precious father the saint San Miguel, for we want to put up a little thatch house there. I don't have many children; the only one I have is little Juan alone. May we?"

Then Juan Francisco said, "Let it be given them. What do you say? Let's give it to them! Juan Miguel, take your cattle prod . . . to measure it with. Let's go, noblewoman, and see where you would like it to be."

Then they went. "Where would you like it to be? Here, or maybe over there? Say where you would like it to be."

Then the woman said, "Let it be here."

Then the lords said, "Then let it be there."

Then Juan Francisco said, "Who is going to measure it out?"

Then the lords said, "Who indeed? Other times, wasn't it dear old Juan? He'll measure it out."

Then they said to him, "Come, good Juan, take the cattle prod in your hands and measure it out. Measure out six lengths on all four sides."

And when he had measured it, then they said, "That's how much land we're giving you."

Then Ana said, "Thank you very much; we appreciate your generosity."

Then the lords said, "Let it begin right away; don't let the stone concern you, but let it quickly be prepared to begin the foundation."

Then Ana said, "Let's go back and you must enjoy a bit more pulque."

Then the rulers said, "What more do we wish? We've already had [enough]."

And Ana wept, and her husband wept, when they were given the land. Then Ana said, "Candles will be burnt, and I will go along providing incense for my precious father the saint San Miguel, because it is on his land that I am building my house."

Then Juan Miguel said, "We thank you on behalf of your precious father; let it always be so . . ."

When all five lords had spoken, everyone embraced.

Today, Friday, the 20th day of the month of October of the year 1583. I did the writing and it was done before me, don Juan Bautista, notary. The lords convened here in Amaxocotitlan.

Don Juan Miguel, regidor, don Baltasar Francisco, don Juan Francisco, don Juan Miguel of Pelaxtitlan, don Antonio Miguel of Teopanquiahuac.

5.3. Concerns Over the Sale of Nahua Nobles' Lands, Tlaxcala, 1552[3]

This brief document treats an issue of great concern – the loss of lands by nobles who could no longer count on the labor of local commoners to work them. The indigenous population declined precipitously during this period, and Spanish officials restricted the numbers of people obligated to serve native lords (because Spaniards were competing for that same increasingly scarce supply of labor, especially in this area of central Mexico). Commoners also found it easier to get land of their own as depopulation made land available. Thus, nobles found it more expedient to sell some of their vast landholdings, often to Spaniards who had the money to pay for them. All these developments signified the inevitable decline of the nobility, whose income depended on land and labor. Understanding the gravity of the situation, and perhaps exaggerating the extent to which lords were becoming commoners, the cabildo began to consider taking drastic measures to prevent a process that had only begun and would only get worse.

In the loyal city of Tlaxcala, on the 10th day of the month of May, in the year of the birth of our savior lord Jesus Christ 1552, there assembled and consulted here in cabildo the very honorable lords the governor don Domingo de Angulo; and the alcaldes ordinarios don Diego de Paredes, Félix Mejía, Alonso Gómez, and don Diego de Guzmán; and the rulers don Juan Maxixcatzin, don Julián Motolinia, and don Francisco de Mendoza; and all the regidores, don Julián de la Rosa, Buenaventura Oñate, Antonio del Pedroso, Antonio Téllez, don Domingo de Silva, Hernando Tececepotzin, Baltasar Cortés, don Juan de Paz, Pablo de Galicia, Lucas García, Pedro Díaz, and Tadeo de Niza; not in the presence of don Juan Xicotencatl, who is sick; before us, notaries of the cabildo, Fabián Rodríguez and Sancho de Rozas.

---

3   Translated from Nahuatl by Sousa, based on Lockhart, Berdan, and Anderson (1986: 85–86).

They deliberated about how the lordly houses are going very much to ruin now. Many of the nobles who live as part of them have sold their fields and have been left not as nobles but as commoners. And all the cabildo members said that in the next five or ten years or so the lordly houses' fields will come to an end; perhaps those who are in the lordly houses will become ordinary commoners, and the commoners who are buying the fields will be noblemen. Therefore, the cabildo ordered that the crier proclaim in the marketplace that the cabildo orders that none of the Tlaxcalan nobles is to sell his (or her) fields, and if it is discovered that someone sells them, his relatives are to take his remaining fields from him too; this is to be done before the alcaldes. And the cabildo ordered that if his relatives want to evict a person who has sold fields, it can be done; they can evict him, it is to be done before the governor and alcaldes. And so that it not be misunderstood, it is established that here in the city there may be selling and buying of property. Later it was put before the lord corregidor, Alonso de Galdo, who said, "An inquiry is to be made; then I will issue a decree." All the council members signed. The day, month, and year were given above.

Alonso de Galdo, don Diego de Paredes, Félix Mejía, don Juan Maxixcatzin, don Julián Motolinia, Alonso Gómez, don Diego de Guzmán, don Francisco de Mendoza, Baltasar Cortés, Pablo de Galicia, Lucas García, Tadeo de Niza, Buenaventura Oñate, Antonio del Pedroso, Hernando (Tececepotzin).

Done before us, the notaries: Fabián Rodríguez, notary, Sancho de Rozas.

5.4. Zapotec Land Transfer from Zimatlan, 1565[4]

This lone Zapotec document in our collection, from the Valley of Oaxaca, represents a concerted effort by the cabildo to ensure that Spaniards do not buy or otherwise acquire unused property. Thus, the cabildo is ratifying that a piece of land belongs to one Alonzo Caballero, presumably a Zapotec noble from Zimatlan, who possesses the titles and papers to defend his claim in a Spanish court of law, if necessary. Only a few decades after the Conquest, native cabildos were all too aware of the potential threat that Spaniards could pose when they sought to acquire unused land within or near the borders of a community, and how important writing was in documenting and confirming legal possession. This case also confirms the process glimpsed in

4 Translated by the "Zapotec Texts" group at UCLA, including Xochitl Flores, Brooke Lillehaugen, Olivia Martínez, Pamela Munro, Lisa Sousa, and Kevin Terraciano. We are grateful for Pam Munro's work on the final translation, which is presented here by Terraciano, who found the original document in AGN-Tierras 241: 7, and who prepared the initial transcription and translation for the group.

document 5.2 in which local authorities assigned vacant land to individuals. Finally, it is interesting to note that the writer used the Mesoamerican vigesimal numbering system to write the Christian year (3 × 400 + 300 + 60 + 5 = 1565).

We say this, the governor, alcaldes, and regidores, all of us: we give vacant land, land that cannot be cultivated, land that is not *estancia* (cultivated or pastured) land, land that no person cultivates, because some other Spaniard wants to take the land, having established his estancia. Thus we say that you, Alonzo Caballero, should bring the title, you should bring the *provisión* (legal document of entitlement) so that you will take the land, and it will be yours. You have put an estancia there. You will have the land that is under the hill [named] Quialaiocotopa, at the edge (or mouth) of the river Quiquela, because your land, your property, is there, and because the land and the property of your father is there. Thus we say to you, Alonzo Caballero, you will have that place now because of the documents. We all agreed upon it; we give you all of our signatures, the said governor, the alcaldes, and the regidores. Thus it was written, today, Saturday, 23 [of the] month of November, today, 1565 years [since] the son of God was born here; it was said in the seat (or altar) of the audiencia.

Lorenzo de Figueroa; Gaspar López; Joseph Hernández
Melchor Pérez, alcalde, Juan de San Andrés.

I, the escribano, heard all these words; thus this decree was spoken in the seat of the audiencia. Thus I have placed my signature on this paper.
Lazaro Jiménez, writer (escribano)

5.5. Nahuatl Testament of Doña María Juárez, Culhuacan, 1577[5]

The noblewoman doña María distributes her tecpan (palace) lands, chinampas (raised, irrigated fields) and the "woman land" between her children and sisters. It remains unclear what the category of "woman land" means, a term that appears in other documents. She wants to sell one piece of land but forbids any Spaniard from buying it. This latter provision was common in Mesoamerica; as we saw in documents 5.3 and 5.4, many native communities prohibited the sale of land to Spaniards in the colonial period.

Doña María Juárez
Here in the altepetl of San Juan Evangelista Culhuacan, the 17th of April of the year 1577, in the name of the Most Holy Trinity, Father, Son, and Holy

---

5   Translated from Nahuatl by Sousa, based on Cline and León-Portilla (1984: 246–51).

Spirit, I order my testament. Let all those who see this document know that I, named doña María Juárez, am a sick person, whose home is in the *tlaxilacalli* (subunit of an altepetl) of Santa Ana Caltenco Tecpan. Although my body is sick, my spirit and soul, my will and understanding are sane and sound through our lord God. When I die, first I place my soul entirely in [God's] hands, because it is his image and his creation. May he take it and have mercy on it, and may he pardon all my sins with which I have offended him. Here is what I guard on earth for our lord God (i.e., my property).

First, concerning my two children, I declare that Juan Juárez has always been looking around and has not come to settle down anywhere; and the other, doña Ana Cihuanenequi, is sick; but I do not take from them all their inheritance that belongs to them, that my lord (husband) don Andrés Juárez, their father, left to them. Perhaps it is true that someone will object to the first testament that I made. Everything is my own; it is my property and my inheritance and it belongs to me. And now again I set in order the *tecpancalli* (palace); it is to be as in the testament, with all the house chinampas of the tecpan, and the fields in Tlallachco, and the chinampas here in Quauhtenanco and in Amaxac, and the woman land in Huixachtlan, and the other land in Huixachtlan Ocelotepec, and the wet sandy land in Coatlan next to the field of don Juan Téllez, who sows his part of it, and cultivated land in Tomatla, and the other lands in Tociçolco; all will belong to the tecpancalli.

And as to my two older sisters, Ana Teicuh, widow of Gerónimo, and Magdalena Tiacapan, wife of Pedro de la Cruz, I declare that I give each one forty [units of measure] of land in Tociçolco. And this land I give to them is my property and my inheritance, as it is written in the testament.

Third, as to the house chinampas of the tecpan in Çacaapan that the judge Juan de los Angeles declared to be its house chinampas, there are twenty of them, each one twenty [units of measure] long. I have divided them; ten of them I gave to people, as all the tlaxilacalli authorities of Santa Ana Cal[tenco] know, and the other ten still belong to me, for they are my property and my inheritance.

Fourth, I mention again the piece [of land] in Tomatla. All the chinampas are to be sold in order to pay the fifteen pesos that belong to Diego Ramírez, the inspector. And since he has disappeared, I order that the money be delivered to the church in order to acquire and buy things for the church. And if any money is left over, it is to be given to the poor and to the hospital to cure the sick. And if it is not possible to give it to them, it is all to be delivered to the church to say masses for us. And Spaniards are not to buy these chinampas that I have mentioned, but only the inhabitants of the altepetl here.

Fifth, I declare that that my field in Coatlan, with peach trees on it, is to be sold in order for masses to be said for me, for me in particular. No Spaniard is to buy [the field], but likewise only the inhabitants of the altepetl here.

Sixth, I declare that my field in Tlallachco is not to be sold, rather it is just to be rented out each year, and with the money that is acquired there, masses are to be said for me. This is all the land with which our souls will be helped. I mention, appoint, and request two people to speak for us, the executors Miguel García, [notary of the] church, and Martín Lázaro, deputy. If they die, other people are to be named again to look after it. This is my entire declaration, I, doña María Juárez, the sick person, whose home is here in Santa Ana Caltenco Tecpan. It was done before those who heard it, the tlaxilacalli authorities: Francisco de San Gerónimo Xochicozca; Juan Vázquez Callal; Francisco Tlamaceuhqui; Pedro Chicotl; Martín Lázaro, deputy; Miguel García, [notary of the] church; and Alonso Jiménez; and the noblewoman doña Ana Tiacapantzin.

Juan Bautista, notary.

5.6. Last Will and Testament and Inventory of Goods and Properties of the Mixtec Lord of Yanhuitlan, Don Gabriel de Guzmán, 1591[6]

Here is the quintessential Mixtec lord who has managed to adapt to the changing times in order to protect and to even extend his vast estate in the colonial period. The previous ruler of Yanhuitlan, don Gabriel's uncle, was interrogated and imprisoned by the Inquisition for allegedly continuing native sacred practices and for defying the friars. In contrast, don Gabriel, who was tutored by the friars as a young boy, is the consummate Christian cacique. He gives very detailed and explicit directions in the religious preamble of his testament, practically showing off his knowledge of the faith in front of the friars and other prominent people who are present to hear it, and requests to be buried in a special sepulcher of the great church of Yanhuitlan. The religious and all the church singers need not walk very far to accompany his body to its burial, for he lives in a sprawling palace across the street from the church. As cacique of Yanhuitlan and other places, his landholdings extend to many parts of the region, and he is able to refer to each one by its Mixtec name. He also possesses many European goods and has invested in various Spanish-style enterprises; in fact, he is able to speak Spanish so well that he gave his testament in that language, rather than his first language of Mixtec. Note that he makes careful provision for his inheritance, naming multiple potential heirs in response to the possibility of disease and death.

In the name of the Holy Trinity, the Father, Son and Holy Spirit, three persons and only one true God in whom I truly believe as a faithful Christian, and of the glorious and blessed Virgin Holy Mary, mother of Jesus Christ, my Lady and advocate, and of the glorious Saints Peter and Paul Apostles of Jesus

6 Translated from Spanish by Terraciano. The original document is in AGN-Tierras 985, 2: ff. 26–28.

Christ and of the blessed male saints and female saints of the celestial court to whom I pray and request that they might be advocates before Him, the most high reverence of Jesus Christ, son of the living God, who died for me on the cross and redeemed me from sin, so that through his grace my sins would be pardoned and my soul be saved, Amen.

Let all who read this last will and testament know that I, don Gabriel de Guzmán, cacique and governor of this pueblo and province of Yanhuitlan, fluent in the Castilian language which I speak and write and understand well, my body being ill from sickness that Our Lord God has set upon me, and in my sane judgment and understanding, such that Our Lord God has wished to grant me, and fearing death, which is a natural thing for all living men, and wishing to place my soul on a course to salvation, I know and consent to making and ordering my testament in the following form and manner.

First, I entrust my soul to God Our Lord Jesus Christ, Son of the Living God, who redeemed it through his precious blood, and the body to the earth from whence it was formed.

And I declare that if it were the will of Our Lord God to take me from this present life, from my present sickness, that my body is to be buried in the church and monastery of Our Lord Santo Domingo of this pueblo of Yanhuitlan, in the sepulcher where my first wife, doña Isabel de Rojas, is buried, and that twelve pesos of gold be given in alms for the sepulcher.

And I declare that my body be brought in a litter, with a high cross, from my house to the said church in order to be buried and that some religious should come for my body, and that all the church singers should accompany my body, that they should bring wax (candles) from all the *cofradías* of this pueblo of which I am a member, and that they should pay the church singers four pesos from my property.

And I declare that on the day my body is buried, that a high mass be sung before the body if it is the hour for it and, if not, then on the following day, and that it be with deacons, and that they should be paid twenty pesos of gold for the first mass, to be given to the religious from my property. And I beg and ask fray Pedro de Vicuña, vicar of this pueblo, to say mass on that day for me.

And aside from me and my goods, for the compulsory Orders and the redemption of captives, four *reales* of silver are to be paid from my property.

And I declare that one peso of gold be given to each of the cofradías of this town, to be paid from my property.

And I declare that they say fifty high masses for my soul in the monastery of this town, and to pay from my property the customary alms, and that it be done soon.

And I declare that I owe to Pedro Díaz, a Spaniard who has a store beneath the portals of the town, 113 pesos that he gave me in reales and in merchandise from the store, I order to pay him from my property.

And I declare that I owe Diego García, an Indian trader of this town, 120 pesos that he loaned me in reales. I order to pay him from my property.

And I declare that I owe the community of this town sixty pesos in reales, I order to pay it from my property.

And I declare that I owe Juan López, juror, twenty-five pesos that he loaned me in reales, I order that they pay him from my property.

And I declare that I owe Juan Pérez, an Indian from the barrio of Ayusi, thirty-five pesos. I order that they pay him from my property.

And I declare that I owe the traders of this town, creditors of Ana Macías, six hundred pesos. I order that they be paid from my property, and each one should have what belongs to him, according to their accounts . . . three hundred of the total should be paid from my property because it is my debt; the community should pay the other three hundred because it was used to pay the tribute owed to don Francisco de las Casas. Thus, it is the responsibility of the community to pay the three hundred pesos that I paid to José de Vitansos, for the part that they owed him as one of the creditors, from the letter of payment that I have.

And I declare that the community of this town owes and is obligated to pay María García and her husband, Gregorio, 240 pesos for the money that they loaned to Gregorio de las Casas when he went to Spain; the community collected it from them and has never repaid them. I order them to pay it.

And I declare that the community of Achiutla owes me forty-five pesos and two *tomines*. I order that the money be collected.

And I declare that the cacique of Mistepec, don Diego Montero, owes me thirty pesos, and that he left a borrowed silk vestment in the possession of don Baltasar de Chávez, governor of Tlaxiaco. I order that the money be collected and the vestment returned.

And I declare that Juan Benítez Farfán, resident of Mexico, owes me ninety pesos for the public document that he made before the notary, Juan de Ramales. I order that it be collected.

And I declare that Gabriel de Chávez, resident [Spaniard] of Mexico [City], owes me fifteen pesos that I loaned to Miguel García Rengino plus an article of clothing, which is a skirt, which Gabriel de Chávez has in his possession. It's made of wool, the color I cannot remember. And also there is a brown taffeta tunic. I order that the articles of clothing and money be collected from the said Gabriel de Chávez.

And I declare that don Antonio de Velasco, cacique of Nochistlan, has in his possession a silver plated cup, and two pepper shakers, and he owes two hundred pesos to the alcalde mayor (Spanish official) of this pueblo. I order it to be collected from him.

And I declare that don Baltasar de Chávez owes me six pesos. I order it to be collected from him.

And I declare that Antonio de Ramales owes me fifty pesos, and that he has a silver pitcher of mine; I order that the fifty pesos be collected and that the pitcher be returned.

And I declare that Francisco de Salinas owes me four pesos and four reales. I order it to be collected from him.

And I declare that I possess two jewels, which are gold cascabels, [used] for dancing, which are now in the community of Achiutla. They are worth forty-five pesos and two tomines. I order that they be returned [or give me the money for them].

Francisco de Salinas owes me another twenty pesos which I let him borrow to pay don Francisco de las Casas (the encomendero) for the musket that he owed him. I order that the twenty pesos be collected. He owes me another four and a half pesos that he borrowed for a musket.

And I declare that I owe Domingo Hernández, Indian of this pueblo, ten pesos. I order that they pay him.

Silver

And I declare that I have for property: a gilded silver goblet with four little dents; a plain silver vessel; a vessel with its cover; another small silver pot with a handle; a plain gilded silver mug with a decorated border; another gilded silver mug with an inscription; six fluted, silver spoons; another spoon with a tortoise-shell handle; an antique gold cup; a mug with a decorated cover; a tall, plain silver mug with a Roman [figure]; a silver cup made by Indians; four black coconuts adorned with silver.

Jewelry

A large gold piece with the figure of an eagle and twelve cascabels; another piece with Santiago printed on it with six cascabels; another piece with the royal arms and seven cascabels; another gold piece in the form of a pelican; another gold piece in the image of Our Lady; an alligator with ten gold cascabels and some jade; a gold piece containing the figure of Christ; eleven cascabels and a cherubim; another gold image of the Boy Jesus; a gold piece with the royal arms and eight cascabels; a piece of low-graded gold, with the image of Our Lady and five cascabels; two pieces with figures of Our Lady and seven cascabels; a large Spanish piece with a half-moon and rays in the middle, with twelve cascabels hanging from a gold fish; a round, flat silver medal.

Livestock

And I declare that I have two estancias of *ganado menor* (sheep and/or goats), in the place called Yucunixaacuiaa, with its titles of possession, and another Yendechaio, between the road that goes to Teposcolula and the road to Texupa. And I affirm that I have as property 1,340 goats in the abovementioned sites, and two hundred kid goats of less than two years, of which twenty of them belong to María de Chávez, my wife, who bought them with her money, and should be given to her.

Animals

And I declare that I possess a gray horse; a stallion; a colt; a sorrel horse which belongs to my wife, María de Chávez, and she is to be given what is hers, according to my will.

And I declare that in this house where I live, I have a quantity of maize in two places which is mine.

And I declare that Tomás de la Torre, who lives in San Francisco . . . Tecomatlan, has a quantity of maize which belongs to me.

And I possess a book *Flor Santorum* and another small book which is called *Contemptus Mundi*.

And I declare that Luis, whom my wife María de Chávez knows, owes me ten pesos. I order that they collect it from him.

And I declare that I have as my legitimate children don Francisco de Guzmán, and doña María de Guzmán, who is married to don Miguel de Guzmán, and doña Inés de Guzmán, who is married to don Francisco de Mendoza. I declare that all three are my legitimate children. Doña Isabel de Rojas, who is deceased, is my legitimate wife.

Also, I declare that I am cacique and lord of this pueblo of Yanhuitlan and its sujetos, by direct descent, and I have peacefully possessed such title for thirty-five years. I order that I bequeath it to don Francisco de Guzmán, to whom it rightfully belongs, with all that is connected and concerned with it, and the lands contained in this account.

[In the community of] Yodzocahi

the field [named] saha yucu tnoo
the field yucha nama
the field tiyoco
the field tiquaha
the field toto coo
the field yuhui yoco
the field ytnu anino
the field diyeca
the field yucha niñe
the field yucha yete
the field toto ñaña cuiñe
the field dzuma yuu
the field yuhui yaca
the field yucha yuhui

the field cha dzoco
the field dzini coo
the field yucha yahua
the field atucu
the field ñucahua
the field yuqh dzuñu
the field yuhui tinana
the field chaco nuhu
the field saha yuqh
the field tiyahui
the field yucha vaya
the field yucha taha
the field cha tiyoho
the field yucha vico

the field ticacuiy
the field andeye
the field dzeque chicha
the field ytnu caca
the field cha yoo
the field tnu dzidzi
the field nduhua ytnu yuhua
the field yucha ndehe

the field yuhui dzoco tende
the field yodzo tahuayu
the field yodzo chisi yucu sayu
the field andeye
the field yuhui dzahua
the field ñoho saha ñuto
the field saa ndza caha

Tiyaha

the field yodzo nohuico
the field yucha nitnaa
the field cahi ydzo
the field nu tnuni
the field njaa huico
the field yucha ndodzo

the field diyeca
the field yuhui cahua
the field yuhui njiyo
the field andaha
the field cahua quaha

Yuqhduchi

the field dzuma ndacu
the field ytnu toto
the field tinduu

the field yodzo cuhua
the field yucha ñucuisi

Yodzocoño

the field noquaa
the field chiyo ndacu
the field yucha coyo
the field ytnu tacu
the field yuhu yuhua
the field achacu
the field ticuiy
the field njica yucu
the field duhua tutnu
the field sique ndacu ñuu
the field chayoo

the field tindudzi
the field yni yuhua
the field tandoho
the field nuunduhua
the field ducha yuhui cani
the field duhua techi
the field dzeque yucu añahi
the field yodzo tanjaa
the field nuu yutnu cate
the field ducha yuhui cani
the field yuvi dzitoñaña

Yuchatnoho

the field nducha dzoco
the field yucha ñunduu
the field yodzo cahi
the field njisi nuu
the field mini yodzo dzaa

the field andudzu
the field yodzo tinono
the field yucu oco dzana
the field yuhui ndaya
the field maa yucha

the field chiyo ndica huaco
the field dzuma yuhui toco ndeye

the field tutnuñu
the field yucha nicatni

Ñutuhui
the field cahuandoco
the field cahua techi
the field saha cahua tedza yehe

the field yodzo ticaha
the field ñutuhui

Yucunjiy
the field tisiy

Atoco
the field dzuma ñuquaha
the field yucha tiñoo
the field tinduchi

And I declare that at the same time I am lord and native cacique of the pueblo of Achiutla and its *sujetos*, and that the said *cacicazgo* and *señorío* by law belongs to the said don Francisco, my son. I give possession to him. I married the said doña María, my daughter, with don Miguel de Guzmán. It is my will that the said doña María should enjoy the cacicazgo and señorío in her lifetime. After her death, it is my wish that my son don Francisco will inherit it from doña María, his sister.

And I declare that I have as goods three iron brands for cattle, two pliers, two hammers and hoes, a desk and a writing place and other jewels that I have in my house where I live. I order that they be divided among my heirs.

And I declare that if the said don Francisco, my son, should die without heirs, then doña María de Guzmán, my daughter, should inherit and succeed to the cacicazgos and señoríos of Yanhuitlan and Achiutla. After her and her children, my daughter doña Inés [should inherit]. And after them, their children and heirs and successors [should inherit] through direct lineage. And the same goes for Tlaxiaco and Atoyaquillo, in whose possession is the said don Francisco, because it is my will to avoid the legal suits and differences, which follow one after another.

And in order to carry out and pay for my last will and testament, I appoint as executors don Francisco de Guzmán, my son, Cristóbal Pérez, resident of this pueblo, and Tomás de la Torre and Bartolomé de Espinar, Indian nobles of this pueblo. To each and every one of them, I grant the necessary power that the law requires; they will take my goods and sell them in a public auction and what is necessary to comply with this testament in all that it says and contains.

And I leave the remainder of my goods to my universal heirs, the said don Franciso de Guzmán, doña María de Guzmán, and doña Inés de Guzmán, my legitimate children, and to doña Isabel de Rojas, my legitimate wife. All of them should inherit equal parts, one no more than the other. And I entrust and pray that they look after and sustain Mariá de Chávez, my (second) wife, that they honor and respect her as a mother. And I declare that the said María de Chávez should be given a sorrel horse as I have ordered, plus twenty goats and a colt that my son-in-law don Miguel gave me, and a saddle in order to get around. I give these in return for the service that I have received from her. And thus I entrust my children to guard and fulfill the wishes of my last will and testament, and that all other testaments and statements that I have made in the past be null and void. So it is done in Yanhuitlan, the 28th day of the month of August, 1591. I sign my name and order that it [the testament] be closed.

> Don Gabriel de Guzmán.
> And all the said witnesses sign. Gonzalo de Ovando Guzmán, Andrés de Azevedo, Bartolomé Velásquez, Tomás López del Río, Juan Rodríguez, Lázaro de Santiago.
> And I, Juan de Ramales, public notary.

5.7–5.9. Maya Testaments of Juan de la Cruz Coba and Mateo Canche, and the Settling by the Cabildo of the Estate of Josef Cab, Ixil, 1766[7]

Compared to Spaniards living in colonial cities or to Mesoamerican nobles such as don Gabriel de Guzmán (document 5.6), the Maya inhabitants of the cah (Yucatec town, or in this case, a village) of Ixil were poor. Yet although the peso value of their possessions may have been low, it is clear from their wills that the men and women of Ixil in the 1760s placed an economic, cultural, and sentimental value on their material goods, one that transcended the market values of the outside world. Ixil's testators took care to designate particular items to named family members, thereby offering us hints as to the nature of relationships within and between families – and how Mayas in Yucatan conceived of family. Testators also paid attention to the accurate description of their most valuable category of property – land – locating house plots, cultivated and forested land using cardinal directions, and the named owners of adjacent plots; this was the way Yucatec Mayas had been describing land for centuries.

As we have seen in this and the previous chapter, colonial Mesoamerican documents tended to be community products, written by the town notary and witnessed by the town governor and council – even if the documents were concerned ostensibly

---

7   Translated from Yucatec Maya by Restall. Versions of these translations, complete with transcriptions of the Maya originals, are in Restall (1995b; 1997: 329–30). The originals are part of *The Testaments of Ixil*, archived in CAIHY-CCA, ff. 17r, 20r, and 22v, respectively (catalogued in Restall 1995b and 1997 as documents 36, 41, and 45).

with the business of individuals. Those who lay dying in Ixil in the 1760s thus dictated their wishes before an array of town councillors, including the batab *(cah governor) and others with both Spanish and ancient Maya titles of office. Individual business in a cah was also town business, especially when a testator sought to clarify the details of a property dispute (as in document 5.8) or when he died before he could make a will (as in document 5.9). In the latter case, the council was able to consult not only the surviving relatives of the deceased but also the testament of his grandfather, made forty years earlier and preserved in the town's book of wills.*

5.7. Will of Juan de la Cruz Coba, Ixil, 1766

Juan de la Cruz Coba, child of Catalina Coba, died on 12 November of 1766.

In the name of God the Father, and God the Son, and God the Holy Spirit, three persons, one God almighty. This will be made public, the document of my final statement in my will, inasmuch as I who am Juan de la Cruz Coba, I the child of Catalina Coba, although I am dying, content is my heart and my understanding is sound. I wish my body to be buried there in the holy church. Likewise I supplicate our blessed father Padre Guardian that he say one said mass and that he send up for me a prayer in the mass so that my soul be aided by our lord in God through the suffering of souls in purgatory. Likewise, the mass fee of six tomines will be given, with two tomines for Jerusalem. Likewise, one house-plot share with its well I leave in the name of my daughter, Pasquala Coba; as it was my inheritance from my mother, Catalina Coba.

Likewise, one share of a forest with one well inside it; the cah is to its north; it's called Cudzila; it's for Pasquala Coba and my grandson Nicolás Couoh. Likewise, here is the other portion of the forest, which is for my younger cousin Felipe Coba and my uncle Agustín Coba. Likewise, here is my forest jointly-inherited from my mother, Catalina Coba; Tixculix is to its north; I leave it in the name of my daughter Pasquala Coba, with my younger cousin Felipe Coba, and Nicolás Couoh, and my uncle Agustín Coba, their inheritance, the four of them together; the adjacent forest to the south is Agustín Ake's, to the north Juan Matu, to the east Nicolás Coba; to the north is the town, which is adjacent on its south side to Josef Pech. Likewise, one table with our holy virgin and her tabernacle, for Nicolás Couoh. Likewise, seven beehives for my wife and one sapling sapote tree – the beehives will go to my infant, Marcela Coba. This is the truth, the end of my statement in my will. I designate one [*sic*] noble, Pedro Pot and Diego Pech, as executors; they will request my wish for a mass for my soul. Before these the batab and magistrates: Eight reales.

Don Ignacio Tec, batab; Pablo Tec, public notary; Josef Pech, Diego May, alcaldes; Antonio Tec, Francisco Canul, Antonio Pech, Pedro Canul, regidores.

[different hand:] Eight reales; I said this mass and signed, fray Juan de Hoyos.

5.8. Will of Mateo Canche, Ixil, 1766

In the name of God the Father, God the Son and God the Holy Spirit, three persons, one true God, almighty. The document of my last will and testament will be made public, inasmuch as I am Mateo Canche, the son of Francisco Canche and María Tec, residents here of the cah of Ixil. Wherefore I supplicate our blessed lord the Padre that when my life here on this earth ends, I wish my body to be buried in the holy church; and that one low mass be said, the fee for which will be given, six tomines, and one tomin for Jerusalem; and that a prayer be said for me in the mass so that my soul be helped in the suffering of purgatory.

Item: There is a forest at the entrance to the town, a league along the Chicxulub road, adjacent to the forest of the Poot family, my share of which I leave in the hands of my daughters, Luisa Canche and Marta Canche; likewise one chest for my daughter Luisa Canche; likewise two machetes and one spoon for my daughter Marta Canche. This is the end of my statement – also I remember a forest. I sold it to Josef Canul. It is at Tixcacal. However, I returned three tostones to Josef Canul's son, Martín Canul. Then that Martín Canul ran away. On this day let it be recorded that when Luisa Canche and Marta Canche have fully returned his money, the three pesos, to the aforementioned Martín Canul, then this forest will be placed in the hands of these daughters of mine. This is the end of my final statement in my testament. I appoint a nobleman, Jacinto Pech, as executor.

Six reales, with one real for Jerusalem.

Don Ignacio Tec, batab; Andres Tec, lieutenant; Marcos Poot, notary; Diego Coot, Gaspar Yam, alcaldes; Gaspar Chan, Gaspar Ek, Sebastián Chim, Cristóbal Na, regidores.

I said this recited mass and signed, fray Juan de Hoyos

5.9. Settling of the Estate of Josef Cab by the Cabildo, Ixil, 1767

Testimony regarding Josef Cab, who died on May 30th, 1767. He had *not* made his statement. He died in Tihó [Merida]. We who are the batab, lieutenant, magistrates, regidores, and notary are now gathered together, all of us, in court, in order to deliver this house-plot with its well to the children of Josef Cab and to his younger siblings; to all his children and the daughters of Marcos Cab, as their fathers are dead. Marcos Cab had no testament. His son, this Josef Cab, also died without making his statement. Therefore, we have just seen the desires of their ancestors with respect to this house-plot – in the testament of Josef Cab, who died in the year 1726 – that it belonged to their ancestors, their fathers. For whosoever thinks this is not good, let them see Josef Cab's will. His children will affirm it. All of them use this house-plot: Dominga Cab and María Cab, Francisca Cab, Rosa Cab, and Francisco Cab; and the daughters of this deceased Joseph Cab – Isidro Cab, Ana Cab, and Simona Cab. Also one axe, one blanket, one machete, one shirt, one pair of trousers, and one belt, [now] the property of Isidro Cab. This is the truth, the end of the arrangement of everything by us, the batab, magistrates, regidores, and notary, today, May 30th, 1767.

Captain don Ignacio Tec, batab; Andrés Tec, lieutenant; Diego Cot, Gaspar Yam, alcaldes; Gaspar Chan, Gaspar Ek, Sebastián Chim, Cristóbal Na, regidores; Marcos Poot, notary; Josef Mis, *ah cuch cab.*

5.10. Testament in Kekchí Maya of Magdalena Hernández, Cobán, 1583[8]

Whereas Ixil's Mayas in the 1760s gave small sums of money to pay for posthumous masses, this Kekchí Maya woman leaves a huipil, *a traditional Mesoamerican dress, and a grinding stone or metate, to be sold to pay for masses, in addition to some coins. The difference is probably less a regional one than a question of time. In the late sixteenth century, when Magdalena died, cash and coinage had not fully permeated economic relations in colonial Mesoamerica. Goods were still exchanged through barter, and taxes and tribute were paid primarily in goods. In highland Guatemala, where cacao had been grown for centuries and its beans used as a form of coinage, the practice continued into the colonial period, complete with vigesimal counting – as Magdalena's will illustrates.*

In detailing her possessions, Magdalena reveals to us something of the activities that occupied and supported her in life. In and around her house in Cobán she tended fruit trees and planted other things, she ground corn to make tortillas, she weaved cotton, she may have made wooden chests, and she probably made chocolate.

The testament of Magdalena, wife of Hernández, deceased.

In the name of the lord God, God the Son, and the Holy Spirit. I now begin my testament; I declare my heart's feelings, my heart's desire, concerning all I have that is to go to those I leave behind when I die.

One huipil and one stone, for two masses to be given for me. I give one sum of five tostones, for which three masses are to be said for me, with the

8   Translated from Kekchí by Restall, from the transcription of the original document found among the Dominican papers in the Cobán church in 1921 by Erwin P. Dieseldoff and published with a note by William Gates in 1931, drawing on the Dieseldoff/Gates translation in Dieseldoff (1931). Cobán is in the Kekchí-speaking region of eastern highland Guatemala.

harp; and may they bring in the candles. With these things, I have asked for five masses altogether. And all the corn goes to God's home, with one curved axe, one axe; for which she asks two masses, "one for me," the sick woman says, "one for my husband," says the sick one, already named.

"One planting spade," she also says, "to go to Luis Caal, so that he can eat," says the sick one. "One planting spade," she says too, "for Gumercindo Yat, as my husband ordered when he died," says the sick woman. "One curved axe," she says, "for Luis Caal," says the sick one. "One more," she says, "to replace it," the sick one says. "I have already given him one large weaving comb. Now I give him one curved axe," says the sick one. "Also to Gumercindo Yat one chest, which is finished," says the sick woman, "and an unfinished chest," she says, "for Luis Caal," the sick woman says.

"Now my huipil, for which I owe Gumercindo Cuz ten tomines in cacao; [a debt of] eight times twenty [cacao beans] in my husband's name. For one turkey, [a debt] was entered with Gaspar Tun, for which I paid a hundred [beans]," she says. "Sixty more was the price of the dog; all accounts were in cacao. Also three measures of my cotton, which is mine and, if well, I'll weave," the sick woman says.

"As for this my home, on the street," she says, "with its six trees – of camelia, banana, avocado, guava, peach, and melon – is to help me when I also go before God, with my deceased husband," says the sick Magdalena.

Before us, the principal men, the alcaldes and regidores, as witnesses to the sick woman's declaration. Before Luis Caal, as witness. I wrote down her words on Tuesday, the third day of the month of December, the year 1583.

Gonzalo Metez, alcalde; don Domingo de Guzmán, alcalde; three regidores; the alguacil mayor; Lorenzo, the mayordomo.

Gumercindo Metez, notary.

5.11. Acknowledgment of a Maya Land Sale, Ebtun, 1769[9]

As we have already seen in this chapter, Mesoamericans conceived of land ownership in complex terms. Some land was privately held, some land was community property, and some land was conceived as both private and communal – meaning, as in the example of Pasquala Chi's forested land given here, it could be inherited and sold but only to residents of the same town. In fact, Pasquala was able to alienate her plot – that is, sell it to an outsider – but only by presenting a rationale to the town council. Her rationale was need; she needed the money to survive during a period of drought and famine, and nobody in Ebtun was willing to buy the plot. The council then granted her permission to make the sale, although damage to the original manuscript has

---

9   Translated from Yucatec Maya by Restall, from the transcription of the original document (now lost) by Roys (1939: 288–91).

destroyed the document's final lines, including the ratifying signatures of the town councillors.

In demonstrating that she truly owned the plot of land being sold, Pasquala describes its history, thereby revealing to us the persistence of an old custom. The land had once been owned by Pasquala's mother's father, don Pedro Noh (a "don" because he was batab of Ebtun earlier in the eighteenth century). According to early colonial Spanish sources (such as the Franciscans Diego de Landa and Diego López de Cogolludo), it was an ancient Maya custom for a man to work for his father-in-law for a number of years after marriage (five or six years, according to Landa). Here we see that custom still in use in late-colonial Ebtun (a village in northeastern Yucatan); don Pedro had obliged his son-in-law, Pasquala's father, to work the plot for him, only giving it to him as an inheritance when don Pedro died. The description of the forested land also hints at an older history, as the plot seems to contain part of a long-abandoned settlement, perhaps an ancient Maya site of the kind that pepper the Yucatec countryside.

An acknowledgment, Oxtun.

I who am Pasquala Chi, resident in the cah of Ebtun, in the municipal jurisdiction of our holy lord the blessed saint San Bartolomé, I sell the forest given to me by my father, Gervasio Chi, given to him by my maternal grandfather, don Pedro Noh. This is the forest that he gave to my father when he got married to my mother; and he came to it under the hand of my maternal grandfather in order to work for him. Then, when that grandfather of mine died, he delivered all his forests to them and all his house-plots and everything that belonged to my grandfather at that time; he made it clear that he delivered it to my dad and my mom. It was also seen by the elders of the town how they worked for my grandfather during the many years that my father, Gervasio Chi, was given use of the forest.

Now therefore I am selling that forest to a certain nobleman, Marcos Mo, resident of the town of Dzitnup, because it borders on his forest. For the following reason, I announced it [was up for sale] – three times I announced it, until he purchased it from me – so that I may sustain myself during this great famine. Thank God he bought it from me, when I was supporting myself, for nobody was buying forests and house-plots, as at that time they were dying of hunger. It was then that I went to get the approval of the elders of my town, that they might therefore take pity on me. For I saw that everyone had died, and that those that were left had gone into the forests in order to sustain themselves from the fruits of the trees. Thus I went to that other town to sell this forest.

This is how much I sold it for: three pesos. The forest I am selling is to the northeast of the Oxtun savanna. Its first stone-mound marker is on the red earth south of the road; this large stone mound is also the stone mound of the forest of don Antonio Pat of Dzitnup and also the people of Dzitnup. Then [the boundary] runs to the east alongside the road until it reaches the second large stone mound at the foot of an ancient house platform; on the south side of the road is the large stone mound of Marcos Mo, the purchaser of this forest. Then [the boundary] turns and goes northward and passes a line-mound to the west of the entrance to an old cistern, crossing over it and arriving at the third large stone mound to the west of the hollow, the large stone mound of this purchaser of the forest, [part of] the line-mound of the forest of Sahcaba. These, then, are the stone mounds.

Not only were they given by our lord the Señor Juez [Spanish judge], named Miguel, who confirmed the large stone mounds of the forest, but also present was Marcos Mo and the other petitioners, Lorenzo Ah Chelen Ek and Francisco Canche; and it was under the orders of our lord Señor Alcalde Captain Vetia that the judge came and confirmed this large stone mound at the entrance to the hollow to the west of the border of the Sahcaba forest. Then [the boundary] turns and runs westward along the break in the Sahcaba forest and passes a line-mound on red earth, continuing west until arriving at the fourth large stone mound at the gap, the split in the great, ancient house platform; the fourth large stone mound is at the base of this old stone platform, in the gap that is there, and this is also a large stone mound of the Ucan family. Then [the boundary] turns . . .

5.12. Mixtec Litigation over Land in Yanhuitlan, 1681[10]

The proliferation of native-language writing in the second half of the seventeenth century is exemplified by a case that was adjudicated by the cabildo (Spanish-style municipal council) of the yuhuitayu *(Mixtec term for a complex community, sometimes simply* tayu) *of Yanhuitlan (Yanhuitlan was derived from the Nahuatl name; the place was called Yodzocahi in Mixtec). Representatives of two* siña *(Yanhuitlan area term for a constituent part of a* ñuu *or Mixtec community; the siña was often called* barrio *or* sujeto *by the Spaniards) presented complaints to the cabildo of Yanhuitlan over some disputed lands. This case illustrates the ability of the native cabildo and its notaries to apply Mixtec-language writing to a specific Spanish model, with separate presentations, petitions, notifications, testimonies, and decrees. The plaintiffs presented a last will and testament, written in 1642, to support their claims. The native cabildo resorted to this practice because its members sought to resolve their own disputes involving corporate landholdings without involving Spaniards. Basically, this complex dispute focused on the question of whether the lands belonged to one of the siña (called Ayusi and Yuhuyucha) or to the palace of a lord. In the end, the representatives from the prominent siña of Ayusi found a testament that indicated that it belonged to the governor of Yanhuitlan, don Domingo de San Pablo Alvarado, and dropped its claim. But they also spoiled the claim of the siña of Yuhuyucha,*

10   Translated from Mixtec by Terraciano. The original document is in AJT-Civil 4, 467: ff. 40–45v. See also Terraciano (2001: 384–95) for a transcription and translation of this lengthy case.

whose members were working the land in question. Toward the end of the case, representatives of Yuhuyucha placed a thinly veiled threat on the table when they said to the lords of the cabildo: "If all our lords do not intend to do as we ask, we ask all the officials to permit us to present testimonies, petitions, decrees, and testaments before the lord alcalde mayor (Spanish official) so that he may see our concern here." Indeed, this case did go before Spanish officials. Thus, this case reminds us that there were at least two levels of local justice in the colonial period, and factions within a community could and did resort to involving Spaniards, even when the matter did not concern them.

Presentation

In the *tayu* of Santo Domingo Yodzocahi, today, Wednesday, the 30th of July, 1681, we officials, the governor, don Domingo de San Pablo y Alvarado, the *alcalde ordinario*, don Pedro de San Miguel Mejía y Guzmán, and the *alcalde*, Juan Miguel, saw this petition. Thus we look after the concerns of all those who make requests in this petition.

[signatures] don Pedro de San Miguel Mejía y Guzmán
Governor don Domingo de San Pablo y Alvarado

Petition

Agustín Andradas, regidor, Gerónimo Pérez, Domingo de Tapia, Baltasar Gómez, all of us appear before you, the governor, don Diego de San Pablo y Alvarado, the alcalde ordinario, don Pedro de San Miguel Mejía y Guzmán, and Juan Miguel, and all the *regidores*, according to the royal law of our lord God, first of all, and for our lord King don Carlos the second, who looks after our fathers and mothers and all of us commoners of the *ñuu*, here in this *audiencia* (used here as cabildo meeting place) of Yanhuitlan, where the Royal arms of our lord King and those of all his subjects are located. Today, we officials ask about Domingo Ramos, Gaspar Ramos, and Pablo de Ramos, who were born in the *siña* of Yuhuyucha, who have knowingly encroached on lands belonging to the people of the siña of Ayusi, which were given to us by our fathers and mothers [ancestors], those who are living on the alluvial, cultivable fields of the siña of Ayusi, and all those who are tributaries of the siña of Ayusi and who also perform labor duty for the *ñuu tayu* [Yanhuitlan]. Let it be said that the testament made by Juan López, from the siña of Ayusi, speaks the truth. Let the testament or other writings be read and examined in order to show whether the fields that they have forcefully seized really belong to the siña of Yuhuyucha. The fields of Ayusi are called Yuhuicani, and those in the plain of the ñuu are called Ytuniñe ("fields of the palace"). There were two plots of land. Now they want to take away the fields there that are named Yuchayeye and the lime furnace [which is located on the land]. We commoners of the *ñuu siña* of Ayusi appeal to all you officials of the *yuhuitayu* of Yodzocahi. We have made this petition today, Wednesday, the thirtieth day of the month of July, in the year four [x] four hundred [+] four [x] twenty [+] one [= 1681] years since our lord was born. We kiss the feet and hands of the lordly officials.

[signature] Agustín de Andrada, Gerónimo Pérez, Miguel de Espinal, Baltasar Gómez, Juan de Espinosa

Decree

We, the governor and alcaldes, have seen this petition. Thus I order you with this warrant, Domingo Ramos and Pedro de la Cruz, you are notified by this warrant of mine to obey and to comply immediately with the obligation that I order, that you not work the ravine named Yuchayeye, where there is a lime furnace. Now the people of the ñuu siña of Ayusi have come to present a testament and to make this petition. Also, I order that you present testaments or other writings for your lands that you sow [named] Yuhuicani, where there are pitahaya trees and where you sow your beans. If it is not yours, do not sow the land, do not take away what truly belongs to your brothers, your neighbors; and nobody is to touch the land, the royal patrimony, without the license of us officials, the governor, the alcaldes, before you sow the land that you desire. Thus I have imposed a penalty on you today so that you will not enter upon the lands, so that you will not sow them. You will sow the fields of your fathers and mothers (ancestors) and the fields that you have purchased. If you do not obey what I have declared, you will pay fourteen pesos and you will spend thirty days in jail. Thus we declare in this audiencia of our lord King, today, Wednesday, the 30th of July, 1681.

Governor don Domingo de San Pablo y Alvarado
don Pedro de San Miguel Mejía y Guzmán
Before me, Nicolás de Villafaña, notary of the cabildo

Here I have heard, as a poor commoner of our lord God and a commoner of our lord King, and a commoner of all our lord officials, the governor, the alcalde, and the regidores – the precious words of all my lords. I will appear before all the officials and I will respond as to whether we people from the ñuu did this, and all of we people here will speak about the lands of the yuhuitayu of this Yodzocahi. Thus, all will see how they respond to our lord.
Domingo de Ramos

Notification

Today, Wednesday, the 30th of July, at three hours, I the notary read this decree and petition before Domingo de Ramos, who responded in the following manner: he said that he obeys the words of our lord King and the words of the lordly officials, governor, and alcaldes, so that I, the notary, receive it as faithful, true, and certain. Thus I make my signature and the regidor [does the same] to verify that they have responded to this petition with their words. The witnesses signed this paper.

Nicolás de Villafaña, notary of the cabildo

witness Josef de Villafaña, Juan Bautista

Testament in the year 1642

Juan López, [from] the siña of Ayusi, a tributary settlement

By the sign of the cross et cetera. In the name of God the Father, God the Son, and God the Holy Spirit, it will be done in the name of Jesus. I am Juan López. Today, I am very sick. Even though now I am sick, it is certain in my heart that I truly believe in the Holy Trinity, three persons but one true God. And it is certain in my heart that I truly believe in the Fourteen Articles of Faith. And it is certain in my heart that I truly believe that our lord Jesus Christ came into this world as a man to redeem sinners. And it is certain in my heart that I truly believe in the Lady Holy Mary of the Rosary, the precious mother of God. And it is certain in my heart that I truly believe what the holy church believes, and what all Christians of this world believe. And with all my heart I offer my soul to God. And [as for] my body, I ask that my body be buried in the church when I die, I offer one peso.

I offer two reales for the tolling of the bells when God has taken me, when my soul has departed.

I offer two reales for the purchase of the black cloth.

I offer two reales for those who bring the *cruzmanga* (shroud) and accompany my body.

I give two reales for the singers who accompany my body.

I offer two reales to the *cofradía* (confraternity) of the lady Holy Mary of the Rosary and all those male Christians and female Christians who accompany my body.

I ask that a mass be said for my soul nine days after I die, I offer 1 peso.

I, María García, request that a mass be said for this man's soul twenty-nine days after God takes him and he has died, I offer one peso.

For myself I ask that another mass be done [after] forty-nine days, I offer one peso.

I, Diego Hernández, request that a high mass be done for the soul of my compadre, I offer four reales.

I, Juan Gutiérrez, request that a high mass be done for the soul of my compadre, I offer four reales.

I, Sebastián Ortíz, request that a high mass be done for the soul of my father, I offer one peso.

I, Inés López, request that a high mass be done for the soul of my compadre, I offer four reales.

Now I declare what is mine, that which the lord God has given me while I lived on this earth: my three houses that I built with my own hands and the magueys on the patrimonial land, and I give all that is mine to my oldest child named Andrés, so that he might pay my tribute. When God takes me and I die, he will no longer hand over my tribute.

And a field [named] Yuchayeye that goes as far as the lime furnace.

And thus I have spoken. I make my testament today, Thursday, the 11th of December, 1642. Truly and certainly, I have accomplished my desire of writing this document for the sake of my soul and my body. Truly and certainly, let nobody interfere with what I have ordered, and let nobody dispute my words.

Thus it is seen by Miguel Pérez and Juan Gutiérrez and Juan López, witnesses; these three witnesses here see that I make my testament truly and honestly. Now, I appoint Miguel Pérez to be the executor who cares for my soul when I die. Juan López has spoken in this testament that I have made. I, the notary Tomás Sánchez, have written this testament truly and certainly for the named cabildo.

Before me, Tomás Sánchez, notary

Presentation
In this tayu of Santo Domingo Yodzocahi (Yanhuitlan), today, Tuesday, the 12th of August, 1681. I, the governor, don Domingo de San Pablo y Alvarado, the alcalde ordinario, don Pedro de San Miguel Mejía y Guzmán, the alcalde, Juan Miguel, have seen this petition, and thus we will do the justice that this petition requests.

Governor, don Domingo de San Pablo
don Pedro de San Miguel Mejía y Guzmán

Petition
Domingo Ramos, Pedro Ramos de la Cruz, Gaspar de Zúñiga, and Pablo de la Cruz, people who are from the ñuu tayu of Santo Domingo Yodzocahi, who were born in the siña of Yuhuyucha. We appear here in the audiencia of our lord King and the Royal arms, all of our lord officials, the lords who are the head of all of us, the *yya toniñe* (lord ruler) governor, the alcaldes, and all the regidores. We are responding before all our lords and officials by contradicting the petition and testament of the people of the ñuu siña of Ayusi. The testament is null and false because it is obvious to everyone that a line of handwriting was added to the testament; it is the handwriting of the elder noble Domingo de San Pablo. Thus we all ask for justice before all our lords, that Domingo de San Pablo and Gerónimo Pérez be placed in jail, so that we have an investigation [and] witnesses before all our lords. It is true that the person who damages the contents of the testament, and the people who seize and enter the lands of our lord God and our lord King and the lands of their neighbors, that they have made a damaging petition against us, accusing us of seizing the lands of our neighbors. But we will not falsify a testament as they have done, such as the one that they have presented before all our lords. Now, they would rob and harm the lands

of this lord. Thus, we all ask that justice be done to them, for tricking our lord God and our lord King and all our lordly justices, the governor, our alcaldes.

Together we request, we ask for justice, we ask that the accusers be placed in jail and that our good lords hold an inquiry with witnesses. If all our lords do not intend to do as we ask, we ask all the officials to permit us to present testimonies, petitions, decrees, and testaments before the lord alcalde mayor so that he may see our concern here. We do not ask for justice falsely or maliciously; we truly and honestly make an oath of the cross on our petition here, our lords.

They will pay the costs for all the work done by the lords.

Diego de Ramos, Pedro Ramos de la Cruz, Gaspar de Zúñiga, Pablo de la Cruz, Jacinto Ortíz

Decree

I, the governor, and the alcaldes, have seen this petition and I hereby order Domingo de San Pablo and Gerónimo Pérez to obey my decree and to do as I have ordered, so that they will be placed in the jail here. For the sake of justice, I ask that all those who have spoken in this petition give testimony as witnesses, so that what the petition requests will be done by all of us officials, as it is the duty that we are obligated to perform and to which we are sworn. And we will hear the words of all the witnesses, including the words of witnesses who will present the other side, so that you will have a ruling and an inquiry in order to respond. Thus I declare in this audiencia.

don Pedro de San Miguel Mejía y Guzmán
Governor don Domingo de San Pablo y Alvarado
Before me, Nicolás de Villafaña, notary of the cabildo.

Notification

Today, at around two hours, I, the notary of the cabildo, entered inside the jail where Domingo de San Pablo and Gerónimo Pérez are being kept. I read the decree before the two of them and they responded that they obey the royal laws of our lord King and of the lordly officials. This was how they responded. The witnesses heard this and they made their signatures and I, the notary of the cabildo, signed as a witness, also.

Before me, Nicolás de Villafaña, notary of the cabildo.
Domingo de San Pablo, Gerónimo Pérez

Presentation

In this tayu of Santo Domingo Yodzocahi, today, Wednesday, the 17th of September, 1681, they presented this petition before me, the alcalde ordinario, don Pedro de San Miguel Mejía y Guzmán. They are responding to all the people from the ñuu siña of Ayusi. Thus we provide justice to those who appeal to us in this audiencia.

Domingo de San Miguel Mejía y Guzmán
Notary, Miguel Abendaños

Petition

All of us, Agustín de Andrada, regidor, Gerónimo Pérez, Domingo de Tapia, Baltasar Gómez, respond before you, lord ruler governor, don Diego de San Pablo Alvarado, alcaldes don Pedro de San Miguel Mejía y Guzmán, Juan Miguel, and all the regidores who work in your presence. Today we reply to the petition and inquiry given by Domingo de Ramos, which says that we insert things in the testament of Juan López, of the siña of Ayusi, in order to deceive people. Of all the testaments that are kept inside the audiencia, one testament was found today that belongs to our lord governor, don Domingo de San Pablo Alvarado, which shows that the lands of Ayusi belong to the yya toniñe and all his dependents of the siña of Ayusi. This fact is true and certain. We have not attempted to insert things. Before all of you, we perform this important duty, and we have signed the petition. Today, Friday, the 12th of September, in the year 1681, et cetera.

We kiss your precious hands. Gerónimo Pérez, Domingo de Tapia, Baltasar Gómez

Decree

I, the alcalde ordinario, have seen this petition and hereby declare that you, Domingo de Ramos, Pedro Ramos de la Cruz, Pablo de la Cruz, and Gaspar de Zúñiga, have heard this ruling of mine. Know, obey, and comply with the obligation that I command here: that nobody enters upon the land that will follow yours, the land [named] Yuchayeye and those that are above Ayusi, because this petition says that it belongs to the lord governor, don Domingo de San Pablo y Alvarado. Another testament says that the alluvial lands belonging to the lord governor are the lands [named] Yuchayeye, where the lime furnace and all the [land] above Ayusi are located. Thus, I will impose a penalty on those of you who do not leave the land there, the place that belongs to the lord; those who do not obey what I have ordered here in my decree will pay six pesos, and I will place them in jail for fifteen days. This is what I order here in the audiencia of our lord King, in this tayu of Santo Domingo Yodzocahi.

Don Pedro de San Miguel Mejía y Guzmán
Before me, Miguel de Avendaño, notary of the cabildo.

6

SOCIETY AND GENDER

Native societies of Mesoamerica were complex and stratified. Distinctions based on gender, class, and status determined a person's rights, privileges, and roles. Mesoamerican societies were generally divided into two hereditary groups: nobles and commoners. Within these two broad categories there were variations in wealth and status, and in occupations and obligations. Nobles possessed much of the permanent wealth, held high offices, dominated the arts of war, and enjoyed numerous privileges by virtue of their elite status. Normally, they represented roughly ten percent of the indigenous population. Because status was hereditary, a noble was theoretically the child of a lord and, therefore, a descendant of a noble lineage with its own palace, lands, and dependents. The hereditary ruler, called a *cacique* by Spaniards (derived from an Arawak word for ruler which Spaniards adopted in the Caribbean), was the highest-ranking noble.

Elites paid taxes on the basis of their extensive lands, but they were exempt from participating in the rotary draft labor system. Rather than performing manual labor to fulfill their tribute obligations, nobles served the community by holding religious and civic offices. Men and women of the commoner class paid taxes in goods and provided labor to the nobles in exchange for access to land. For example, women often spun cotton into thread or wove cloth as part of their tribute payments. Commoner men labored on agricultural lands and construction projects, and they served in the military. In pre-Conquest times, warfare was one of the few avenues of social mobility for commoner men who excelled in battle.

There were several other subgroups of commoners in Mesoamerica, including merchants, artisans, dependents, and slaves. Professional male and female merchants and craftspeople worked in local markets or traveled to distant places to buy and sell goods. Some long-distance merchants had special privileges and ties to the nobility. Dependents were people who lived on the estates of nobles; as they worked plots of land belonging to the lords, rather than their own, they did not pay tribute in labor or goods. Finally, in pre-Conquest times, Mesoamericans practiced slavery; slaves were mainly people who had been captured in warfare, who had been convicted of committing a serious crime, or who had been sold into slavery because of poverty. By the late sixteenth century, the enslavement of natives from the sedentary societies of central Mexico was no longer practiced.

An extensive set of terms to distinguish the various groups reflected the complexity of the societies of the region. A male ruler was called *tlatoani* in Nahuatl, *yya toniñe* in Mixtec, and *batab* in Yucatec Maya. A female ruler or the wife of a ruler was called *cihuatlatoani* in Nahuatl, *yya dzehe toniñe* in Mixtec. A nobleman was identified as a *pilli* or *teuctli* in Nahuatl, *toho* in Mixtec, and *almehen* in Yucatec Maya, and a noblewoman was designated a *cihuapilli* or *cihuateuctli*, *toho dzehe*, and *colel* by the Nahuas, Mixtecs, and Yucatec Mayas, respectively. The Nahuatl term for commoner was *macehualli*; this term originally meant human being but later came to approximate the Spanish term *indio* or indigenous person. Mayas also used *macehual* for commoner, having borrowed the term from Nahuatl before the Conquest. The Mixtecs called commoners *ñandahi*.

Although the terminology for social differentiation became simplified by the seventeenth century, the basic categories for rulers, nobles, and commoners continued to be used in Mesoamerican languages throughout the colonial period, with somewhat modified meanings. At the same time, a new system influenced by Spanish naming patterns emerged in which numerous social distinctions were reflected in one's personal name. In most of Mesoamerica, names were based on the native calendars in pre-Conquest and early colonial times. In addition, people had nicknames or personal names, often based on physical attributes or characteristics. By the mid-sixteenth century, indigenous people at all social levels adopted Spanish first names, often keeping a native last name. For example, Mixtec commoners continued to add calendrical names to their Spanish first name through the first half of the seventeenth century and beyond in some places. Over time, saints' names became the most common type of surname among the indigenous population in central Mexico and Oaxaca; the typical name of a person of humble origin might be Juan Domingo, for example. Somewhat more prestigious would be a name that was religious, but not specifically that of a saint, such as Juan de la Cruz (of the Cross). Next higher was a humble Spanish surname, mainly the patronymics (especially the names ending with *-ez* that mean "child of someone," such as Hernández, son of Hernando). The highest members of indigenous society took more distinguished Spanish surnames, often those of local high-ranking Spaniards and conquistadors. They also adopted the Spanish practice of placing the noble title of *don* (masculine) or *doña* (feminine) before their first names. The Maya were exceptional in that, although they adopted Spanish first names and titles of nobility, they maintained their own system of patronymic surnames, based on male lineage, which has persisted widely until today. The documents throughout this book reflect the persistence of native social categories and the complexity of the naming system that evolved during the colonial period.

Like class and status, gender shaped one's roles and responsibilities in Mesoamerican societies. Men and women each had clear responsibilities and obligations, which were symbolically assigned at birth by a midwife when she performed the bathing and naming ritual (see the Nahua midwife's speech in Chapter 9). Although gender ideologies associated men and women with certain tasks, in most cases these were not inflexible divisions. Men were generally the agriculturalists and warriors, and they practiced trades having to do with building and transporting goods. Men also held nearly all the high political offices. Women maintained the household, prepared beverages, cooked food, and wove textiles. Women also exercised important roles as producers and vendors in the markets and as midwives and healers. And like their male counterparts, native women participated in the civic and sacred life of the community (see Chapters 4 and 8 on political and religious life, respectively).

Tribute obligations and property rights were intertwined. As tribute-paying citizens of their communities both men and women could own property. In marriage, men and women kept their properties and belongings separate, so that a husband did not control his wife's property. She could buy and sell land, and borrow and loan money as she wished. In the colonial period a native woman also made her own testament, in which she designated her choice of heirs to inherit her lands, houses, and other possessions. Like men, indigenous women also could serve as witnesses to legal transactions, such as the writing of a testament, and as witnesses in criminal and civil investigations. Furthermore, women also could initiate criminal and civil suits, and during the colonial period, women sued over a variety of issues, including inheritance disputes and wife-beating.

The sources in this chapter illustrate the significance of class, status, gender, and ethnicity in colonial Mesoamerica. Document 6.1 discusses the assessment of tribute and document 6.3 describes the assets and privileges of a Nahua noble; both sources represent the reciprocal rights and obligations of nobles and commoners. Colonial land records and testaments inform us about men's and women' s property rights and inheritance patterns (see documents 6.4 to 6.8). Several of the documents also betray social tensions that existed within the community: document 6.2 involves resentment over the apparent social mobility of commoners who profited from the cochineal trade; document 6.9 presents accusations of misconduct leveled at a governor and refers to a disgruntled Maya woman who allegedly put a curse on her town governor. Several of the native-language records translated here offer insights into gender relations, gender expectations, and gender-based social networks.

Finally, document 6.10 comes from the hand of a Franciscan-educated Nahua noble named Chimalpahin, who lived in Mexico City for most of his life. His *Diario* follows in the tradition of a Nahua genre of writing called the annals. He recorded the notable events of his own day, focusing on the 1590s to 1614, in his native Nahuatl language. His perspective represents a Nahua writer's view of the people and events of Mexico City in this period. But Chimalpahin was no ordinary Nahua: he is arguably the most prolific Mesoamerican writer of all time. As with all the documents in this section, Chimalpahin's *Diario* reveals both profound cultural changes and surprising continuities in Mesoamerican societies during the colonial period.

6.1. Assessing the Maize Tribute in the Nahua Cabildo of Tlaxcala, 1548[1]

This early colonial document demonstrates how Spanish tribute collection was affected by indigenous practices that were based on a graduated taxation system, a progressive system that distinguished differences in the amount of wealth and property among the residents of Tlaxcala. Nobles were expected to give more than commoners gave to the altepetl because they owned more; the highest nobles were expected to give the most. The amount was not fixed but negotiated and, in general, the lack of rigid distinctions between the social categories suggests that the social hierarchy was more of a fluid continuum than a fixed order. In contrast, Spanish nobles were exempt from taxation, a system that enabled the Spanish nobility to amass great fortunes. By the end of the sixteenth century, the payment of royal tribute became more standardized and was assessed according to the size of a community's population, and nobles and officials were exempt from contributing. As in most early colonial documents, the mixture of Spanish and native surnames reflects the coexistence of two traditions.

In the loyal city of Tlaxcala, on the 27th day of the month of January of the year 1548, there consulted and assembled the governor, Alonso Gómez, the alcaldes, Gaspar de Luna, Félix Mejía, Pablo de Galicia, Alejandre Tlapialtzintli, and the regidores, don Juan Xicotencatl, don Juan Maxixcatzin, don Julián Tlapitzahuacan, don Francisco de Mendoza, don Antonio Calmecahua, Juan de Avalos, Calisto Portugués, don Martín Coyolchiuhqui, Antonio Téllez, don Francisco de Tapia, Tiburcio Albino, don Diego de Paredes, Antonio Flores, Lucas García, and Diego Cihuaintecuiyo. They agreed how the maize tribute belonging to our ruler the emperor is to be paid. A commoner who is somewhat well off is to pay as tribute half a *fanega* (Spanish unit of dry measure, equal to about one and a half bushels). If someone really appears like a commoner and is very poor, he is to pay as tribute one-fourth a fanega of maize. But one who is wise and very well off is to pay a fanega or a fanega and

1 Translated from Nahuatl by Sousa, based on the transcription and translation in Lockhart, Berdan, and Anderson (1986: 67–69).

a half of maize. And the rulers who are very wealthy, don Juan Xicotencatl and don Juan Maxixcatzin, are to give as tribute seven fanegas of maize each, and don Julián Tlapitzahuacan and don Francisco de Mendoza are to give as tribute six fanegas of maize each. And the other nobles who are very wealthy will either surpass or perhaps only equal the four rulers in paying tribute. And for all the other nobles it is to be seen; he who is somewhat wealthy will perhaps present three or four fanegas, or only two fanegas. The alcaldes and rulers who are to look after the maize will decide [the actual amount]. And if it fails to reach eight thousand fanegas, a bit [more] will be given as tribute; or if it should exceed eight thousand fanegas, the maize tribute will be reduced a little. Then they placed their signatures and names. The day, month, and year were mentioned above.

> Don Francisco de Mendoza, don Juan Xicotencatl, Alonso Gómez, Félix Mejía, don Julián Motolinia, Alejandre (Tlapialtzintli), don Juan Maxixcatzin, Gaspar de Luna, Pablo de Galicia, don Francisco de Tapia, Antonio Flores, don Diego de Paredes, don Antonio Calmecahua, Juan de Avalos.

6.2. Debate in the Nahua Cabildo of Tlaxcala on the Cultivation and Sale of Cochineal, 1553[2]

The dye called cochineal was a valuable product in Mesoamerica before and after the arrival of the Spaniards. Before the age of synthetic dyes, Spaniards and other Europeans prized the bright red dye of cochineal, and demand for the product increased after the Conquest. In the early colonial period, the area of Tlaxcala was one of its greatest producers. As this debate demonstrates, the impact of the introduction of a money economy was already evident by the 1550s; nobles complained how anybody – even commoners – could make a great profit from selling cochineal. It was not the first time that the cabildo took up the subject of cochineal production. According to the Nahua lords who sat on the municipal town council, macehuales and others were collecting the dye, which comes from the tiny insects that cling to a particular species of the prickly pear cactus, and then selling it to buyers on their own. As a result of this newfound wealth, they neglected their other duties such as maize cultivation, they squandered the profits on luxury goods and conspicuous consumption, and, in general, they subverted the natural social and moral order of the community. Thus, the cabildo members proposed to limit and control its production. It is very likely that these nobles tended to exaggerate the situation while neglecting to mention that many of them cultivated cochineal for their own profit. But the fact remains that money is power, and these lords could see how their own positions of rank and authority were being undermined by Spanish demands for a product and a changing market

---

2   Translated from Nahuatl by Sousa and Terraciano, based on the transcription and translation in Lockhart, Berdan, and Anderson (1986: 79–84).

situation. The moralistic language of the discussion is reminiscent of documents in Chapter 9 of this volume.

In the loyal city of Tlaxcala, on Friday, the 3rd day of the month of March of the year 1553, they assembled there in the cabildo the magnificent lord Alonso de Galdo, corregidor in the province of Tlaxcala for his majesty, and the interpreter, Miguel Cardenal, Spaniard; and in the presence of the very honorable lords don Domingo de Angulo, governor; and the *alcaldes ordinarios* don Diego de Paredes, Félix Mejía, Alonso Gómez, and don Diego de Guzmán; and of the four rulers, don Juan Maxixcatzin, don Julián Motolinia [are present], don Juan Xicotencatl is sick [and absent], and in the presence of don Francisco de Mendoza; and the regidores don Julián de la Rosa, Buenaventura Oñate, Antonio del Pedroso, Antonio Téllez, Hernando Tececepotzin, don Juan de Paz, Baltasar Cortés, Pablo de Galicia, Pedro Díaz, and Tadeo de Niza; absent are don Domingo de Silva, who is sick, and Lucas García, acting as judge in Coyoacan. It was done before us, Fabián Rodríguez, Diego de Soto, and Sancho de Rozas, notaries of the cabildo of Tlaxcala.

The cabildo deliberated about how everywhere throughout Tlaxcala the cochineal cactus, from which cochineal comes, is being planted. Everyone does nothing but take care of cochineal cactus; no longer is care taken that maize and other foods are planted. For food – maize, chiles, and beans – and other things people need were once inexpensive in Tlaxcala. It is because of this neglect that the cabildo members saw that all the foods are now expensive. The owners of cochineal cactus merely buy maize, chiles, etc., and they definitely feel that it is with their cochineal, by which their money, cacao beans, and cloth are acquired. They no longer want to cultivate their fields; they just stopped doing it out of laziness. Because of this, now many fields are overgrown with grass, and already famine has arrived. Things are no longer as they were long ago, for the cochineal cactus is making people lazy.

Our lord God is extremely offended that these cochineal owners devote themselves to their cochineal on Sundays and holy days; no longer do they go to church to hear mass as the holy church commands people, but they are concerned only with their food and cacao, which makes them feel superior. And then later they buy pulque and then get drunk; all of the cochineal owners gather together. They buy a turkey and then give it away for less than its price, and pulque too; they indiscriminately give away their money and cacao. They do not remember how our lord God mercifully gave them all their wealth; in vain they squander it. And he who belonged to someone [dependent or slave] no longer recognizes whoever was his lord and master, because he is seen to have gold and cacao. It makes them arrogant and deluded so that it is clear that they esteem themselves only through wealth.

And also the cochineal dealers, some of them nobles, some commoners, and some women, line up here in the Tlaxcala marketplace and await the cochineal. When they are not rushing to collect cochineal, they go around entering the various homes of the cochineal owners. And there many things happen; there they get the women drunk, and there some commit sins. They go entering the homes of the cactus owners; they already know those from whom they customarily buy dye, and sometimes they also go on Sundays and holy days, so that they miss attending mass and hearing the sermon. They go around wanting only to get drunk. And these cochineal dealers act as if the women who gather dye have been made their mothers. Some of the men hire themselves out to Spaniards to gather dye for them, and they give them money and cacao. And later they distribute the women to them, as though they were their mothers; to some they assign seven or eight women, or thereabouts, who gather dye for them. Because of this many improper things are done. And of those who hire themselves out, many are likewise ruined, because some are now slaves in the hands of the Spaniards. If it were not for cochineal, they would not turn out this way.

And both the cactus owners and the cochineal dealers who do this only in vain begin to ally with each other, or take each other as co-godparents (compadres), or just feed each other, gathering and collecting together with their women. They feed each other, however many of them there are; they give each other a great deal of food, and the chocolate they drink is very thick and full of cacao. When they find the chocolate just a little watery, then it is not to their taste and they do not want to drink the chocolate. Some pour it to the ground, so that whoever has given his perfectly good cacao to someone is insulted, but they are very proud because of it. And also then they buy pulque or Castilian wine; even though it is very expensive, they pay no attention, they just give it [the money] to the person selling it. And then they become really drunk with their wives; they fall down drunk one at a time where they are gathered. Many sins are committed there, and it is all because of cochineal. Also these cochineal dealers no longer want to cultivate the soil; although some of them own fields, they no longer want to cultivate them; they do nothing but seek out cochineal. And some of the cactus owners and the cochineal dealers sleep on cotton mats, and their wives have great skirts to wear, and they have much money, cacao, and clothing. The wealth they have only makes them vain and swaggering.

Before cochineal was known and everyone planted cochineal cactus, it was not this way. There were some people who clearly lived in humility, but just because of the cochineal now there is much drunkenness and swaggering; it is very clear that cochineal has been making people idle for the last eight or nine years. But back before that there was a time of much care in cultivation and planting; everyone cultivated the soil and planted. Because of this, the cabildo members said it is necessary that the cochineal cactus decrease; no longer should so many be planted, since it causes idleness. It is greatly urged that everyone cultivate and plant; now let much maize, chiles, beans, and all edible plants be grown. Because if our lord God should wish that famine come, will money, cacao, and cloth be eaten? Will there be salvation through them? It cannot be. Money, cacao, and cloth do not fill one. But if much food is kept, with it they will save themselves, since no one will starve; no one will die being wealthy.

Thus two or three times the lord viceroy who presides in Mexico City, don Luis de Velasco, has been told and it has been brought before him how the dye inflicts suffering, and he has been informed of all the damage done. And then the ruler viceroy gave orders in reply; he ordered the lord corregidor that in his presence there should be consultation here in the cabildo to approve how many plantings of cochineal cactus are to be kept by each person; it is to be a definite number, and no longer will there be planting indiscriminately. And during the discussion, some of the cabildo members said that five plantings of cochineal cactus should be kept by each person, and others said that fifteen should be kept. But when the discussion was complete, everyone approved keeping ten plantings of cactus, and the [Spanish] lord *corregidor* also thus approved it. No one is to exceed the number. And the women who gather dye in the marketplace are to gather dye no more.

Nevertheless, it is first to be put before the lord viceroy; what he orders in reply will be made public. Then in the cabildo were appointed those who will go to Mexico City to present before the lord viceroy what was discussed above. Those who will go are Alonso Gómez, alcalde, and the regidores Antonio del Pedroso, Pablo de Galicia, and Pedro Díaz, with the escribano of the cabildo, Fabián Rodríguez. It is by order of the cabildo that they will go to Mexico City. The most illustrious lord viceroy will decide how to reply; then it will be announced throughout Tlaxcala how cochineal cactus is to be kept.

Alonso de Galdo, don Domingo de Angulo, don Diego de Paredes, Félix Mejía, Alonso Gómez, don Diego de Guzmán, don Juan Maxixcatzin, don Julián Motolinia, don Francisco de Mendoza, Antonio del Pedroso, don Juan Xicotencatl, Hernando (Tececepotzin), Baltasar Cortés, Pablo de Galicia, Lucas García, Miguel Cardenal, Tadeo de Niza, Buenaventura Oñate, [and other rubrics].

Done before us, escribanos of the cabildo. Fabián Rodríguez, escribano, Diego de Soto, Sancho de Rozas.

6.3. Privileges and Assets of Don Juan de Guzmán, Nahua Governor of Coyoacan, c. 1550[3]

Here is the quintessential lord, the governor and highest-ranking person in the prominent altepetl of Coyoacan, with all his far-flung landholdings, properties, privileges, servants and dependent laborers. Even the marketplace is considered part of his

---

3 Translated from Nahuatl by Sousa, based on the original Nahuatl transcription and translation in Anderson, Berdan, and Lockhart (1976: 150–65) and in Carrasco and Monjarás-Ruiz (1978: 184–85, 192, 210–11).

patrimony. His lands are recorded and enumerated according to native custom and units of measurement. Judging by his opening remarks, he adopted the role of a Christian native lord who actively sought to retain much of his estate.

[Statement to the Cabildo:]
Praised be the name of our redeemer, Jesus Christ, Amen.

I, don Juan, governor of Coyoacan, who guards our Lord God's altepetl for him, present here before you who guard the altepetl of Coyoacan – you rulers, nobles, and lords. This is what our ruler the lord viceroy and your father the vicar want the assessment of the Coyoacan lordly tribute to be, what is to be given to me and what is needed daily: three hens; two baskets of shelled maize; four hundred cacao beans; two hundred chiles; one piece of salt; tomatoes; gourd seeds; ten men as servants; eight women as grinders of maize; six loads of wood; five loads of grass for horse fodder. These [goods], which are greatly needed, are to be delivered daily.

And it is required that fields in four places be looked after, the first at Ocoçacapan, the second at Milpolco, the third at Coyotleuhco, the fourth at Tochco. It is necessary to see to it well so that it will be done.

And it is required that a separate house be built; it will be don Juan's house. The commoners are to make it for him. It is to be seen to.

And it is required that ten carpenters be assigned to him, and also ten stonemasons, who are to do what is needed.

And the market is to belong to don Juan, it is to pertain to the royal palace household.

And as to all the artisans and craftsmen, it is required that they all be assigned to the palace to do what is needed.

And it is required that every 180 days two tomines be given to don Juan; all the commoners will give it to him so that he will rule. It is to be given to him twice a year.

Here is what really needs to be done. Will it be thus, or not? Confer together, you regidores and alcaldes, you don Pablo Çacancatl and you, don Luis, lord of Acuecuexco, and you, Juan Tlailotlac, all five of you consult and determine whether it is to be done or not. This is all that I say in your presence.

[Number and Location of Dependents:]
There belong to don Juan 29 persons of his royal household, plus widows.
- At Chimaliztacan are 7 persons.
- At Atlauhcamilpan, 7 persons.
- At Mixcoac, 4 persons.
- At Xochitenco, 4 persons.
- At Chinancaltonco are 4 persons.
- At San Gerónimo are 12 persons.
- At Tlaçoiyacan are 18 persons.

- At Hueicalco are 8 persons and 2 young men.
- At Ahuacatitlan are 21.
- At Acopilco are 25 and 6 young men.
- At Pachiocan are 2 persons.
- At Chimalpan are 4 persons.
- At Amantlan are 6 persons.
- At Coatzonco, 13 persons.
- At Tecoac, 6 persons.
- At Acolco, 80 persons.
- At Tlamimilolpan, 51 persons.
- At Çacamolpan are 29 persons.
- At Ocotitlan, 30 persons and 6 young men.
- At Tepechpan are 6 persons.

And it all totals 380 plus widows.

[Some Duties of the Dependents:]
As to the *macehualtin* (commoners) of lord don Juan who are to work the land and clear the ground in San Agustín, those of Xiuhtlan begin, then those of Çacamolpan, Ocotitlan, and Coatzonco, and the people of the household, and the Ahuapoltitlan people, for a week each; Diego is to supervise them.

And the Acopilco people are to give wood – planks and cut wood – to Pedro de Vergara; Huitznahuatl is to supervise them.

And the people of Atlauhcamilpan are to feed people for a week; they will do it under Domingo.

And the fieldworkers at Cimatlan and Mixcoac are to reap wheat at Atepocaapan for a week; Juan Tlanahuahua will supervise them.

And the artisans and privileged people will also farm; they are to work all the purchased land that lies scattered about, beginning at Neçahualcaltitlan; Antón Huixtopolcatl is to supervise them.

The people of Chimaliztacan are to guide the oxen working the land for a week.

[Lands of don Juan:]
Memorandum: the lands of the ruler and governor don Juan in the lower region are recorded here, beginning first with:
- At Tlacomolco, at the palace, land 60 *quahuitl* long, 40 quahuitl wide.
- At Tepancallo, with a patrimonial house (*huehuecalli*) on it, 63 quahuitl long and 40 quahuitl wide.
- A lot outside the palace, 11 long, 10 and 1 *matl* wide.
- At Acuecuexco a patrimonial field (*huehuetlalli*), 55 long, 37 quahuitl wide.
- At Tletlepillocan Tlillac patrimonial land, 94 quahuitl long, 20 wide at the bottom and narrowing to only 8 at the top.

- At Atlhuelican, with a palace on it, 27 and 1 matl long, 24 quahuitl wide.
- At Atlhuelican Tlacopantonco, 84 quahuitl long, 37 wide at the bottom and narrowing to 25 wide at the top.
- At Xochac patrimonial land, 111 quahuitl long, 38 wide at the bottom, toward the edge of the main road, and narrowing to 25 wide at the top.
- At Quauhcuezcontitlan, in the place of chinampas, 149 long, 123 quahuitl wide at the bottom, narrowing to 98 wide at the top.
- At Amantlan, in the place of chinampas, 181 long, 140 wide.
- At Atecontonco, in the place of chinampas, 95 long, 10 wide.
- At Coatzonco, 200 long, the same wide.
- At Tecoac rocky land, 130 long and 27 wide, and the cultivated fields above the rocky land, 30 long, 25 wide.

Purchased lands belonging to don Juan:
- Next to the palace at Xocotitlan, 16 quahuitl long, 14 quahuitl wide.
- Outside the palace at Teçoncaltitlan, 19 quahuitl long, 7 quahuitl wide.
- At Acuecuexco Amaxac, 6 quahuitl long, 3 quahuitl wide.
- Also at Acuecuexco, 6 long, 5 quahuitl wide.
- At Nexpilco, outside the place of Pedro Coacuech, 24 long, 13 wide.
- Also at Nexpilco, 7 long, 4 wide.
- At Atenco, outside the place of Mecatzin, 6 long, 3 wide.
- Also there, next to the reservoir, 9 long, 5 wide.
- Outside Santiago, at Huexotitlan, 13 long, 3 wide.
- At San Agustín Teocalçoltitlan, 100 long, 34 quahuitl wide.
- At Apçolco Chiquiuhchiuhcan, 15 long, 10 quahuitl wide.
- Outside the palace at Atlhuelican, 12 long, 3 quahuitl wide.
- Also at Atlhuelican, 12 long, 6 quahuitl wide.
- Also at Atlhuelican, with a chalk adobe house on it, 9 quahuitl long, 6 quahuitl wide.
- Also there, next to the chalk adobe house, 7 long, 3 wide.
- Also there, next to the ash heap, 9 and 1 matl long, 3 and 1 *tlacotl* wide.
- Also there, facing the place of Pedro Tetometl, 16 quahuitl long, 7 and 1 *yollotli* wide.
- At Acalopan, 20 long, 2 quahuitl wide.
- At Texomolco, 11 long, 2 quahuitl wide.
- At Xalpan, outside the place of Macahual, 10 long, 4 quahuitl wide.
- At Tenexcaltitlan, rocky land, 14 long, 9 quahuitl wide.
- At Cueçalco, 16 long, 3 quahuitl wide.
- At Xancopincan, 12 long, 1 and 1 matl wide.
- At Tlalxopan, 11 long, 3 quahuitl wide.
- Also at Tlalxopan, 4 long, 3 wide.

- Also at Tlalxopan, 5 quahuitl long, the same wide.
- At Cueçalco Xalpan, 71 quahuitl long, 32 wide.
- Right next to it, at Xalpan, 84 quahuitl long, 35 wide.
- At Atlixocan, 105 quahuitl long, 100 quahuitl wide.

Don Juan's purchased lands in the upper region are recorded here, beginning with the first:
- At Atonco Xochicaltitlan, 17 quahuitl long, 14 wide.
- At Ahuatzalpan, outside the place of Juan Hueiteuctzin, 13 quahuitl long, 3 wide.
- At Çacatetelco, outside the place of Marcos, 5 quahuitl long, 1 and 1 matl wide.
- At Yecapan, outside the place of Huecamecatl, 10 quahuitl long, 3 wide.
- At Quauhtlapetzco, outside the border, 6 long, 3 wide.
- At Tolnahuac Tenanitlan, 20 quahuitl long, 10 quahuitl wide.

[Some lands given to or taken by don Juan's dependents:]
Voluntarily I gave away land of mine at Coatzonco and Çacamolpan; I gave it to my fieldworkers. As to how it was counted, it was counted with the twelve-foot rod.
- At Çacamolpan, 280 long, 100 wide.
- At Coatzonco, 340 long, 40 wide.
Without my presence land was given out at Axochco, Ocotitlan, Tecoac, Amantlan, Chimaliztacan, Atlauhcamilpan, Ameyalco, and Tianquiztonco.
- What they took at Axochco is 90 long, 40 wide.
- What they took at Ocotitlan is 500 long, 40 wide; the fieldworkers took it.
- What they took at Amantlan is 140 long, 40 wide.
- What they took at Chimaliztacan is 130 long, 40 wide.
- What they took at Atlauhcamilpan is 120 long, 40 wide.
- What they took at Ameyalco and Tianquiztonco is 100 long, 40 wide.
The fieldworkers of lord don Juan de Guzmán who were given land on his fields totaled 109 people.

6.4. Nahuatl Testament of Ana Juana, Culhuacan, 1580[4]

In contrast to the previous document, Ana was no lord, but she was not poor, either. She used the last will and testament to settle her estate before her death. She had other matters to settle, as well, including her relationship with a deadbeat husband.

---

4   Translated from Nahuatl by Sousa, based on the transcription and translation in Cline and León-Portilla (1984: 80–85).

Clearly, Ana is a very capable woman who owns a good deal of property, separate from her (third) husband's estate. She chose to bequeath it all to her son.

Ana Juana of Santa Ana Tlacuilocan

In the name of our lord Jesus Christ and of his precious mother, the heavenly lady Holy Mary, may all persons who see this document know that I, Ana Juana, whose home is here in San Juan Evangelista Culhuacan, in the *tlaxilacalli* of Santa Ana Tlacuilocan, first place my spirit and soul entirely in the hands of our lord God, because it is his creation. When I die, let him take it, and let him pardon me of all my sins. As to my earthly property that I keep for our lord God, it is my property. Let all who are my relatives know that it is my testament. Let no one invalidate my statement that I put on paper.

Thus I begin my statement: there is an enclosure of mine standing beside the road that is not yet roofed. I give it to my son named Juan Francisco. The houselot on which [the enclosure] stands is fifteen matl wide toward Xochimilco and toward Mexico City, and in length, toward the east, it is only ten matl. And I also give my son an old house that stands there facing toward Xochimilco. And there are three chinampas of mine next to the house, each one twenty [units of measure] long, next to the field of Martín Tlacochcalcatzintli. And there in the place named Quauhtenanco there are two chinampas of mine, each one twenty long, at the edge of the canal, next to the field of the late Francisco Yaoxomol. And there is one chinampa at the entrance that is ten matl, and three "Mexica lands" in the place named Ayoc. And I give all of these chinampas that are written here to my son, Juan Francisco, because he already pays tribute on them. Let no one ever take them from him.

And in Apilco there are seven chinampas of mine, each one twenty [units] long. I declare that as long as I am ill they are to be used for me, and when I die, let them be sold, and I will be buried from the money in proceeds.

And in Santiago Tetla there are sixty [units of measure] of dry land of mine; the first is in the place named Iççotitlan Ohuicanpolco, next to the field of Mateo Ilamatzin, and the second is in the place named Texalpan, next to the field of Pedro Guillermo, a poor person from Amantlan. And the third is in the place named Temamatlac, next to the field of Pedro Itztolcatl, and here in Huixachtlan there are twenty [units of measure] of dry land of mine, next to the field of Miguel Coltzin. I give all of this dry land of mine that I record here to my son Juan Francisco. Let no one take it from him because he will pay tribute on it, he will perform community work duty on it, the hay tribute and all the various tributes.

And here is what I say concerning my husband named Gabriel Itzmalli, who is a great villain. Let him never bother my son, nor accuse him of anything. I do not know how many debts he has. He never gave me anything at all, not money nor telling me "poor you," as did the three who died, two of whom were my spouses, because we worked together to make a living. But this one, if he went to collect fruit or if he went to get maize, he would sell it himself without showing me how much he had bought. But as to the maize he just measured it out and gave it to me. Thus I say that I am afraid [of what he will do]; I declare that he should not accuse my son of anything; I beg lord don Francisco Flores, the alcalde, to speak for [my son] and to take him, because he is his godchild. Let him not abandon him.

And I said above that I gave to my son, Juan Francisco, a house that faces Xochimilco; it was the inheritance of my late sister-in-law who died. And I declare that they are not to tear it down. Let my son Juan Francisco pay something for it; he is to offer a little money to the church so that she will be helped before God our lord.

And here are the debts of my husband that I have paid, as I very well know: one peso which belongs to don Francisco Flores, alcalde, and four tomines that belong to his younger sister named Juana Xoco, and four tomines that belong to someone whose home is in San Mateo. And my husband asked me for a peso and said "I am going to get fruit with it," and he just collected it and didn't buy the fruit. In all I paid four pesos.

This is all that I have written and put down on paper, in my testament. It was done before the *tlaxilacalli* (subunit of an altepetl) authorities as witnesses: Pedro Tecpanecatl; Martín Tlacochcalcatl Xochicuetzin; Diego de Tapia, church attendant; Domingo Çannen; Pedro Xochinanacaz; and before the women: Juana María, widow of Pedro Tepanecatl; Magdalena, wife of Pedro Tecpanecatl; Juana Tiacapan, wife of Diego de Tapia; Ana Tiacapan, wife of Tlacochcalcatl; Magdalena, wife of Domingo; Ana Xoco, widow of Juan Atonemac.

Done before the executors Martín de Santiago and Anton Jacobo, alguaciles. And I, Juan de San Pedro, wrote the testament. And before Diego de Tapia. It was done the 16th of the month of September of the year 1580.

6.5. Mixtec Testament of Don Gerónimo García y Guzmán, Teposcolula, 1672[5]

This Mixtec lord is the husband of doña Lazara, who wrote her testament nineteen years later (see document 6.6). Although he is a yya (lord), he never attained the rank of yya toniñe (ruler) of the yuhuitayu of Yucundaa, which was called by Spaniards the cabecera of San Pedro y San Pablo Teposcolula. (In the Mixtec language, people called the place Yucundaa or "blue hill"; Teposcolula is a name based on the Nahua word for the place, which the Spaniards adopted, and then attached saints' names to it.) He never became the hereditary ruler of Yucundaa because he comes from a neighboring community called San Juan Teposcolula; he even mentions the siqui or barrio to which he belongs, which also has a name (Yaacahi). In any case, he leaves everything,

---

5 Translated from Mixtec by Terraciano. The original document is in AJT-Civil 4, 417: 16–16v. See the transcription and translation of this document in Terraciano (2001: 376–79).

including his palace complex, in his wife's hands, who will then pass it on to their surviving children. Finally, his pious bequests to the church are very interesting. He gives money to the various images inside the great church of Teposcolula, including a Spanish Christ and a Christ of the Mixtec (Ñudzahui) people. Most likely, the different images of Christ correspond to the cofradías or confraternities that maintained the images; often, these cofradías were organized along ethnic lines, representing the parish members. This is a very good example of how native people appropriated Christianity to the extent of keeping their own image of Christ within the Church.

In the name of God the Father, God the Son, God the Son [sic], and God the Holy Spirit, three distinct persons, but one true and good God in whom I believe, I, don Gerónimo García, from the siqui [named] Yaacahi. I am a poor man who guards all the commandments and articles of the faith, the ten [commandments] of our true lord God, so that good will be done in the name of the lord Jesus.

Today it will be known to all the lords, nobles who are present and to all who will see this testament of mine that I now make. Whether I die or I am saved, I truly desire only that I obtain complete satisfaction in my heart, despite this sickness that is the justice of our lord God. My body is sick but I am clear hearted. I speak with certainty, I speak honestly and with God's will I put down my words on this paper. This will be done, all will be recorded and written. Nobody is to obstruct it, nobody is to deny it, nobody is to change it.

Thus I now arrange things for my soul and my body. Now first and foremost, I offer my soul before our lord God, whom I have served as a slave. Second, I give my body to the earth, the mud. All that I have possessed, while living in this world, I have borrowed. I ask that my body be buried in the great church. I offer ten pesos. Then, when nine days have passed, and my body has been cared for, I request that a high vigil mass be said on behalf of my soul. I offer two pesos. Then when forty days have passed, and my body has been cared for, I ask for a vigil and a mass to be said by three priests for the benefit of my soul. I offer four pesos.

Then, I offer to our lord God and also to the sacraments two reales; before San Pedro [and] San Pablo I offer one real; before the lady of Soledad I offer half a real; before Santo Diego Soriano I offer a half a real; before the holy Spanish Christ I offer half a real; before the Spanish Lady of the Rosary I offer half a real; before Jesus of Nazareth I offer half a real; before San Raimundo I offer half a real; before San Jacinto I offer half a real; before San Miguel I offer half a real; before Santo Domingo I offer half a real; before the Holy Christ of the Ñudzahui (Mixtec) people I offer half a real; before San Diego I offer half a real; before the lady below the choir I offer half a real; to the souls I offer half a real. This I offer before our lord God. If I am worthy, may you collect my soul.

Now as to the things of the world that our lord God bestowed upon me as I have lived with my wife, doña Lázara de Guzmán: my same wife will hand over the tribute to our lord king. And in her hands I place my house plots and all the patrimonial lands and the houses of my palace, where my children live together in the complex. Thus, now I appoint the elder noble, Pedro de Andrada, and the alcalde, Lorenzo González, to be my executors. So that my soul will be taken, take care of things quickly. Take care of my body. Keep my wife company and see also to my worldly obligations when I die.

May our lord God guard my wife until her final day, and may she consult with the executors who will divide the patrimonial house plots between each child. Each child will have some of it. Thus, I order before all the officials who are now in attendance, and all the lord nobles who are witnesses to this: Sebastián de Palma, Andrés de Tapia, Gerónimo Bautista.

True and certain are the words and speech of the lord, which I have written, the named notary. Today, Friday, three hours in the afternoon, on the 6th of May, in the year 1672, here in the yuhuitayu of San Pedro and San Pablo Yucundaa (Teposcolula).

Domingo de Velasco, Notary

6.6. Mixtec Testament of Doña Lázara de Guzmán, Teposcolula, 1691[6]

As mentioned earlier, doña Lázara inherited her husband's palace and estate and now divides it equally among her sons. Here we see that the palace has a specific name, which can be translated as "place of the jaguar," and that there are many lands attached to the palace. The aged noblewoman reminisces that she enjoyed the "gift of life" with her husband for sixty years and bore him twelve children. One has a sense of the high and early mortality rate in this period, in that only three of the children survive. She gives all the properties, including some other houses and lands that are separate from the palace, to her three sons and beseeches them not to fight over who gets what. She leaves it to them and hopes that they will continue to reside in the palace complex. Note that doña Lázara, like her husband, very carefully makes many pious bequests and preparations for a Christian burial in front of the highest lords and elders of the two communities – San Juan Teposcolula, and San Pedro y San Pablo Teposcolula.

In the name of God the Father, God the Son, and God the Holy Spirit, three persons but only one true God in whom I believe. I, the person named doña Lázara de Guzmán, who comes from the *siqui* (Mixtec term for the subunit of a ñuu) *barrio* (Spanish term for a section) of Yaacayhe, and who guards all the Commandments and Articles of Faith, the ten laws of our lord God and

6 Translated from Mixtec by Terraciano. The original document is in AJT-Civil 4, 417: 18–19. See the transcription and translation of this document in Terraciano (2001: 380–83).

that which is declared by our precious mother Holy Roman Church, and all the mysteries of the lady ruler Holy Mary, and the cofradía of our lady ruler Santa María to which I belong.

Now let it be known by all the *yya* (lords) and *toho* (nobles) who see this, my testament, that today I am clear in my heart and in my five senses. I speak truthfully, I speak honestly, that I have received the seventh sacrament with my deceased husband, don Gerónimo García y Guzmán, lord of the palace named Ñuuñañu, which belongs to this *tayu* (yuhuitayu) *cabecera*. I had the gift of life with him, I lived with him in the world for sixty years. I lived with him in the presence of our lord God, who gave us twelve children, seven daughters and five sons. Our lord God took all seven daughters and two sons, so that three male lords remain. The first lord is called don Domingo García y Guzmán, the second lord is called don Josef García y Guzmán, and the third lord is called don Pedro García y Guzmán. All three of these lords have received the favor of our lord God and the deceased don Gerónimo García y Guzmán. These three lords here, my children, are to take care of and look after my soul, and they are to be my executors as long as they live in this world. Likewise, I appoint all three as my heirs. They will take in their hands all the fertile lands and everything that belongs to the lord don Gerónimo García y Guzmán, my deceased husband.

I ask the holy father priest to bury me in the sacred ground inside the church, to see to it that I am buried in this way, as a poor person who awaits the hour when God will take my soul. Let all the yya and toho know that I am a humble person who has lived humbly on this earth. Thus I give alms. I ask for a vigil mass for the burial of my body when I die; I offer two tomines. And I offer alms to pay a vigil mass of the holy cross, and also I offer to pay the instructor of the church singers for singing when God has taken my body, four tomines. And on the ninth day I request a vigil mass for my soul, I offer two pesos tomines in alms. Also I offer alms to our lord of the Holy Sacrament, one tomin. I offer alms to the lady of the Rosary, one tomin. I offer half a tomin to our lord holy Christ. I offer half a tomin to San Miguel. I offer half a tomin to San Diego. I offer half a tomin to the souls. I offer half a tomin to our lord Jesus of Nazareth. I offer half a tomin to our lord the holy Spanish Christ and I also offer alms to our lord God.

As for duties of the world, I say truthfully, I say honestly, I make clear that all which our lord God gave to me and the deceased don Gerónimo García y Guzmán, my deceased husband, the palace Ñuuñañu and all the palace lands and all the lands belonging to the palace called Ñuuñañu, I declare that it all be placed in the hands of my three children, don Domingo, don Josef, and don Pedro, so that all may share it and work it as three forever. Let nobody contest it or fight over it. Also, there is a purchased house, which is located in the siqui called Dzumañuu, with a plot of house land behind the house, a plot of land above the house, and a plot of land below the house, which are all together.

Also I say that there is a lot of patrimonial land behind the palace named Duhuandoo, which is at the edge of a canyon named Ndicuana, next to the house of the deceased Petronilla and a lot of land. I place all of it in the hands of my children, and the three of them will have what belonged to their grandparents.

Also there is a house in the same siqui as the house of Dionisio Delgado, an uncle of my deceased husband. I possess a testament [for it]. I place it in the hands of my three children, don Domingo García, don Josef García, and don Pedro García. All the lots of land and all the adjoining houses I place in the hands of my children. Thus I say it in my testament.

These words of doña Lazara de Guzmán are heard clearly by the governor, alcaldes, regidores, fiscal, and the four elder noble witnesses whom I designate: Lorenzo González, governor of the yuhuitayu of San Juan, who has had the gift of life in this world for eighty years; and the maestro Domingo de Zelís, who has had the gift of life for fifty years, is a witness; and the noble Juan de Santiago y Cortés, who has lived for thirty years, is a witness; and maestro Nicolás Clemente, who is twenty-six years, is a witness. What is said in this testament is true and certain. Thus all the officials make their names on this paper, the governor, alcaldes, regidores, and the fiscal. Today, Tuesday, the 9th day of the month of January, in the year of one thousand [*sic*] 1691, in this yuhuitayu of San Pedro San Pablo Yucundaa (Teposcolula).

Governor don Gabriel Ortíz de Tapia
Alcalde Gerónimo Miguel de Zárate
Domingo de la Cruz
Fiscal Juan Nicolás
True and clear are the words of the lord, which I have written, Juan Domingo.

6.7. Mixtec Testament of Lucía Hernández Ñuquihui, Tepsocolula, 1633[7]

Lucía has both Spanish and Mixtec surnames, indicating that Mixtecs were still using the 260-day sacred calendar at this time, which was forbidden by the friars for its association with pre-Conquest rituals. But what is most interesting about this testament and inventory is all the cloth and money that Lucía possesses or is owed. Here is a lesser noblewoman who was involved in cloth production and selling. The cloth goods that male Mixtec long-distance merchants brought to Guatemala and Mexico City were produced or managed by women like Lucía; often, married couples collaborated, one producing and the other transporting and selling. The fact that Lucía's husband owned three mules suggests that he used them to

7   Translated from Mixtec by Terraciano. The original document is in AJT-Civil 3, 287: 24–26v.

transport goods. Eventually, in the latter part of the seventeenth century, Spaniards took over this trade, as they did with every other profitable sector of the economy. The cloth trade was a pre-Conquest tradition that now involved pesos of silver. Because Mixtec women kept their property separately from their husbands, Lucía possessed a considerable amount of wealth (especially for a native person), which she distributed among her children and grandchildren. The writer of the inventory employs both the introduced Arabic and the Mesoamerican vigesimal counting system.

This is what I declare, I who am named Lucía Hernández Ñuquihui of this *ñuu siqui* [named] Dzumañuu, my ñuu siqui. In the holy name of the Father God, and the Son God, and the Holy Spirit God, it will be done in the holy name of Jesus.

Let all the officials see this document of mine, Lucía Hernández Ñuquihui, of this ñuu siqui [named] Dzumañuu that is attached to this yuhuitayu of San Pedro y San Pablo [Teposcolula]. Today, I make my testament; now I am suffering the pain and justice and pain of our lord God, but I am clear in my heart and I know that I have loved our lord God, and so now I will speak truly about what will be seen on this paper because nobody should contradict the document, nobody should obstruct anything which I order today.

First, I believe in the one true god, the Father God [who is] one person, the Son God [who is] one person, and the Holy Spirit, three persons but one sacred spirit God. And I believe all that my precious mother holy Church of Rome believes. First, I declare that I offer my soul to our lord God, the lord who made me, and I give my body to the earth from whence it came. Also, I declare that on the day when my body dies I request that an eternal mass be said by the precious father, [for this] I offer three pesos to the precious father lord who says the mass for my soul; one peso for the vigil and four tomines for the salaries of the cantors, thus I pay twelve tomines. I request that my body be buried inside the church, next to the altar of the holy sacrament, next to Santa Ynez, I pay four pesos. I request a silver *cruzmanga* for which I pay four tomines. I pay four tomines for the ringing of the bells. I request a little wax from the [cofradía of the] Holy Cross and the [cofradía of the] black Santa María when my body dies. Also, I order that a sung mass be said by my precious father nine days after my death, and I also request a mass be said to San Miguel, and I offer a peso to pay for it.

And also I order that an eternal mass be said by my precious father in the church twenty-nine days after my death, and I offer three pesos and one peso for the vigil and four tomines to pay for the cantors; I offer a half peso to [the cofradía of] Santa María, a half peso to San Pedro, a half peso to San Pablo, a half peso to San Diego, a half peso to the souls in purgatory. And this is what I give on behalf of my soul.

And also I order that my oldest child named Pascual Sánchez will have eighty pesos that I have because his father [Lucía's husband] sold three mules;

but I spent some of the money when he was sick, so he will get the remaining twenty pesos. And I have some land that the deceased Ana García sold to me; I order that my child Pascual Sánchez use it to pay the tribute of our lord king. And I also order that masses be said for my soul on the feast days of saints.

I give to my child, Pasqual Sánchez, and Pedro, my grandchild, the child of Pasqual, some lots of land [named] Dzinisaha and Yuhuyahy. They will divide it equally between them.

Also I declare in truth that my grandchild named Pedro Sánchez, child of Pascual Sánchez, will have sixty pesos and thirty magueys and a field [named] Tadzahua, a field that the deceased Domingo sold, and a field [named] Yodzohuaya that Francisco García sold for ten pesos.

Also I declare that my child named Petronilla Sánchez, will have sixty pesos and a field [named] Yuhundiye, and a field [named] Yodzoyuhusichi, and also a field that Juan Bautista sold for five pesos, and a field that Diego Camaa sold, and also a house that she is to receive.

Also I declare that my two children, Clemente Ramírez and his own child, the little girl named Juana Ramírez, will have five houses and a steam bath (temascal) and its patrimonial land in back of the houses and the magueys that are there on the [following] four lands are for masses for my soul: a field [named] SahaYucundaa, and a field [named] Cahuacundi, and a field [named] Nduhuaychi, and [a field named] Dzahuayaha, and my child named Juana will have them. My child, Clemente Ramírez, is not to sell them [the lands]; I give him nothing more because he has already spent eighty pesos when he wounded with a knife the person [named] Juan from the coast.

Also I write my inventory concerning the money of mine that María López has, twenty-two pesos; Lorenzo de Chávez [owes me] fourteen pesos; Juan Gómez [owes me] three pesos; Francisca Conchi has two pesos [of mine]; María Nacusi [owes me] six pesos; Sebastián Qhñoo from the ñuu of San Juan [owes me] two pesos; and my executors will collect all that is mine and arrange for masses to be said for my soul.

Also I name as my executors and I give power [of attorney] to Pedro Mariscal and Dionisio Delgado so that these lords will work on behalf of my soul, and that all my goods and what is owed to me will be collected and divided among my children by the executors, and the father (priest) should say masses. This is my last will and nobody should contradict it. This is all that I declare in the presence of all of us, Pedro de la Cruz, alcalde, Bartolomé de Velasco, regidor, the witnesses Bartolomé de Velasco and Juan Bautista, saw this paper testament today, on Sunday, 22nd of May, 1633 years, I wrote the words before me, Andrés de Jeréz, escribano. Inventory of all the cloth, cotton yarn, and wool yarn of the deceased named Lucía Hernández Ñuquihui, of the *siqui* Dzumañuu. Today, Sunday, 26th of June of [the year]1633.

- Ten pounds of [white] cotton yarn and cloth.
- Seven pounds and eight ounces of blue and black wool yarn. Goods of the deceased Andrea Camaa, grandmother of Petronilla, who is the child of Pascual Sánchez.
- Six pounds of cotton yarn.
- Four pounds and eight ounces of blue and black wool yarn.
- Three silk cloths, two maguey cloths.
- Two cloaks and one shirt.
- Some old trousers.
- A blue woolen cloak.
- One colored skirt.
- One *huipil* of poor cloth; one woolen *sayal* skirt.
- Three new woolen skirts.
- Six collars and one large collar.
- One white damask huipil.
- One white huipil.
- One cloak of poor cloth.
- Three pieces of yellow taffeta.
- Three jackets and one cloak.
- Forty-two *cascabeles* (little bells).
- Four pounds of blue woolen cloth.
- One pound of white cotton cloth.

Money that was presented today, Sunday, on June 26, 1633.
- 202 pesos and two tomines.
- Isabel Delgado has 100 pesos.
- That makes 303 pesos and 2 tomines.
- The money of the deceased person named Andrea Camañe, child of Andrés Cahui, which amounts to 118 pesos.
- Also the 25 pesos that María [of] Tilantongo has, which belong to Pascual Sánchez.

Total = 446 pesos

6.8. Maya Testament of Juan Cutz, Motul, 1762[8]

This testament, although representative of colonial Yucatec Maya wills in many ways, is unusual in not including an opening religious formula (for examples of this formula, see the preceding four documents, as well as documents 5.5 through 5.8). Perhaps Juan Cutz was in a hurry to dictate to the notary of Motul his wishes with respect to his main house-plot; he seems anxious to ensure that his son Andrés will

---

8   Translated from Yucatec Maya by Restall. The original document was in the ANEY, 1796–97: 205 (in one of the volumes stolen in 2001, located by the Mexican authorities, but as of 2004 not yet turned over to the AGEY). A version of this translation appeared in Kellogg and Restall (1998).

inherit the plot unchallenged and be able to enjoy the fruit of Juan's hard work. This will is also noteworthy for the detailed comments that Juan Cutz makes on each parcel of land that he owns. It was normal for Maya testators to describe the location of a plot of land, either by naming the owners of adjacent plots or identifying adjacent landmarks (examples of both are in Cutz's will). But Cutz goes a step further by recounting something of the plot's history and even stating how a plot is to be used – note that one house-plot is to be reserved for two young daughters to inherit and "to spin thread there" when they come of age. In addition, Cutz states the specific size of his milpa, *or maize-field, lands, using the Maya measurements of the* bak, kal, *and* kan *(1* bak *equals 20* kal *equals 400* kan, *and as a* kan *is equivalent to the Spanish* mecate, *the translation below uses mecates). This attention to detail, as well as the use of native-language terms of measurement, although common in Nahuatl wills (see document 6.3, for example), is relatively rare in Maya documents, especially this late in the colonial period. The point, therefore, is not just that native ways of counting were replaced by Spanish ones – be it in the form of money, the calendar, or land measurements – but that such a transition was stretched out over the colonial centuries.*

I who am Juan Cutz, I am a citizen here in the *cah* (town) governed by our lord the blessed San Juan Baptista, here in the town of Motul, where I make my true statement and affirm that I give this house-plot of mine to my children and this forest of milpa lands that is mine. Therefore first I give away this one house-plot where I reside to my son, Andrés Cutz. This house-plot has a well of mine. I made the well hole; thirteen pesos and one toston I paid for the well construction. Here too is the stony ground around it. It was Tomás Aguilar's stony ground, because he used to live there when it was the property of my father, Pablo Cutz. I didn't take it from this Tomás Aguilar; I paid him bit by bit. The price of this stony ground came to eight pesos; a resale payment of four pesos was also made by me. The cost, the price of the resale of this stony ground was therefore twelve pesos. Thus I leave it to my son here with all these planted palm trees and all its other trees. Nobody shall have much to say about it. Whoever does come out with words about it, at that time let them come out with forty pesos for my son here. This is how expensive this house-plot of mine is because I made it what it is. This is my true statement, before my lord the *batab* (governor) and my lord the magistrates. I now deliver this house-plot to my son here, as is my wish. Likewise I give to my son here one mare bought with my mother's corn field; and one cow with its calf which I bought for five tostons; and one house-door with its frame which I bought for one peso of henequen; and one chest, inherited from my mother; and one silver spoon, also inherited from my mother, which I also give to this son of mine, Andrés Cutz. Nobody shall say anything about it.

Likewise I give to my son, Josef Cutz, one house-plot without stony ground. His children shall live there in time. This particular house-plot I inherited from my mother; it is to the east of the town on the road to Cibalam, as is well known.

Likewise I give to my daughters, Luisa Cutz and Josefa Cutz, one house-plot that is to the east of the town on the road to Cibalam. It shall go to both of them at the time when they are ready to spin thread there; then they will take possession.

Likewise I give to my daughters, Antonia Cutz and Rosa Cutz, one house-plot for both of them. This house-plot has a well; it is near the town's entrance, on the road to Cibalam. These house-plots we are neither to sell nor to give away; they dictated this impediment in the time of our ancestors.

Likewise I leave in the hands of my sons, Josef Cutz and Andrés Cutz, four milpa fields. Here is one of them, of one hundred mecates, to the east of the town and to the north of Bom. There is a well dug in it. Here is another one of them at the corner of the town *estancia* (cattle ranch); it is known to be one hundred mecates. Here is another one which is to the west of Yaxleula and the twenty-mecate forest-plot of don Francisco Ake – it is well known to be one hundred mecates – and the other one hundred-mecate field, a forest-plot my mother bought from the notary Lorenso Kuh, which is to the north of Chenkelem. The cultivated area of this forest-plot is known to be four hundred mecates. I leave the whole field with its contents in the hands of my sons Josef Cutz and Andrés Cutz. Thus my wish at this time is just. I make this my true statement, as a testament, that I swear by the word of our lord God whereby I passed my tribute collection, according to my appointed office, on to our lord the *encomendero*. This true statement I make before my *batab* and my lords the magistrates and *regidores* and notary. This is the truth. Today, on the 13th of August of the year 1762.

I, Juan Cutz.

We who are the *batab* and magistrates, *regidores*, and notary here in the town of Motul, to whom Juan Cutz gave his true statement. He now makes his true statement; he hereby swears by the sayings of our lord God regarding where he stands in his tribute collection. He made his true statement. This is the truth. We now give our signatures below. Today, on the 13th of August of the year 1762.

Don Mateo Koh, *batab*; Pasqual Pech, lieutenant; Ambrosio Kuh, notary; Nicolas Balam; Bernardino Pech; Santiago Koh, *alcaldes*; Julian Tzek; Sebastián Chan; Mateo Ake, *regidores*.

6.9. Lawsuit by Diego Pox Against Don Jorge Xiu, Maya Governor of Dzan, Over Alleged Judicial and Sexual Misconduct, c. 1580[9]

This fascinating document offers a window, as tantalizing as it is revealing, onto a complex dispute in the Maya village of Dzan, located in a region of northwest Yucatan

---

9 Translated from Yucatec Maya by Restall. The original document is in TULAL, *Tierras de Tabí* papers: 32v–33r; a few lines of the document are translated in Restall (1995a: 577).

that a half-century earlier had been a small polity or kingdom under the rule of the Xiu dynasty. Here the community's Xiu governor meets resistance to his alleged attempts to (mis)use his authority to acquire a valuable orchard owned by the Pox family. According to Diego Pox, don Jorge Xiu has waged a three-pronged campaign of harassment – trying to have Pox declared illegitimate, inducing his sisters to sue him for the plot, and trying to seduce or rape Pox's wife. Clearly, class and gender intersected at the very heart of this conflict.

Note that two of the four Spanish settlements founded in the Yucatan peninsula are mentioned here – Merida, the sole city and the provincial capital, and Bacalar – but that both are still being called by their Maya names of Tihó and Bakhalal. Diego Pox has traveled to Merida to present this testimony, but he has also been to Bacalar. The small and isolated port-town of Bacalar was located far from Dzan, across a region that lay outside colonial control and at the other end of the Yucatan peninsula. Bacalar was a gateway to trade, mostly illegal, with the English and Mayas in Belize, and with the Spaniards and Mayas in Guatemala. Some of this trade existed before Bakhalal became Bacalar, and indeed Diego Pox's statement is evidence of the perpetuation of long-distance Maya trade between northwest Yucatan and the cacao-producing regions of highland Guatemala.

I, Diego Pox, householder in the cah of Santiago Dzan, having appeared in person before my greatly respected lord, the *halach uinic* (chief ruler), governor, here in the city of Tihó (Merida), having prostrated and abased myself beneath his foot, beneath his hand, while I recite my statement before him according to my ability. Here is the judgment that I received here before the lieutenant general here in Tihó. It is concerning a planted orchard of mamey trees, red mameys; my father and I too planted them with my own hands. This father of mine was Juan Pox, the elder. He died without composing a testament, his last will, because he died suddenly. But he was going to make it to me [make me his heir], the eldest of his sons, I, Diego Pox. There are also my younger sisters, the three women, Mençia Pox, María Pox, Beatriz Pox, married also. They were ordered by don Jorge Xiu, our governor in the town, to divide up the household goods of my father among themselves and with my mother-in-law and my younger brother, Francisco Pox, now deceased – as shown in the inventory written of the household goods of my father. There are also the debts of my father, which I paid myself also. They were ordered ... in order that ... (document damaged) [Although] I have previously paid it, they [the trees] were not made over to me. This is the reason that I have appropriated half the mamey trees; this was formerly the property of my younger brother, this deceased Francisco Pox, the four mamey trees were his property as written in his testament. Then it was redeemed at auction [and became] my property, but today I do not have it. He did not wish to execute it, the nobleman don Jorge Xiu, our governor here in the town. He was given a notification along with the judgment, which was in my favor. But in no way did he honor it. He did not fulfil what was ordered in the judgment, for he has broken up my mamey orchard among my younger sisters. It is only his word by itself. These younger sisters of mine, they do not say that they dispute my ownership, because I myself paid the debts of my father. For this reason our mamey orchard is my property entirely.

The nobleman don Jorge Xiu does not wish this, because he hates me. This is I, who am known to be the eldest son of Juan Pox, the elder, deceased. I have also supported my father. Four times I have gone to buy and sell at Bakhalal (Bacalar) that I might bring cacao, half of which I gave to my father. This is known by the principal men in my town. This nobleman, don Jorge Xiu, has been asking to take from me the land that I own today. But I will not go because he tells me to. He will bear witness either that I am not the legitimate son of Juan Pox or that I am a minor under his guardianship. Then it will be taken from me as he declares it will.

My second petition before our lord – and may he pardon my fault in petitioning – is that the worst of the deeds committed by this nobleman don Jorge Xiu was when he came four times into my house to grab my wife by force to fornicate adulterously with her. He wished it in vain. He was not to fulfil his desire. I then told this official, don Jorge Xiu, that it was not right for him to act like that with us, so that we might obey him. This is all I said to him, but he would not stop. This was the cause of the quarrel. But today I wish to get a judgment again, within one day, for the fulfillment of everything that is ordered in the judgment. He did not fulfil it as ordered before. This is what I want. Here also I have the judgment with me today, the one I got here before. There are also the witnesses from the town of Dzan and all around it who know I am the eldest son of Juan Pox. This is my petition before our lord that he may grant it in his mercy and that he will make it in my favor. And my name is given by the writer of my words:

Diego Pox, of Dzan.

We now also make our true statements before Francisco Tamay, Francisco Euan, Francisco Xool, Pedro Tzuc, householders here in the town; Mençia Pox, María Pox, Beatriz Pox have no dispute with our elder brother, because we took no part in the paying of the debts of our father. It was don Jorge Xiu who forced us to sue our elder brother. This is our true statement. This is the reason why our declaration is written down at the end of our elder brother's petition.

6.10. Excerpts from Chimalpahin's *Diario*, 1604–1614[10]

One of the most prolific Nahua writers of all time was born in Amecameca in 1579 and moved to nearby Mexico City when he was very young. He called himself don

---

10 Translated by Lockhart, Susan Schroeder, and Doris Namala in a manuscript titled "Annals of His Time: Volume Three of the Codex Chimalpahin." The excerpts presented here have been modified slightly by Sousa and Terraciano, with the authors' consent. We are grateful to the authors for this contribution to our volume.

Domingo de San Antón Muñón Chimalpahin Quauhtlehuanitzin; we know him best today as Chimalpahin. Both of his last names refer to native lords to whom he traced his roots. His writings treat both the pre-Conquest past and his own present times, focusing especially on events in and around Mexico City. He is known especially for his annals, a genre of Nahua writing that survived the conquest. The present work, called the Diario, *is not a diary but rather a Nahuatl-language commentary on events of interest to the public, a selective and at times personal rendering of references to the people, places, and events of his day.*

His purpose for writing was to convey to future generations the way things were in his altepetl. The coverage is organized into year entries that refer to both the Christian calendar year and its native equivalent, based on the Nahua version of the Mesoamerican calendar. The content of Chimalpahin's Diario *is typical of the genre, including: public ceremonies involving high officials; religious feasts and processions; plagues and epidemics; storms, floods, earthquakes, solar eclipses, comets, and other natural events; crimes and public executions, including inquisitorial autos da fe; labor projects involving large numbers of native workers from multiple communities; and other noteworthy events and scandals of the day. Although he refers to many events that seem to interest primarily Spaniards in the city, including the death of a Spanish king and reports on events in the Philippines, he is also very attentive to activities that concern native people, in general, and in particular many communities in and around the Valley of Mexico. We can see from his writings that the four-part complex altepetl of Mexico Tenochtitlan did not disappear with the decision of the Spaniards to make Mexico the capital city of New Spain. As a native noble who was educated by and lived with Franciscans in the San Antonio Abad church in Xoloco, he had a foot in both the Spanish and the indigenous worlds.*

As the reader can imagine, this is an extraordinary source for cultural and intellectual studies of Nahuas in an urban setting in the late sixteenth and early seventeenth centuries. The Diario *consists of 284 pages. The following selections represent some of the many themes that are covered in the work, which focuses on the period from the 1590s to 1615, when the last entry was recorded. The selections provide glimpses of how Chimalpahin viewed the people and events of his own day. Most need little explanation; the final selection, however, refers to Spanish attempts throughout much of the colonial period to drain the lake surrounding Mexico Tenochtitlan in order to alleviate the floods that were so common in the city, a situation that was undoubtedly made worse by the deforestation of nearby mountain slopes.*

Floods and Processions, 1604

Today, Friday, the 15th of October of the year 1604, was when there was a procession and penitence here in Mexico, just as is customarily done on Holy Thursday. The reason for the procession was the water, that every part of Mexico (Tenochtitlan) was flooded. And all the Spaniards went in procession; they assembled at the parish of Vera Cruz; all the *cofradías* assembled there. And we commoners (*macehualtin*, plural of *macehualli*, used by Chimalpahin here to refer to indigenous people, in general) assembled at San Josef, at San Francisco. Thereupon everyone set out and departed; at Ayoticpac, outside the house of Agustín Guerrero, the commoners and Spaniards joined, so that there the procession became one. Then everyone went to the nunnery of Concepción, then to Santo Domingo, then to Encarnación, then to Santa Catarina de Sena, and outside the palace at the cathedral. A carrying platform belonging to the district of Santa María went in procession, a crucifix. They went along sheltering our lord with a canopy. Next to him went the crucified thieves, then also a *guión*, a small banner, then also crosses with cloth decorations, and then also three large black banners went ahead. The Tlatelolca (people from the altepetl of Tlatelolco) just came last. They brought out three of their large banners, a cross of Soledad, a processional cross, and a decorated cross. And a true cross, a cross with a relic of the original cross, went standing on a large carrying platform, they went sheltering it with a canopy. And our precious mother, Our Lady of the Rosary, went standing on a large carrying platform; priests carried it, and many priests went in procession. During the procession the penitents scourged themselves. Perhaps there were some twenty-four thousand [participants] counting everybody, commoners and Spaniards. But many more Spaniards scourged themselves than commoners. Thereupon they returned once again and went where the procession had started.

It was in the same said month of October that the Mexica Tenochca began, at the order of the viceroy don Juan de Mendoza y Luna, to perform work duty, so that they built, fixed, and renewed the walls which had been damaged and were full of holes everywhere. They had first been built during the time of the lord viceroy, don Luis de Velasco the elder, in 12 Flint year (according to the Mesoamerican calendar), the year of 1556. At that time the said viceroy was ruling here in Tenochtitlan, when because the Mexica were flooded then too, forty-nine years before now, since the same thing happened, that everything was flooded, therefore because of that also the dikes that had holes in their sides were fixed and all closed up everywhere. The cleaning up and fixing began at Coyonacazco, then San Sebastián, then San Pablo, then Mixiuhcan, then at Acachinanco. They were busy at it the whole month of October until it was fixed. And it was the lord viceroy, don Juan de Mendoza y Luna, in person who saw to it and supervised the workers so that the walls would be repaired; he went about accompanying them in a boat. He was also pondering how to he could protect the altepetl of Mexico Tenochtitlan, since it was already very much flooded and the water came into it from everywhere, descending from the forests. It greatly worried the lord viceroy how the altepetl of Mexico was about to perish from water. When the Mexica had finished building and repairing all the said walls, thereupon the Tenochca were assigned a different task.

And in the same said month of October of the year 1604, the people of the four parts of Chalco were given tasks by order of the lord viceroy. Bringing down logs from the forest began everywhere in Chalco. The Chalca were assigned the wooden beams called *morillos*, because of which they suffered greatly. They went to get them and take them out from the slopes of [the volcanoes of] Iztactepetl and Popocatepetl, and the Amaquemeque went there to cut them, and they brought them to the shore at Ayotzinco. Of the wooden columns or morillos that were brought here to Mexico, a total of six thousand were the exclusive responsibility of the Amaquemeque.

Japanese Come to Mexico City, 1610

Today, Thursday in the afternoon, the 16th of the month of December of the year 1610, at six o'clock, was when perhaps as many as nineteen people from Japan, in China, arrived and entered here in the city of Mexico. A noble, their lord, the ambassador from the court of the great ruler, the emperor of Japan, who brought them, came to make peace with the Christians so that they would never make war but always be at peace and esteem each other, so that Spanish merchants will be able to enter Japan and none of the people there will be able to impede them. And also the people of Japan will be able to come to Mexico to do business, to come here to sell their goods that are made there, and no one will be able to impede them, for thus the lord viceroy don Luis de Velasco, marqués of Salinas, whom they came to see, informed them. Don Rodrigo de Vivero brought them here; they all had landed together; he had gone to be governor in the city of Manila in China [i.e., the Philippines] and was the nephew of the ruler don Luis de Velasco, marqués, viceroy in Mexico; he was his nephew through his spouse. The said don Rodrigo de Vivero had gotten lost on the ocean as he was coming here to Mexico, as became known today. A year ago, in the year 1609, when he was already expected, no one came. Later it was said that perhaps the ship was lost, or broke up somewhere on the ocean, or sank in it with the goods as happens sometimes. It was really thought that the ship in which don Rodrigo was coming was lost and sank. It turns out that a sea storm arose over them in the ocean, and they went along driven by the winds of the storm, and they took their goods and threw them all in the water, and in that condition the storm carried them to where they landed in the great royal altepetl of Japan, where the people of Japan met them in peace; the ruler, the emperor of Japan [and don Rodrigo] met one another. It became known that he went to reside at his palace; he made much of him, fed him, and there don Rodrigo borrowed from the emperor of Japan; he borrowed many thousand [pesos] of his that don Rodrigo brought here to Mexico.

And also, because of that don Rodrigo came bringing people of Japan to collect the many thousand pesos that he had borrowed. And some of the said people of Japan who came here were already Christians and others still idolaters who were not yet baptized. And they were all dressed up as they are dressed up there [in Japan]; they wear something like an ornamented jacket, a doublet, or long blouse, which they tie at their middle, their waist; there they place a *catana* (Asian cutlass) of metal, which counts as their sword, and they wear something like a *mantilla* (headdress for women). And their footwear is soft, softened leather called chamois, like footgloves that they put on their feet. They seem bold, not gentle and meek people, going about like eagles. And their foreheads are very bare because they closely shave their foreheads, making the shaving of their foreheads reach to the middle of their heads. Their hair just begins at the temples, all going around toward the nape of their necks. They are long-haired; their hair reaches to their necks from letting it grow long. They cut only the tips; they look like girls because of the way they wear their hair. Their hair is rather long at the neck; they put together something like a *piochtli* which they tie in twisted, intertwined fashion, reaching to the middle of the head with close shaving. It really looks like a tonsure that they display on their heads, because long hair goes around from their temples to the nape of their neck. And they do not have beards, and they have faces like women, and they are whitish and light, with whitish or yellowish faces. All the people of Japan are like that, that is how they look, and they are not very tall, as everyone saw them.

When they entered Mexico here, the nobleman from there who came appointed as the leader of the Japan people was greatly honored. The carriage of the viceroy, his very own property, went to Chapultepec to meet him as he was passing by on the road. He sent to him, sitting in the coach together, a discalced friar whom they brought from Japan, who came to interpret for them, and a judge of the Audiencia who went to Chapultepec to meet him, when the Japanese came by on the way here. And when they came from Chapultepec, inside the carriage rode all three of them, the nobleman from Japan, the discalced friar, and the judge. When they entered the city of Mexico, they came to establish themselves at the Augustinian church, and not until the next day did they see the lord viceroy; and while they stayed here in Mexico, it was the viceroy who fed them.

An Earthquake, 1611

Today, Friday, the 26th of the month of August of the year 1611, at three o'clock in the morning, was when there was a very strong earthquake such as had never happened before, so that the earth here in the city of Mexico actually moved, and the water of the great lake at Tepetzinco, going toward Tetzcoco, made great noises as it boiled and stirred, and the other waters surrounding Mexico City all made large noises as they boiled and flew up. The water slapping made a sound as though something were falling to the ground from a precipice; it cannot be said or expressed how wide the great stream became and how frightful the slapping of the water was. And all the wells in people's homes everywhere stirred as though someone were taking a bath in them, the way the water flew, boiled, and splashed, hitting and throwing itself against the cistern walls.

And everyone was sleeping in their beds. When they realized there was a strong earthquake, they all got up and ran out of the bedrooms where they were sleeping and came running outside. The Spanish men and women, too, all came out just as they had been sleeping. Some were just in shirts, some came out naked into the patios, some then came out into the road. It was as though we were all drunk, we were so afraid when we saw how houses were collapsing and falling to the ground, for in people's homes everywhere much stone, adobe, and earth came falling in all directions from the tops of the houses. The houses were damaged everywhere; the walls all ripped open even if they were new houses just built; those especially were all damaged and cracked. And at the Theatine college of the Company of Jesus, the stone vaulting above the church ripped in two, and the Franciscan church, as was said, sank into the earth a distance of two inches; and the new church in Santiago Tlatelolco cracked in quite a few places; and the walls of two small churches fell; at the first one, Santa Catalina Zacatenco, the chapel collapsed; the other one was at Capoltitlan de los Reyes. And in many places houses of Spaniards, old and large houses, collapsed, covering people underneath. And some walls in many places came falling down all the way to the ground; some also fell on people, from which there were fatalities. In quite a few places in Mexico people were buried in houses and died from it.

And in the whole chinampa district, in Culhuacan and Cuitlahuac and especially in the city of Xochimilco, there was damage. The churches broke in half, and fell right to the ground. And it came to be known here in Mexico that ten people were buried there, in their homes, when their houses collapsed on them where they were sleeping, who died right away without confession. And small churches in quite a few places there fell in and collapsed with the shaking of the earth. What happened was very frightening and pitiful; cries arose that such a thing should happen to us; the earth went this way and that and we could not stand, we just kept falling down when we stood up, and people really thought that the world was ending. No one remembered what money and property each person had in his house, everything was left inside the house, no one looked at it or saw after it while fleeing; everyone fled outside into the road as long as the earthquake lasted, and many people were hurt running out into the night, as the Spaniards came rushing out of their homes.

But the earthquake lasted for only a very little while. Right away it stopped, but as was said, it was very frightening when it happened and while it lasted. When dawn came and it became fully light, everything appeared and was seen, and all the different things that the earthquake had damaged everywhere here inside the City of Mexico became known. People were frightened, and we feared that as the earthquake happened at three o'clock at night and we thought the earth was going this way and that, it may happen again, as people think.

And after dawn came on the said day of Friday, nothing worried the ruler don fray García Guerra, who is appointed archbishop of Mexico and viceroy; he did not say that there should be prayers or processions or that a litany should be said because such a very frightening earthquake had taken place. For such is the great obligation incumbent upon priests. It is really their duty; they are not just keepers of sheep. Bishops and archbishops are shepherds when something like this happens to people, very frightening and shocking; as long as they are at the head, they lead and guide in the holy Church, they are the ones who should first cry out, give instructions, warn people about things, what and what kind of thing is really needed: that their flock, those guided by them, the residents of the altepetl, should perform prayer, penitence, processions. Penitence should begin first with the rulers, so that their subjects will see it in them and follow them, so that by penitence, tears, sorrow, fasting they will placate our lord God, because perhaps what is happening to people, disease or something else, or whatever it should be that is frightening and shocking, wherever such things happen to people as have happened to us here in Mexico now, happens because of our sins, perhaps through his anger, and is fitting.

And because the ruler don fray García Guerra, archbishop and viceroy, thought nothing of what has happened to us here now and was not afraid of it, he gave orders that there should be bullfighting in his presence in the palace corral, because he is a great lover of bullfighting, so that everyone assembled and went into the corral, where there was bullfighting all day Friday; there the lords judges of the Royal Audiencia assembled. They were enjoying themselves here together with the archbishop and viceroy, watching the bulls, when an earthquake befell them again, at three o'clock in the afternoon, the second time that it happened that the earthquake returned and broke out. And although it was strong again, it was not quite as strong as when it first occurred at night, it just passed quickly and damaged only a few things. At that time the wall of the church of San Juan Bautista of Moyotlan, called San Juan de la Penitencia, cracked in two, and also at that time a Spanish woman and her children were buried in a house which fell in; they did not die because the beams of the house just fell gently on them inside the house, at the wall, so that the beams lay sideways, by which our lord God helped her. The beloved of our lord God, the lord San Nicolás de Tolentino, in his name performed a miracle for the Spanish woman. It was said that this woman, when she realized the earth was shaking and saw that her house was coming down on her, was falling in on her and she could no longer be saved, cried out to him to help her. And it came to pass that he helped her, so that she did not die; they pulled her from the ground. Because this happened, San Nicolás was worshipped even more here in Mexico.

Right after the second time there was an earthquake, in the afternoon, the bells pealed everywhere in mourning; they rang for what are called public prayers at all the monasteries in Mexico. In all the churches absolutely everywhere the bells pealed in mourning because of the earthquake; they began to ring first at the cathedral. And because of this mournful pealing of the bells everywhere in Mexico, the ruler, the archbishop and viceroy, became very sad and worried when he heard it, for he was really enjoying himself among the lords watching the bulls. He was greatly concerned by the pealing of the bells that he heard spread all around, showing sadness, worry, fear, and prayer to our lord God to aid us, because during this second time that there was an earthquake, there was a sound, and everyone heard what kind of sound it was; it sounded like a cart grating along; it sounded like running. Where the sound came from, whether from inside the earth or from the sky could not be established, but it was heard clearly, as though something were running, so that everyone was very frightened again because of that.

But the archbishop and viceroy did not stop watching the bulls because of it; even though he was sad when he heard the bells ringing, he did not therefore halt the bullfighting, but the bullfighting kept on until nightfall. But it was said that he began to get ill as soon as he entered his bedroom in the palace when the bullfighting ended; at that time it began that the archbishop was constantly sick and no longer healthy. And at that time many Spaniards and priests there got angry at him because he did not order prayers said for us because of what just happened to us, and especially he wanted to go about enjoying himself with bullfighting on this Friday, so that they heaped shame on him, especially the inquisitors, so that afterward they prohibited bullfighting in the corral any longer and tore down all the wooden enclosures he had set up there; they removed them all.

The Great Excavation, 1614

On the same said day of Saturday was when licenciado don Pedro de Otalora, president of the Royal Audiencia here in Mexico, left Mexico to go to inspect and to go all around the great lake that surrounds us. He began in Xochimilco, inspecting the level of the water; then he passed through Tolyahualco; then he passed through Cuitlatetelco; then he passed through Ayotzinco; then he passed through Chalco Atenco; then he passed through Chimalhuacan Atenco; then he passed through the great altepetl of Tetzcoco. He went slowly because he went inspecting the waters in each place everywhere, until finally he stopped at Citlaltepec to inspect the water excavation (drainage) being done there. The poor commoners were excavating a mountain there, making a hole in the side of it; where the said waters that surround us and are about to flood the City of Mexico cannot find a channel to come out. It was halted, and the excavation was done no more, because, it was said, a great many poor commoners from far away, a full fifty thousand, died at the place of excavation; people from everywhere were greatly afflicted. And it was said that a million [pesos] of the king's assets was spent there. . . .

7

CRIME AND PUNISHMENT

New Spain was governed by a complex legal system that incorporated both indigenous and Spanish laws and customs, and involved various types of courts with overlapping jurisdictions. Native officials continued to handle many conflicts according to local custom, often without a written record. But the *alcalde mayor* (chief Spanish administrator and first-instance judge in a given jurisdiction) would get involved if the crime was of a violent or serious nature, if a Spaniard was involved, or if the aggrieved party chose to approach him with a complaint. In handling a legal dispute, whether civil or criminal, the alcalde mayor and his staff began a formal investigation by assembling evidence and obtaining preliminary declarations from the parties involved, making arrests, if necessary, and scheduling a hearing with witnesses. Thus, criminal proceedings involving native peoples often originated at the level of the local cabildo and proceeded to the alcalde mayor. When a serious crime such as homicide was committed in a community, the nearest cabildo officials investigated the crime, made arrests, and sent the Spanish alcalde mayor a brief written report of the crime. Thereafter, the entire proceedings were recorded in Spanish by notaries attached to the staff of the alcalde mayor with the aid of translators (as in documents 7.2 and 7.8).

Spanish criminal investigations followed specific rules and guidelines, often structured around a set of questions prepared in advance by lawyers and other colonial officials. But sometimes the native officials recorded confessions or statements from victims and suspects. Documents 7.1 and 7.2 offer excellent Nahuatl and Mixtec examples of testimonies and permit a rare and intimate insight into personal relationships. Documents 7.5 and 7.9 narrate and summarize testimony made by Mayas to their town councils. Document 7.3 is an especially rare type of testimony – a murder note that the assailant himself wrote before fleeing the scene of the crime. In all these examples, we can see how native testimonies take us closer to the crime itself; they are the first written step in an investigation.

In some respects, the alcalde mayor, with his legal advisors and staff, personally administered justice at the provincial level. But native individuals and groups – men and women, nobles and commoners alike – could appeal provincial decisions or move the entire proceedings to either the *Juzgado de Indios* (General Indian Court) or the *Audiencia* (viceregal council and judicial body of New Spain) in Mexico City. Both courts exercised overlapping and supercessory jurisdiction over provincial cases involving native peoples. They could appeal a case in one court and then, if necessary, approach the other. Even if the case were tried at the provincial level, the alcalde mayor consulted a lawyer from the Audiencia or Juzgado who reviewed the complete dossier on the crime and ratified, overturned, or issued a sentence. In fact, provincial courts in criminal proceedings could not impose sentences of death, mutilation, or slavery on assailants without consulting Audiencia officials. Sentences passed by trained agents of the court might be influenced by several factors: early Spanish American precedent and law; the concerns of the colony or province; and the Castilian code of law promulgated in 1567 which applied to the Indies as well as Spain (drawing on a medieval Castilian compilation called the *Siete Partidas*). In theory, local native custom also merited consideration as long as it did not conflict directly with "natural law" or Christian precepts. In reality, although it allowed a range of checks and appeals, the legal system was vulnerable to corruption and prejudice.

Other documents in the chapter reveal some of the personal and political dynamics between Mesoamericans and Spaniards. In document 7.4, a Nahua family attempted to use colonial law to prohibit Spaniards from bringing weapons into their communities. In particular, the Maya documents included here show how personal relationships could also have political implications. In document 7.8, Spaniards are treated as enemies or allies according to the roles and positions they take within a complex factional dispute in a Maya town, a dispute triggered by issues of political legitimacy both within Tekax and in the larger colonial system. In document 7.9, the dividing lines of conflict are likewise based not on Spanish or Mesoamerican identities, but on factional affiliations and perceptions of local interest.

Finally, these documents convey something of the heterogeneity of definitions and conceptions of criminality in colonial Mesoamerica. For Pedro de Caravantes, the real crime committed in Yanhuitlan in 1684 was not his murder of his wife, but Domingo's alleged seduction of Pedro's wife (document 7.3). For Agustín and Andrés, who nearly killed each other in Chalcatongo in 1581, their fight was not criminal, but merely a quarrel that got out of hand – and could be resolved by the protagonists themselves (document 7.2). For the rioters of Tekax, don Pedro Xiu was the town's criminal, but his loyal town councillor, Andrés Chan, saw the rioters as thieves, vandals, and would-be murderers (document 7.8). At least, that was how Chan portrayed them to Spanish investigators; note that the allegation that rioters threatened to cut out Xiu's heart and eat it would have resonated strongly with Spanish notions of native barbarism. The possibility that local Maya rulers presented Spanish officials with one definition of criminality while holding another among themselves is also raised in the testimony against Juan Pablo

Poot; the cabildo of Hoctun may have privately sympathized with Poot, or at least with the cause for which he had tried to recruit co-conspirators, but fear of Spanish reprisals inspired the town councillors to denounce Poot in strong terms, even recommending death as the relevant punishment (document 7.9).

In cases in which Spaniards were the alleged criminals, especially an encomendero (document 7.5) or a priest (documents 7.6 and 7.7), a distinction between native and Spanish conceptions of criminal behavior emerges in the documents. It is perhaps not surprising that powerful colonial officials imagined they could abuse indigenous subordinates with impunity; for every case like the ones included in this chapter, there must have been dozens, if not hundreds, that went unchallenged and unreported. But what is noteworthy is the way in which indigenous governors and councillors responded to the complaints of town residents and employed various strategies – including the shock tactic of document 7.7 – in their efforts to secure justice in the colonial legal system.

7.1. Nahuatl Petition of Simón de Santiago before the Cabildo, 1584[1]

This case illustrates how native authorities in Tulancingo attempted to resolve a petty crime that turned violent: by allowing the aggrieved to prescribe the punishment. The following statement against Cristóbal, recorded in the form of a dialogue, was made before members of the native cabildo, in the absence of Spaniards. Although native authorities handled this case on their own, European introductions are evident.

My lords, my rulers, in your presence I testify about Cristóbal, who is in jail; may you listen well. On Tuesday night he stole a turkey from me; when he made the turkey cry out, my wife awakened and quickly went in to where the turkeys are. She saw that he had already wrung the turkey's neck. Although Cristóbal came running out quickly, my wife was able to see him as he rushed by the grain bin. Then my wife cried out to me, she said, "Wake up, Cristóbal is carrying off a turkey!" Then I got up and came out and went to his house; when I arrived he and his wife were warming themselves by the fire, and I said to him calmly, "Where's my turkey? Give it to me." He said, "What turkey? I will kill you right here. Who will speak for you?" Then he picked up an iron-tipped digging stick and cut open my head, and then he threw me down to the ground, and all I heard him say to his wife was, "Grab the knife on the chest and I'll spill his guts." Then his wife quickly gave it to him; he threw himself on top of me and I couldn't move. I was just lying in the blood from the cut on my head. Then he started trying to stab me, but I pushed

1 Based on translation from Nahuatl by Lockhart (1992: 460–62), modified slightly by Sousa with Lockhart's consent.

aside his hand so that the knife barely entered my back; then I hung on to him and his cloak, which was not strong, was torn to shreds, and also his old shirt and old loincloth, and he was left naked. Then he ran and quickly entered my house, and when he arrived he beat up my wife and told her, "Come get your husband, I've beaten him."

As to the woman, my wife, who was beaten, I say to you, in the presence of you rulers, I ask where am I to get the money [to care for her]? I am a poor person. Cristóbal's wife is healthy; let her come and take care of the person that he assaulted. Let her be there [attend to her] if she recovers. If she dies, let Cristóbal pay the money I have already spent, the two pesos that I have borrowed at the houses of the merchants, and a Spaniard will be demanding more money. So I ask in your presence, let him [Cristóbal] provide the money. He always lives this way, going around stealing and always beating people up and living in idleness. Let the *topiles* (native officers) of Santiago verify the truth of what I say.

Simón de Santiago; my wife is Magdalena.

7.2. Mixtec Testimonies Recorded After an Attempted Homicide in Chalcatongo, 1581[2]

This case elicited three testimonies about an attempted homicide involving two men and a woman in 1581. The text amounts to a fascinating "archival narrative" of infidelity and intrigue, as told by young commoners in their own language. As night turned to day, Andrés and Agustín nursed their serious wounds and tried to come to terms with what had transpired, whereas María had nobody to blame but herself and the devil.

Today, Friday, the 22nd day of the month of September, of the year 1581, we, the *alcaldes* don Alonso de Castilla and Diego Ortiz, came here to San Andrés to speak of the investigation of Agustín García, as to how he fought with a man named Andrés Trujillo.

We asked him: "Why did you fight with Andrés?" He replied: "You will know, lords, that the man named Andrés came to my house in the hills, where I was tending to my fields. It was already very dark. I am asleep, lying with my wife. He came, entered and stood at the doorway; he held an iron-blade knife in his hand. He gave it to my wife. Then she took the knife and dropped it on my chest. I awakened and I grabbed the knife. I attacked him and fought with him as he stood in the doorway. First, I cut him. I injured him so that Andrés began to flee. And then I stabbed him with the knife in the neck and

---

2   Translated from Mixtec by Terraciano. The original document is in AJT-Criminal 1: 35. See
    Terraciano (2001: 372–75) for a transcription and translation of the original.

I stabbed him again with the knife above his ear. So Andrés was in pain, and he cried out to my wife: 'María, grab a rock, grab a stick and smash this devil's head.' Then she took an axe and struck me on the head. This is how it happened nobles, truly and honestly. He arranged with my wife to kill me. I tell you the truth, nobles. I did not have any quarrels with him that would cause him to hate me. I do not know why he would kill me. Thus I declare it, nobles."

Then we asked the man named Andrés Trujillo: "Why did you attempt to kill Agustín? Tell us clearly what is true; did you perhaps have a quarrel with him?"

Then he responded: "It was a pity, nobles. I tell you the truth, my lords, alcaldes. His wife, María García, said to me on Monday, when she came to the river, she said, 'Andrés, come on Thursday night to my field to kill my husband.' This is what she said to me. Then I said, 'all right, good.' That is what I told her. When the Thursday of Saint Matthew came, I went to get a knife from my brother Andrés. 'Lend me your knife, I am going to cut branches,' this is what I told him. Then I took the knife that was given to me and went away. I went to his field, and then I waited nearby until it was dark, whereupon his wife came. She came to tell me, she said: 'Andrés, he is already sleeping now. Come in a little while.' That's what she said. Then I went to the doorway, I gave the knife to his wife. She took it and then she dropped the knife on his chest. So he awoke and attacked me. I fought with him and then he stabbed my neck with the knife and then he also stabbed me above my ear, so I was in pain. Then I cried out to his wife, 'María grab a rock, grab a stick and smash this devil's head.' She then took an axe and struck his head and I fought with him and struck his face. And then I said to Agustín, 'Why are you fighting? I will back down, I will retreat, I am weak, brother. If you want to kill me, then just be done with it. I will die. You are suffering and wounded as I am wounded and suffering. I will cover it up, I will say to my brother and my uncle 'I fell down,' that is what I will tell them. 'But the woman's husband would not consent. So I broke away and fled. This is how it happened, nobles."

"Then I arrived at the house, next to Diego's field. Diego's boy came and found me and I said to him to go call for my brother Simón, who came to carry me."

"I could no longer walk. Then I met the man who had fought with me; his uncle Mateo Sandoval was carrying him. We sat by the road and the people who carried us ate tortillas. Then, Agustín said: 'Andrés, you know, brother, that we must forgive each other, we must cleanse ourselves of this. We are badly hurt. I will give you my shirts[s], and all my capes for you to wear. We must forgive one another and be reconciled. We are both suffering from wounds,' he said. Then I said to him: 'Last night I told you that we should forgive one another but you did not agree.' That is what I said to him in the presence of Simón López, Tomás Pérez, and Mateo Sandoval. So this is what happened nobles, I have recounted this truly and honestly before you justices."

And we asked María García: "Speak truthfully and honestly: why did you attempt to kill your husband Agustín?"

She said: "It is truly cruel, nobles, the devil deceived me. It is true that on Monday, I went to the river and I met the man named Andrés on the road. I said to him: 'Andrés, come on Thursday night to kill my husband.' And he said, 'all right.' When he came, he came right up to my field and then I went to meet him, I said to him, 'Andrés, my husband is already asleep now. Come in a little while.' That is what I said. He said 'all right.' Then I lay with my husband. Then he came and stood in the doorway, he gave me the knife and I took it but I dropped the knife and then he awoke and they came together, grabbed, and fought one another. He stabbed Andrés' neck with the knife and he also stabbed him on the side of his face. Then he was in pain and he cried out to me, 'María, grab a stone, grab a stick and smash this devil's head,' he said. So I took an axe and struck his head, and then I ran away and came to the house [on] María Sandoval's field. Then I did not know what had happened, whether or not they had separated. Later, my husband came and found me at María Sandoval's house and then my uncle Mateo Sandoval came to get me and I went away. This is what happened. I have spoken the truth before you officials. And Andrés has said since that time: 'When your husband has died, then find a good man that you desire, I will not be yours for someone has already informed the officials about us.' That is what he said, and I replied 'all right, that would be good,' I said. Thus, I have spoken the straight truth, so that you will know what happened, lords."

These were all the words spoken truly by all three persons who fought with one another: Agustín García, Andrés Trujillo, and María García. True and honest are the words from the mouth of each man and the woman who appeared before the *alcaldes*, don Alonso de Castilla and Diego Ortiz.

I wrote this document, Lucas Maldonado, notary.

7.3. A Mixtec Murder Note from Yanhuitlan, 1684[3]

Pedro de Caravantes, a toho or nobleman from Yanhuitlan, killed his wife and pinned a murder note to her body before fleeing from the community in 1684. Pedro addressed the three-page letter to both Ñudzahui (Mixtec) and Spanish officials because he knew that both would be involved in the subsequent investigation. The murder note was inserted into the legal dossier as evidence. Pedro claimed to have caught his wife,

---

3 Translated from Mixtec by Terraciano. The original document is in AJT-Criminal 5: 581. See Terraciano (1998) for a full transcription and translation of the murder note and an analysis of this case and similar cases involving violence and adultery.

a mestiza named María Montiel, with the sacristan *(native church attendant), and to have grabbed his cloak as he was trying to flee. Later, he killed her and wrapped her body in the alleged lover's cloak, binding her corpse with rope in a sitting position, according to Mixtec burial practices. Then he pinned the murder note on the cloak. In the note, Pedro tried to justify his act by claiming that he flew into a rage when he caught them together again. In his self-defense, he seems to invoke the Spanish law that absolves a man from killing his unfaithful wife if he loses his senses and harms her in a fit of rage. He even tried to conclude his note with a few lines in Spanish. Indeed, the trial did focus on whether his deceased wife actually did have an affair with the sacristan; although many witnesses testified that their affair was public and well known, the accused lover was rescued in the end by his wife, who claimed that he was a loyal, faithful husband. The record of the case ends with Pedro as a fugitive from justice.*

I am responding before all you lords who are officials, the lord lieutenant, or the lord alcalde mayor, or the Ñudzahui (Mixtec) officials, concerning what I have done because of the crime of someone named Domingo, the son of people who live behind the church of Santa Cruz, the sacristan and husband of Juana, who lives behind the church of Santa Cruz. Because of him I have killed my wife, for I caught both of them together again. Once I caught him with her on the day of Good Friday, and when I caught them on another day I grabbed his cotton cloak from Yodzocoo (Coixtlahuaca, a nearby community). Let the cloak be evidence.

And it is so. If he says that it is not true that I caught him, then the *burro* (torture device) will make him confess the truth. I caught him. Take him to the rack, there he will confess it, he will swear to it. And if he should say "why didn't he kill me when he found me," let it be known that he is a great thief, and thus I did not kill him. I was ashamed because he is such a thief. Though I did not kill him, I now swear on this paper that the sin on my soul is truly his fault. Thus, I demand that justice be done to him, that he be sold to the sugar mill (hard labor), for this Coixtlahuacan cloak, this evidence that I snatched from him, belongs to him.

Let this letter in the Ñudzahui (Mixtec) language be read by don Tomás; he should read this paper and then translate it into Spanish for the lord alcalde mayor to hear, so that justice will be done. By God let it be done.

I will wait over there in a field house and señora Cotita (a Spanish title and a native calendrical name) will look after all her [his dead wife's] things so that it is not said by anyone that I took anything from her. The señora [Cotita] will come here to pick up the title to the house, which I bought for the price of twenty-five pesos. Nobody should try to take it, it will be given to the lady so that she will sell it for her [his wife's] burial.

Thus I request that all you officials do this, sell everything so that nothing remains. And let it not be said by any of you lords "why did he not kill him when he caught him" for I was not about to be shamed by such a thief. Thus her things are to be sold.

You will know lord lieutenant what to do, so that justice will be done. Do not favor him, you who bear the staff [of justice]; see to it that your work is done, be sure to do it. You, too, will learn that he was with her, that this is his cotton cloak, that I caught them myself. Torture will make him confess to the truth of having sinned with that woman.

In truth I swear on this paper and I make a cross here.†

[In Spanish] Let the officials do all that I request, that my writing requests. There in a field house I wait. I do not bear [false] witness. Know that I swear as to how I seized this cloak from Juxtlahuaca [*sic*].

7.4. Petition of a Nahua Family Concerning the Death of a Son, Malinalco, 1641[4]

In 1641, María Salomé, a Nahua woman, filed this humble petition on behalf of her family asking that Francisco Torres, a Spaniard, be prosecuted for the death of her son. Interestingly, Torres was not the person who fired the arquebus (musket) that killed Rodrigo, but he did own it. This case sheds light on indigenous conceptions of blame and on popular understandings of royal decrees that attempted to regulate interaction between Indians and Spaniards. As in document 5.2, a woman speaks on behalf of her family.

My lord Alcalde Mayor, we have come here in your presence, I, María Salomé, my spouse, Agustín Juan, and my mother-in-law. Our home is there in Ocuila. We have come here in your presence to ask for justice. It is because of Francisco Torres that my child died. If he had not brought the arquebus into the altepetl, my child, the late Rodrigo, would not be dead. We request justice. Let him be punished, and [that way] he will pay for the death of my late child. It is the King's order that no Spaniard is to enter the altepetl with an arquebus loaded with gunpowder and shot. Even though he says that the arquebus is not his property, he lies. I need help. That is all that we say in your presence, we who are poor people.

María Salomé   Agustín Juan

7.5. Maya Testimony by the Cabildo of San Román Campeche on the Alleged Rape of a Maya Girl by a Spaniard, 1766[5]

It was one thing for a Spaniard to introduce a gun into a Mesoamerican community, leading to the possibly accidental death of a child. But it was quite another for a

---

4   Translated from Nahuatl by Sousa. The original document is in AGN-Criminal 39: 5.
5   Translated from Yucatec Maya by Restall. The original document is in AGN-Civil 283, 3: 369v–370v.

Spaniard to rape a native girl – especially if the Spaniard was the town's encomendero and the girl a teenage virgin assaulted on her very first day of domestic service in the Spaniard's house in the city. Yet, although the Spaniard's clear criminal intent might make this a serious offense in our eyes, the colonial context denied the victim effective recourse and offered no precedent in the way of punishment for the rapist.

Don Diego Rejón was a wealthy and powerful member of one of Yucatan's oldest Spanish families, and one of a handful of Spaniards who dominated the city of Campeche in the mid-eighteenth century. Although the encomienda system had technically been abolished two centuries earlier, it survived in Yucatan, permitting Rejón privileged access to labor from San Román, one of the Maya villages that lay immediately outside Campeche's city walls. The fact that he sexually assaulted Josepha Ueuet on the first day she was obliged to make the short walk into the city from San Román suggests that he considered such an act his lordly right or droit de seigneur (a medieval European tradition in which feudal lords took the virginity of peasant women). Furthermore, the fact that the Maya governor or batab of San Román insisted that a midwife verify the rape, thereby incurring the wrath of the girl's mother, suggests a skepticism on his part not as to whether the rape occurred but as to the purpose of filing a complaint. If so, the batab was right; the complaint was immediately buried in the local church bureaucracy.

But, as chance would have it, the story did not end there. According to Rejón's wife, doña Antonia Manuela Barranca, she, too, had suffered for years from the man's abusive nature and violent attitude toward women. Her attempts to divorce him (which in colonial times meant separation only and the division of assets) provoked twenty years of legal conflict. Halfway through this bitter and protracted battle lawyers working for doña Antonia discovered the accusation translated here. It was copied into the record of the divorce proceedings, further testimony was solicited, and the details of the rape became public knowledge. Thus, in her campaign to humiliate her husband and destroy his reputation, doña Antonia, unwittingly or not, brought some semblance of the justice that Magdalena Chi had requested for her daughter from her town council.

Here in the courthouse of San Román, today, the 11th of September of the year 1766, appeared Magdalena Chi, the wife of Tomás Ueuet, with her daughter, Josepha Ueuet, virgin, whom she [Magdalena] brought before me, the batab, and the magistrates, regidores and notary. Having gathered together here in the courthouse, she asked justice from us, because when doing her weekly service at the home of our lord señor don Diego Rejón – this was on the very first day this young girl was snatched away to do this weekly service there – this señor don Diego slammed shut the door and windows of his home and began to put his hands all over her, to rape her and do harm to this young virgin. So this was what the two of them [Josefa and her mother] told us here in the courthouse. And I, who hold the office of batab, with the magistrates, then informed this Magdalena Chi that I would call a midwife in order to discover if this señor don Diego had truly ended and forcefully taken the virginity of this maiden. Her mother, this Magdalena Chi, did not want this done. So she went to her home, in a bad mood, saying that she was going to have the gods put a curse on me. Then, later on, we discovered that she called on a *comadre* of hers, Fabiana Gómez, a mulatta midwife, to discover whether her daughter's virginity had been taken; and that having examined her, she [the midwife] told her that it had not been a week since this young virgin had been ruined. This is the truth to which we give our signatures below. Both of them told the truth.

Don Pedro Poot, batab; Manuel Ku, Manuel Cituk, alcaldes; Juan Benito Chan, Juan Pol, Juan Couoh, Lucas Cen, regidores; Antonio Ku, notary.

7.6. Maya Petition of Complaint Against a Spanish Priest by the Towns of Oxtzucon, Peto, Tahdziu, Tetzal, and Tixmeuac, 1589[6]

Occasionally, Spanish officials treated their Mesoamerican subjects so abusively as to provoke riot or revolt; in other cases, native towns engaged in prolonged legal campaigns to have particular administrators or priests removed. The Maya parishioners from a dozen Yucatec towns appear to have suffered the sexual predations, physical abuse, and economic exploitatation of their priest, an Andrés Mejía, for most of the last three decades of the sixteenth century. Repeated complaints and petitions resulted in Mejía being temporarily removed from his parishes – and even from Yucatan – amounting to a tacit recognition by church authorities that their definition of priestly criminality overlapped with that of Maya parishioners. But Mejía was from a prominent conquistador family, and his connections in Mexico City and Merida spared him serious punishment or permanent removal from the colony.

In this petition, the governors and ruling councils of five Maya towns or cahob submit a plea for support from the head Franciscan in the nearby head-town of Tekax. The Maya leaders of the region were clearly counting on the sympathies of this friar, and on those of the chief Franciscan in the colony, whom they name (fray Hernando de Sopuerta). Their hope, expressed later in the petition, that Sopuerta will send another Franciscan to investigate reflects the Maya understanding of church politics in colonial Yucatan, where Franciscans were often at odds with the secular clergy, of which the accused priest, Mejía, was one.

Note that the Maya nobleman who reached out to the unnamed Franciscan to whom this petition is addressed is named don Pedro Xiu. At this time he was batab of Tixmeuac, but he later became batab of Tekax, where he was almost murdered by the townspeople there in 1610, saved only by the intervention of a Franciscan friar – a story told in document 7.8.

God keep you on this the last day [of the month]. You, our father, know we come to Tixmeuac with the nobles. When don Pedro Xiu, governor here in the

---

6 Translated from Yucatec Maya by Restall. An earlier version of this translation appeared in
   Restall (2000: 25–26). The original document is in AGN-Inquisición 69, 5: 277.

cah, told us of your greetings, of the happy tidings you gave him, we were persuaded that your words were good. God be blessed, you know how you protect us. Regarding the statement you made to the nobleman [don Pedro Xiu]: He told us all that you took care of things for him here. We are asking you, then, for God's sake, will you protect us, as you say you will, so that we can carry out our desire to tell the truth about the deeds of the padre Mejía and what he does in the town? So that you will thus hear the story of it, we write this letter to the lord padre, fray Hernando de Sopuerta. If he takes into account what we now say about this padre, extracting all that is true, then, as you said in your letter, a judge, who is a friar, should come to investigate. For here is our statement to you, lord. As you write in your letter to us, when those of Tixmeuac first heard mass here, it was you who first received us into Christianity. This is the reason that we place ourselves before you, so that you, lord, will satisfy our wish. We who are here in Tixmeuac, we are coming from Oxtzucon, Peto, Tahdziu and Tetzal, we who are here with our principal men. Thus we wrote to you at dusk on Sunday. Give us your written word, lord, to the men we are sending there to Tihó [Merida]. We will wait here. You write the truth. We will hear your word.

This is the truth. When he gives confession to women, he then says, "If you don't give yourself to me, I won't confess you." This is how he abuses the women: a woman is not given confession unless she comes to him; until they recompense him with the sin of fornication, he does not give the women confession.

That is the whole truth of how the women are made to prostitute themselves. May God Eternal keep you, our lord.

We who are your children: don Juan Cool, governor of Peto; don Francisco Utz, governor of Tahdziu; all the alcaldes.

7.7. Anonymous Petition of Complaint Against Four Friars, Over Alleged Professional and Sexual Misconduct, Mani Region, 1774[7]

Whereas in the previous document the accusation of sexual impropriety is made in relatively delicate language and almost buried at the end of the petition, the opposite is true here. Using blunt, explicit language, and referring to sexual acts and parts of the body with vernacular Maya terms, these petitioners seem to take delight in recounting the obscene exploits of four local friars. The document strikes us as both shocking and humorous, which is no doubt what it was intended to be – shocking to the church officials who read it (and complained in turn to their superiors about its scandalous language) and humorous to the Maya cabildo members who chose to adopt the anonymous identity of "the informer of the truth." One reason for the difference in tone between this and the previous petition is the identity of the female protagonists;

7   Translated from Yucatec Maya by Restall. An earlier version of this translation appeared in Restall (1997: 330 [transcription], 331 [translation]). Thanks to Terraciano for locating this document in AGN-Inquisición 1187, 2: 59–60.

the petitioners of 1589 are defending their own relatives, the Maya women of their home towns, whereas the anonymous accuser of 1774 identifies the concubines of the friars as non-Mayas. In the previous case, the alleged crimes are committed against Maya women; in this case, the alleged crimes are virtually victimless.

I, the informer of the truth, tell you what you should know about fray Torres, fray Díaz, squad corporal, fray Granado, sargeant, and fray Maldonado: They say false baptism, false confession, false last rites, false mass; nor does the true God descend in the host when they say mass, because they have erections. Every day all they think of is intercourse with their girlfriends. In the morning their hands smell bad from playing with their girlfriends. Fray Torres, he only plays with the vagina of that ugly black devil Rita. He whose hand is disabled does not have a disabled penis; it is said he has up to four children by this black devil. Likewise fray Díaz, squad corporal, has a woman from Bolonchen called Antonia Alvarado, whose vagina he repeatedly penetrates before the whole town, and fray Granado bruises Manuela Pacheco's vagina all night. Fray Maldonado has just finished fornicating with everyone in his jurisdiction, and has now come here to carry out his fornication. The whole town knows this. When fray Maldonado comes each week a woman of Pencuyut provides him with her vagina; her name is Fabiana Gómez. Only the priests are allowed to fornicate without so much as a word about it. If a good Maya (*macehual*, commoner) does it, the priest punishes him immediately, every time. But look at their excessive fornication, putting their hands on these prostitutes' vaginas, even saying mass like this. God willing, when the English come may they not be fornicators equal to these priests, who stop short only at carnal acts with men's asses. God willing that smallpox be rubbed into their penis heads. Amen.

I, father, the informer of the truth.

7.8. Account of the Maya Tekax Revolt, by Cabildo Member Andrés Chan, 1610[8]

In theory, colonial Mesoamerican town governors enjoyed the recognition both of Spanish officials and their native subjects. In practice, town governors were often squeezed between the needs and expectations of those two groups. The Tekax Revolt of 1610 is a dramatic example from Yucatan of a governor caught in this predicament. Viewed in terms of crime and punishment, don Pedro Xiu was condemned as criminally negligent and exploitative by a faction that opposed him in the town council, was manipulated by a rival nobleman of Xiu's, and that enjoyed support among the townspeople. When that support turned into a riot, the mob decided – not

---

8   Translated from Spanish by Restall; Chan's testimony was spoken in Yucatec Maya but recorded by the interpreter-notary in Spanish. The original document is in AGI-Escribanía 305a: 56–61. Thanks to Elizabeth Wright for her comments on some of the phrases in the Spanish text.

surprisingly – to exact their own violent justice. In contrast, the position of don Pedro Xiu, of his loyal alcalde Andrés Chan, and of Spanish investigators, was that the real criminals were the Maya rioters (here called "Indians," as Chan's testimony was written down in Spanish). Because Xiu, as town governor, was the crown's representative in Tekax, the rioters were classified as colonial rebels and punished accordingly. The leaders, including most of the men named in the testimony below, were hanged in the plaza of the provincial capital of Merida; other participants were sentenced for life to labor on the fortifications that were being built around Campeche.

In the town of Tekax, on the 28th day of the month of February, 1610, I Felipe Manrique, by virtue of the commission given to me by the Licenciado Juan de Arguello, lieutenant general to His Majesty's governor of these provinces, and in order to discharge my commission, I ordered to appear before me Andrés Chan, alcalde, as he says he is, of this town; through Gaspar Ruíz de Sandoval, interpreter, I took and received his swearing in by God our Lord and Holy Mary and by the sign of the cross, by which he promised to tell the truth.

And being asked what he knew and what happened, the witness said, "On Monday, at the hour of the Ave Marías, more or less, twenty two days into the present month, I saw a great many Indians gathered together, armed with clubs, knives, and stones, who were very agitated against don Pedro Xiu, governor of this town. And then together they all went to don Pedro's house to kill him, and him not being there, they tore apart the house and stole whatever he had in it. And they would have killed his wife had the padre fray Francisco Alvarez not defended her and removed her, the father of the woman having taken her into the convent, where they put her in the sacristy so that she would not be killed. And they stole from don Pedro everything he had, including a great deal of money, leaving him no more than what he and his wife had on them.

"Because don Pedro had been warned in the house of the alcalde Tomás Hau, where he had gone for a get-together, he knew that those Indians had been to his house to look for him and kill him, that they had demolished his house and stolen all he had in it. And I saw how afraid he was that they would kill him, so I fled with him into the forest and hills to hide. Then those Indians, still armed, went to the house of the alcalde and my colleague, Tomás Hau, looking for that don Pedro; and him not being there, they beat and hit and greatly mistreated the alcalde Tomás Hau, and they wanted to set the house on fire and burn it down, and it would have been burned had nobody come to save it.

"And at that same house appeared Alonso Xiu, son of don Pedro, coming to look for his father, having been told that he had died. And those Indians charged at him and began to beat him with sticks and throw many stones, and they hit him in the head, from which he was badly wounded, and if someone had not helped him escape, they would have killed him.

"In this riot those Indians raised up as captains and leaders Francisco Cal, Juan May, Juan Tzuco, Juan Tox, Gaspar Can, Miguel Pot, Pedro Can,

Francisco Xix, Hernando Ek, Francisco Hau, Cristóbal Na, Pedro Na, Pablo Na, Juan Miz, Pedro Balam, Francisco Cal, and Martín Na. They were at my house, and my colleague's, and those of other principal men, and they demolished their houses and stole what they had inside, and burned some houses, and committed many other abuses, robbing them of all they had in their houses, leaving them with no more than what they had on them.

"Then the next day, Tuesday, don Pedro came back into town at seven or eight in the morning, and ordered one of the alcaldes to report on what had happened. As that very alcalde, I informed him of the situation. And seeing who was thereby guilty, I and the governor [don Pedro] seized some of them and put them in jail in the town hall of this town. And seeing this, those Indians, on the night of that same Tuesday, came to the jail and the town hall, broke down the doors and untied and freed the prisoners from the stocks; and they took the irons of those who were shackled, and they burned the stocks and the pillory that was on the plaza. And in fear I fled with don Pedro to the convent to hide, so that in their fury and their anger they would not kill us; and there the governor and I hid ourselves.

"Those Indians, making a great riot and noise with horns and drums, then came to that monastery and convent in order to kill us, saying in loud voices that don Pedro should be told that they wanted to kill him and eat him. And with this cry they entered the church and convent, breaking down three doors where many of them entered and others scaling the walls with ladders and poles, all in search of don Pedro; and if the padre fray Francisco Alvarez had not defended him, they would have killed him, and in defending him the padre was struck on the leg by a stone. And all that night they kept the convent closed, making the same cry, and issuing proclamations in the town and in the hills, saying that the magistrates of Tekax were ordering that don Pedro be delivered up, because if he was not, they would have to kill all those who were defending him, including the padre fray Francisco Alvarez for defending him too, and they would open up don Pedro and remove his heart and eat it.

"And with this noise they kept the convent closed until Ash Wednesday, when they gathered together inside the church, the priest having delivered sermons to them. There they were in order to receive mass, and he gave them mass in order to calm and pacify them, for there were many of them with sticks and clubs, knives and other weapons. And he began to preach and to tell them to calm down and be reassured that he would order don Pedro to renounce the office of governor and then they would leave town; and they said that if that happened, they would calm down. And under this agreement, the priest had don Pedro renounce, and he brought the Indians two by two to make peace and friendship with don Pedro, and thus they made friends. Under this friendship, the priest and his companion took don Pedro out to the town square; and having mounted a horse, and with him the priest, and his companion, and Francisco de Aguilar, a Spaniard, they accompanied him in order to get him out of the town.

"But the Indians, with the hate that they had for him, rushed out with much noise and shouting and without respect for the clergymen they began to stone them. And they threw so many sticks and stones that they forced them to flee back into the convent, and the clergymen brought in don Pedro greatly battered and injured, as his son had been. And then they closed the convent so that mass could not be said, nor ashes given, and thus it was until almost noon, when many of them went to eat, leaving their guards and sentries, warning the priest that they would get bows and arrows and would come back and kill everyone unless they gave up don Pedro.

"And when after a while the Indians returned with a great noise and battle-cry, the priest saw this and was afraid lest they enter the convent and kill don Pedro; and so in order to protect him he cleared out and removed the most holy sacrament from the chest, and having placed it in another, he hid and shut don Pedro in that ark of the most holy sacrament. And in order to secure them [the chests], he put them in the Franciscan convent, in case they [broke in and] looked for him.

"At the point, there arrived Gregorio de Sigura with another eight or ten Spaniards, and at the entrance to this town they fired an arquebus shot, at which noise and with the coming of the Spaniards they began to retreat and flee. And the Spaniards chased after them, seeing how large the riot was and in order that the church not be burned; and one of the captains and leaders, an Indian named Francisco Cal, while fleeing threw himself into the well in order to hide, but the Spaniards and the priest found out and made him get out, and he is now imprisoned. And it seems to me that without doubt had the Spaniards not come, they [the rioters] would have entered the convent and committed murder and great destruction. And it is a great service to God our Lord and to His Majesty that the Spaniards have come and are on guard in this town, as thus we have been able to plead to the lord governor and captain general or his lieutenant for a peaceful resolution and tranquility for this town and its residents.

"Everything that I have said in this statement is the truth and what I know and saw, by the oath that I made, and I affirm and ratify it. I declare that I am over thirty years old and have not signed because I do not know how to write."

Signed by the interpreter. Felipe Manrique. Gaspar Ruíz de Sandoval.

7.9. Maya Testimonies Regarding the Seditious Behavior of a *Desorejado* from the 1761 Uprising, Hoctun, 1762[9]

The most significant Maya uprising in colonial Yucatan's history took place in and around the small town of Cisteíl in 1761. Although the uprising never posed a serious

9   Translated from Yucatec Maya by Restall. The original document is in AGI-México 3050: 73–74v.

threat to the Spanish colony, the interrogated leaders captured afterward revealed an ideology of nativist discontent that terrified the Spanish colonists. The leader, Jacinto Canek, was publicly tortured to death in a gruesome execution ritual that lasted five hours in the Merida plaza. Eight others were hanged and their bodies quartered, and hundreds more participants given lashes and suffered the loss of one ear. Spaniards referred to these former rebels, one of whom was Juan Pablo Poot, as desorejados *(literally, "dis-eared ones"). An additional round of sentences, including over a hundred hangings and numerous lashings and ear mutilations, were never carried out; as a result, some Spaniards claimed the "pacification" proceedings had been too lenient.*

When this document was written, just six months after the revolt and three months after Canek's execution, tensions were still high. There were still soldiers in Hoctun, even though the town had not been involved in the revolt at all. Most revealingly, the town elders and two witnesses from Hoctun were willing to come forward and denounce a disgruntled resident of their own town – even going as far as to suggest that capital punishment would be appropriate. For the men of Hoctun, having one ear and loose lips in such troubled times was a crime indeed.

On the 28th of April of the year 1762, here in the cah of Hoctun, appeared Lorenzo Ku, and without being given torture, he told, before my lord the Head Justice and before the magistrates and notary, how Juan Pablo Poot has twice come to the house of this Lorenzo Ku to beguile him with the purpose of making war and of killing our lords the Spaniards, on the day of Holy Friday. And also he told him that he had spoken to Lucas Homa, Nicolás Chan, and to other men regarding this war. Without doubt he revealed the truth, he spoke truthfully, in the presence of the magistrates.

At the same time Pedro Pech appeared before me, the batab, and the magistrates and regidores, and the public notary, and before my lords four soldiers, swearing the oath four of five times, saying that when this Juan Pablo Poot came to him, he said, insisting, "Do not come to say anything to me, because I am in the convent of my lord the Padre." And he said in truth that at that time he was beguiling him to go and burn the homes of my lords the Spaniards, and to kill them at night, solely because of the pain he had from having had his ear cut off.

If it is the wish of our lord God, there is no reason to let him live, for he has been beguiled by the devil, nor does he have faith, and has forgotten the commandments of our lord God.

This is the truth, and we sign to it below, today, the 28th of April of the year 1762. Ambrocio Uicab, alcalde; Lorenzo Coyi and Tomás Dzul, regidores; don Tomás Dzul, batab; Martín Coyi, notary.

8

RELIGIOUS LIFE

As the Spanish conquistadors swept through Mesoamerica, friars and priests quickly followed in their footsteps. Twelve members of the Franciscan order arrived in New Spain in 1524, and many more religious joined them in the following decades. They established parishes that were based squarely on native communities, and directed a part of native labor and tribute toward building the church and maintaining their *conventos* or religious establishments. The religious became involved in every enterprise possible in order to sustain their operations, from producing silk and sugar to selling African slaves. The orders (the most important being the Franciscans, Dominicans, Augustinians, and Jesuits) competed with one another for the best areas with the densest native populations. In the early period, the religious were among the only Spaniards living in the native countryside.

In the early post-Conquest period, members of the orders set out to find and destroy temples, images, and the native priesthood. They confiscated and burned codices (pictographic writings on deerskin or fig-bark paper) and created new sacred texts in the form of native-language *doctrinas* or catechisms. They sought to learn as much as possible about native beliefs and customs in order to identify and extirpate them. They underwent extensive native language-training programs so that they could communicate with people, preach to large audiences in the patios of the new churches, and hear confession. They worked with male nobles and their sons in schools to develop native-language dictionaries and grammars, teaching them how to write their own languages with the Roman alphabet. There were so few priests that they could not have done it any other way. All this activity, designed to replace Mesoamerican religion with Christianity, has been called the "spiritual conquest."

Despite the many differences between European and Mesoamerican sacred beliefs and practices, many aspects of sixteenth-century Christianity would not have appeared entirely unfamiliar or incomprehensible to native peoples. Most Mesoamericans – who possessed their own complex and elaborate state religions – had experienced some sort of conquest and expected to acknowledge the new deity or deities of a conqueror. In pre-Conquest times, a large temple served as the ceremonial center of a community and a symbol of identity and autonomy. After the Conquest, churches were built with the same stones and on the same sites as the old temples. People referred to the new structures in terms of the old ones; for example, the Nahuas called the church *teocalli* or "sacred house," Mayas called it *kuna* or "god-house." A hierarchy of native officials, including sacristans and singers, worked in the new churches. This hierarchy was associated with the male nobility of a community, the same social group that organized activities around the old temple and palace complex. They were not allowed to act as intercessors, however, and thus did not become priests. Moreover, Catholicism excluded women from any official positions within the church, except at the level of the community *cofradía* (lay confraternity).

No Christian introduction was more successful than the cult of saints; the patron saint of the local church became a symbolic head of the community, similar in many ways to pre-Conquest patron deities. Sometimes, people coordinated feast days for saints in the Catholic calendar with feasts for deities in the Mesoamerican calendar, celebrating both simultaneously. Catholicism's collective practices, including public worship, processions, cofradías, and public feasts, appealed to indigenous communities. European introductions worked best when they converged with indigenous practices or precedents, when they made sense to the new converts.

Despite the shared features and possibilities for identification between native religions and Christianity, even if native parishioners wanted to accept the new system, they were likely to misunderstand it or interpret many introductions in terms of deeply rooted cultural beliefs or ideologies. Many fundamental Christian principles simply had no corresponding native equivalent; Christian concepts such as sin, heaven, hell, and the devil had no ready equivalents and were understood in many different ways by native peoples. If Christians succeeded in changing the most outward forms of worship at the corporate level, they could not eradicate beliefs and cultural practices at the household level. Countless local forms of Christianity, reshaped by indigenous beliefs and practices, emerged in the early colonial period and continue to evolve in the present.

Another reason for the incomplete conversion of native peoples was the fact that friars and priests were always a tiny minority, especially in rural parishes, remote areas, and peripheral regions. Despite the writings of many friars who tended to exaggerate their own missionary accomplishments, they could never hope to teach the majority more than the most basic tenets of the faith. Also, to many native peoples, accepting the Christian deity did not signify a rejection of all other beliefs. The continued practice of many indigenous rituals and customs, called idolatries by Europeans, were deeply rooted in daily cultural behavior and lay beyond the control of the policing activities of priests. For example, the use of the ancient calendar in many places during the colonial period suggests a continued knowledge of life cycle rituals and other sacred practices that were not fully replaced by Christianity. However, as Christian practices became the dominant public form of religious expression in many places – centered around the church, the saints, and feasts – many ancient practices were driven out of sight or were combined with Christian forms and structures in new, dynamic ways. Ultimately, native peoples created many local religious practices, which defy generalization and reflect a wide spectrum of responses to Christianity.

The documents presented in this chapter provide very particular views on religious life in early- to mid-colonial Mesoamerica. Most of the documents show local rulers taking active roles in the practice of local Christianity, attempting in various ways to manipulate and control it, always keenly aware of its political and cultural dimensions.

The first three documents are pre-Conquest origin legends (all recorded in the colonial period) that attempt to explain the origins of humankind. The legends are similar in many ways to the Book of Genesis and reveal the complexity and diversity of sacred beliefs in Mesoamerica. Some reflect the impact of European colonization on sacred lore; for example, although we cannot know exactly how the Quiché origin legend (document 8.2) was told before the conquest, we do know that it did not include references to Israel, Abraham, and Jacob, and may not have had one of the Quiché founding fathers parting the Atlantic with his staff in the manner of Moses leading his people through the Red Sea. Likewise, the Mixtec origin legend from Cuilapan (document 8.1), retold by a Spanish priest, ends in a biblical flood and the emergence of a single deity.

The next four documents are from the mid-sixteenth century. In these early decades of colonial rule, we catch glimpses of continuity, crisis, conflict, and accommodation. Document 8.4 reveals a native priest's shocking response to the prying questions of the Inquisition. Here are the friars' worst fears confirmed: a rejection of Christianity and a continuing devotion to the rain deity in the middle of Oaxaca. The conquerors came down hard on such outward "idolatry." The background to documents 8.6 and 8.7 includes the brutal anti-idolatry campaign in Yucatan in 1562. Similarly, we read much earlier in document 3.7 of Spanish priests rounding up and destroying native religious images in the Chontal Maya region in the sixteenth century. Such accounts may have left an impression of native religions rooted out and replaced by Christianity. In fact, the Mesoamerican response to the "spiritual conquest" was far more complex and, to some extent, hidden from our view because many native practices were driven "underground." In document 8.5, we see that the new deity is being worshipped in a very traditional manner, forcing native authorities to regulate Christian practices, probably in response to the demands of friars in Tlaxcala.

The documents in the second half of this chapter represent the ways in which native communities accommodated the presence of the church and adapted to Christianity. In documents 8.6 and 8.7, we see most of the Maya town governors in Yucatan collaborating in an effort to exploit the division between Franciscan and secular clergy in Yucatan in the wake of the 1562 anti-idolatry campaign. Their attempts to play an active role in the selection of parish priests set a precedent that was followed for centuries, as we saw in the previous chapter (see documents 7.6 and 7.7). In document 8.8, two Mixtec cousins swear to reject Satan and receive an ecclesiastical dispensation of marriage, recorded in Mixtec by the native *fiscal* of the church, so that their royal union might be recognized by church and state. The testament of a woman named Angelina (document 8.9) shows how ordinary Nahuas adopted and revered Christian saints. Several testaments in Chapters 5 and 6 contain similar evidence of native piety. Finally, document 8.10 provides an excerpt from the Nahuatl story of the apparition of the Virgin of Guadalupe, the most widespread devotion in all of Mexico.

8.1. A Mixtec Origin Legend from Cuilapan, c. 1600[1]

In the beginning of the seventeenth century, fray Gregorio García wrote down a story in Cuilapan, a community in the Valley of Oaxaca, based on a book in the possession of the Dominican vicar of Cuilapan. According to García, the priest had a "hand made book composed of images, like those written by Indians of the Mixtec kingdom in their books or rolled parchments, with descriptions of what the images meant, relating their origin, the creation of the world, and the flood." The legend from Cuilapan attributes the beginning of life to the time when a female deity and a male deity, both bearing the same calendrical name of 1-Deer, built a palace in which they seated themselves as rulers. This primordial couple and much of García's narrative appear in the Codex Vindobonensis, a pre-Conquest screenfold manuscript that provides the only extensive Mixtec account of the creation of the world. Actually, the pre-Conquest codex is far more elaborate and complex than the colonial legend and conveys much of García's narrative in only a few of its many pages. Whereas the codices convey extended narratives and worldviews, the Spanish storyteller ventured only so far. García decided to spare us from all the "nonsense" by cutting short the legend and bringing the entire sacred realm of male and female deities to an abrupt end with a flood. Perhaps fray Gregorio appended this biblical end and new beginning to the story at the point when he interrupted the narrative. Although floods were a familiar theme in Mesoamerican lore, there is no flood in the Codex Vindobonensis. Or perhaps it is possible that native storytellers of the late sixteenth century incorporated the arrival of the new God into their ancient legend. We will never know for certain.

In the year and the day of darkness and ignorance, before there were days or years, the world being in great darkness, when all was chaos and confusion, the earth was covered with water. There was only slime and mud on the

---

1   Translated from Spanish by Terraciano. The legend was given in Mixtec but recorded and translated into Spanish by García in the early seventeenth century. The original is in García (1981 [1607]: Libro v, cap. iv, p. 138).

surface of the earth. At that time, the Indians imagine, appeared a god who had the name of 1-Deer and the surname of Lion Serpent, and a very attractive and beautiful goddess named 1-Deer, whose surname was Tiger Serpent. These two gods are said to have been the origin of all the other gods that the Indians possessed. The histories of this people relate that when these two gods became visible in the world, when they appeared in human form, with their omnipotence and wisdom, they established and founded a large rock, on which they built some very magnificent palaces, constructed with the finest workmanship, where they took their seat and made their residence on earth.

And on top of the highest part of the house and dwelling place of these gods was a copper axe, with the blade turned upward, and the sky above. This boulder and these palaces of the gods were on a very high hill, close to the pueblo of Apoala, which is in the province called the Mixteca Alta. This boulder was named "Place of the Sky" in the language of these people. By this they meant that it was a place of paradise and glory, where there was great happiness and an abundance of all good things; nothing was lacking. This was the first place where the gods made their residence on earth, where they remained for many centuries in great satisfaction and rest, as in a pleasant and delightful place, the world being at that time in darkness and obscurity. This, the Indians held as certain and true, and their ancestors died in this faith and belief.

Thus these gods, father and mother of all the gods, in their palaces and royal courts, had two very handsome male sons who were clever and wise in all the arts. The first was called Wind of 9-Snake, a name taken from the day he was born. The second was called Wind of 9-Caves, which also was the name of his birth date. These two children were raised in great luxury. The older one, when he wanted to amuse himself, turned into an eagle and flew high in the sky. The second also transformed himself into a small animal, in the form of a serpent with wings, and flew through the air with such grace and agility that he passed through stones and walls and he made himself invisible, so that those below were fortunate to hear the clamor that these two made. They took these forms in order to demonstrate the power that they possessed to transform themselves and to return to their previous state.

These two brothers, being in their parents' home, enjoyed much tranquility, arranged to make offerings and sacrifices to their parents, the gods. They took clay incense burners with coals, over which they tossed a certain quantity of ground *henbane* (plant of the Mediterranean region) in place of incense. And this, say the Indians, was the first offering made in the world. Having offered this sacrifice, these two brothers made a garden for their pleasure, in which they placed many species of flowering trees and roses, others that bore fruit, and many sweet-smelling herbs and other species. In this garden and orchard they were entertained and delighted; next to it they made another very beautiful field where they had all the necessary things for the oblations and sacrifices which they offered to the gods, their parents. Luckily, after these two brothers left their parents' house, they were in this garden, taking care to water the trees and plants, tending to what was grown, and making (as I said above) offerings of powdered henbane in clay incense burners.

At the same time they made prayers, votive offerings, and promises to their parents, asking them that by virtue of the henbane which they offered, and from the other sacrifices they made, that they [the gods] would be gracious enough to create the sky, so that there would be clarity in the world, so that the earth would be created or, better said, that it [the earth] would appear and that the waters would be gathered, since there was no other place for their rest except for that small vergel tree. And to oblige them of their request, they punctured their ears with obsidian bloodletters in order to let drops of blood. They did the same to their tongues, and this blood they scattered and sprinkled over branches of trees and plants with a *hyssop* (a plant in the Bible used in Hebraic purification rites) from the branch of a willow tree, as a sacred and blessed thing. They engaged themselves in such a manner, keeping time as they desired, happy as could be, always subservient to the gods, their parents, and attributing more power and godliness to them than to themselves.

So as not to disgust the reader with these fables and nonsense that the Indians tell, I omit and overlook a great many things. In conclusion, after referring to the sons and daughters that those gods had as husband and wife, and the things that they did, where they had their seats and residences, and the labors and effects attributed to them, the Indians say that there was a great flood in which many gods drowned. After the flood passed, heaven and earth were created by the God whom they called in their language "Creator of All Things." The human race was restored and, in this manner, the Mixtec Kingdom was founded.

8.2. Quiché Origin Legend, from the Title of Totonicapán, 1554[2]

The origin mythology of the Quiché Mayas of highland Guatemala has survived most famously in the form of the Popol Vuh, *a kind of Maya Old Testament in that it tells the story of the Creation, of the early interactions between gods and men, and of the settlement of the land by the Quiché founding ancestors. A shorter variant on this book is the* Title of Totonicapán, *written down in 1554 and signed by ten "of us, the descendents of Balam-Qitzé," including don Juan Cortés Qicab and don Juan de Rojas Qicab, memorialized in the* Popol Vuh *as the last of the Quiché kings. Not surprisingly, the version of Quiché history by Balam-Qitzé's descendents depict him as "the first leader ... by unanimous vote."*

2   Originally in Quiché, translated from Spanish by Restall. The Spanish version was written by Padre Dionisio José Chonay in 1834, from the original Quiché text, apparently no longer extant, and was published in Recinos (1950: 213–42).

Here we present only the first of the Title's eight parts. It recounts how the Quiché nations were founded by Balam-Qitzé and the other nahuales *and ends with the Quichés sharing their discovery of fire with non-Quiché peoples in return for their allegiance.* Nahuales *were guardian spirits in Mesoamerican culture; here the term is used metaphorically, so as to present the leaders as protectors of their people in an almost supernatural way. The text illustrates how the traditional interweaving of religious mythology and history, combined with the cultural accommodations of the early colonial period, facilitated the intrusion of Christian elements into how the Quichés remembered their pre-Christian past.*

The wise men, the nahuales, the leaders and lords of three great peoples and of others who joined them, called The Elders, extending their gaze over the four parts of the world and over all that is beneath the sky, and encountering no obstacle, came from the other part of the ocean, from where the sun rises, a place called Pa-Tulán, Pa-Civán.

The principal lords were four: the first was named Balam-Qitzé, grandfather and father of us the Cavekib; the second Balam-Agab, grandfather and father of those of Nihayib; the third Mahucutah, trunk and root of the Quichés; the fourth was named Iqi-Balam. These were the chiefs of the first nation or first subdivision of Quichés, and the wife of Balam-Qitzé was named Zaka-Paluma; she of Balam-Agab, Tzununi-ha; she of Mahucutah, Cahixa-ha; Iqi-Balam was a bachelor.

The leaders of the second nation or subdivision of Quichés were called Tamub; they made up another four: Qopichoch, Qochohlam, Mahquinalon, and Qoganavil. They were the trunk and root of the princes of Tamub, who were named Cakoh [and] Egome. Together these tribes came from the other part of the sea, from the east, from Pa-Tulán, Pa-Civán.

The leaders of the third Quiché subdivision or nation were also four, and they are Chiyatoh [or] Chiya-Tziquin, Yolchitum, Yolchiramag, and Chipel-Camugel. These were the trunk and root of the houses and families of Gala-Ciha and of Tzununi-ha; but this third subdivision made itself distinct with the name Ilocab.

These, then, were the three nations of Quichés, and they came from over there, where the sun rises, descendents of Israel, from the same language and from the same traditions.

When they rose from there, from Pa-Tulán, Pa-Civán, the first leader was Balam-Qitzé, by unanimous vote, and then the great father Nacxit gave them a gift called Giron-Gagal (the Quiché sacred stone).

When they arrived at the seashore, Balam-Qitzé touched the sea with his staff and at once a way opened, which then closed up again, because that was how the great God wished it, for they were sons of Abraham and of Jacob. So it was that those three nations passed through, and with them thirteen others called Vukamag (Seven Peoples).

Once on this other side of the sea they were obliged to sustain themselves with roots, for lack of food, but they journeyed content. They arrived at the shore of a lake where there was a multitude of animals; there they built settlements, but being displeased with the place, they abandoned it. They came to a spot called Chicpach; they set up camp, leaving as a monument a large stone, then continued their migration, always maintaining themselves with roots. They arrived at another spot which they named Chi-Quiché: there they remained for some time, and, having abandoned it, arrived finally at a mountain which they called Hacavitz-Chipal.

This was where they came to a halt, and this was where Balam-Quitzé, Balam-Agab, Mahucutah, and Iqi-Balam decided to make a home. The three Quiché nations or subdivisions were together, that is, the Cavekib, the Tamub, and the Ilocab, and also the thirteen other peoples, called Vukamag-Tecpam.

And they had been in Hacavitz for some time when they agreed to make fire: "We have suffered too much cold," said Balam-Qitzé, "let us try to make a fire."

"Very well," said the thirteen peoples of Vukamag, "let us establish the kind of prize to go to those who first make it; if it appeals to you, we can commit to giving our daughters to those who first make fire."

"Very well," said Balam-Qitzé.

And beginning to rub wood and stones, those of Balam-Quitzé, Balam-Agab, Mahucutah first made fire; but the peoples of Vukamag were by no means able to make it, and so then the latter said: "Give us a little of your fire."

"Give us," they replied, "what we have won, or give us a pledge or a sign."

"And what sign would you like us to give you?" said those of Vukamag.

"If it appeals to you," said Balam-Qitzé, "we will kiss your chests as a sign that you are in debt to us for your daughters."

"Very well," replied the thirteen peoples, and, letting themselves be kissed, they ratified the agreement.

8.3. The Yucatec Maya Origin Legend and Annals of the Xiu, from the Book of Chilam Balam of Mani[3]

In this version of Maya origin mythology, from the northern Yucatec town of Mani, the religious elements are highly muted, perhaps significantly so. Ostensibly written in or shortly after 1610, the surviving version of this passage dates from a couple of

---

3 Translated from Yucatec Maya by Restall. A photostat of the original manuscript is in TLH, Codex Pérez, pp. 134–37. An earlier version of this translation appeared in Restall (1998: 140–42). There are similar annals passages in the Chilam Balam manuscripts from Chumayel and Tizimin (Roys 1933: 135–44; Edmonson 1982: 3–11; 1986: 51–64), but the Mani version is the most substantial.

centuries later, and may reflect the impact of Christianity on Maya conceptions of their ancient origins – the calendar provides a structure and rhythm to the past, but the pre-Christian gods are missing. The Books of Chilam Balam (i.e., of the Prophet Balam) were community books in which a wide array of information was written and rewritten down during the colonial centuries – from ancient prophesies to historical annals to medicial cures. No pre-Conquest or early antecedents of Chilam Balam *literature survive, so we can only imagine how changing religious and historical perceptions must have been reflected in the editing and recopying process.*

In the passage here, the story of mythical origins of the founding fathers of the Xiu dynasty is highly truncated; within a few lines they arrive in Yucatan, where they then move around the peninsula participating in all the key historical moments of the millennium before the Spaniards arrive. The impression given of pre-Conquest chronological precision may be misleading, as the dating of later events is somewhat muddled; fray Diego de Landa, for example, the second bishop of Yucatan, died in 1579, and his predecessor, fray Francisco de Toral, first arrived in the province in 1562. The two entries recording hangings are accurate, however; those of 1562 were part of Landa's campaign of persecution during that summer (see documents 8.6 and 8.7), and the hangings of 1610 followed the Tekax Revolt (see document 7.8 in the previous chapter). Note how the imposition of Christianity is reflected in the adoption of the Christian calendar, with both calendars used to record events during the mid-sixteenth century transitional generation.

This was the arrangement of the *katun* (twenty-year calendrical cycle) since the departure from the land and home of Nonoual. The Tutul Xiu were at West Zuyua for four eras; the land they came from was Tulapan. Four *katunob* had passed when they journeyed and arrived here with Holon Chan Tepeuh and his subjects. When they set out for this province, 8 Ahau had already passed; 6 Ahau, 4 Ahau, 2 Ahau, making eighty-one years (*haab*), as one year (*tun*) of 13 Ahau had already passed when they arrived here in this province; eighty-one years had passed when they journeyed out of their land and came here to this province of Chacnouitan. This was eighty-one years (*años*).

8 Ahau; 6 Ahau; in the second Ahau Ah Mekat Tutul Xiu arrived in Chacnouitan; they were in Chacnouitan a year short of a hundred years. These years came to ninety-nine years.

Then the district of Ziyancaan, or Bakhalal (Bacalar), was discovered. 4 Ahau; 2 Ahau; 13 Ahau; for sixty years they ruled in Ziyancaan, then they came down here; during the years that they ruled Bacalar, Chichen Itza was discovered. Sixty years.

11 Ahau, 9 Ahau, 7 Ahau, 5 Ahau, 3 Ahau, 1 Ahau; they ruled Chichen Itza for 120 years. Then Chichen Itza was abandoned and they went to the cah of Champoton, where the holy men of the Itza people had their homes. These years came to 120.

In 6 Ahau the land of Champoton was conquered. 4 Ahau; 2 Ahau; 13 Ahau; 11 Ahau; 9 Ahau; 7 Ahau; 5 Ahau; 3 Ahau; 1 Ahau; 12 Ahau; 10 Ahau;

in 8 Ahau Champoton was abandoned. Champoton was ruled for 260 years by the Itza people, who came back to their houses a second time. In this katun [i.e., 8 Ahau] the Itzas went to live beneath the trees, beneath the branches, beneath the foliage, where they suffered. These years that went by were 260.

6 Ahau; 4 Ahau; forty years, in which they came to establish their homes a second time and they lost Chakanputun. These years came to forty.

In katun 2 Ahau, Ah Cuytok Tutul Xiu founded Uxmal. 2 Ahau; 13 Ahau; 11 Ahau; 9 Ahau; 7 Ahau; 5 Ahau; 3 Ahau; 1 Ahau; 12 Ahau; 10 Ahau; for two hundred years they governed along with the king (*halach uinic*) of Chichen Itza and [the king] of Mayapan. These years that went by came to two hundred.

These katunob were 11 Ahau, 9 Ahau, 6 Ahau, and 8 Ahau, in which the king of Chichen Itza was overthrown due to the plotting of Hunac Ceel; this happened to Chac Xib Chac of Chichen Itza, due to the scheming of Hunac Ceel, the king of Mayapan. It comes to ninety years, for after ten years of 8 Ahau came the year of destruction caused by Ah Zuyteyut Chan, Tzuntecun, Taxcal, Pentemit, Xuchueuet, Ytzcuat, and Kakaltecat – these were the names of the seven men of Mayapan. Ninety years.

In this eighth Ahau they went to bring down the ruler Ah Ulmil, because he had feasted with the Ulil ruler of Ytzmal (Izamal). The katun cycle had turned thirteen times when they were overthrown by Hunac Ceel in order to teach them a lesson. It ended in 6 Ahau; thirty-four years; the years that went by were thirty-four.

6 Ahau; 4 Ahau; 2 Ahau; 13 Ahau; 11 Ahau; the territory of the fortress of Mayapan was conquered by those outside the wall, by factional rule within Mayapan cah, by the Itza men with their ruler Ulmil. Eighty-three years. 11 Ahau had begun when Mayapan was destroyed by the foreigners from the hills outside Mayapan cah.

Mayapan was destroyed in 8 Ahau; then came the katun 6 Ahau, 4 Ahau, and 2 Ahau, in which the year came when the Spaniards first passed through and were first seen in the land and province of Yucatan, sixty years after the fortress was destroyed. Sixty years.

In 13 Ahau and 11 Ahau there was great sickness and the dying of the Maya in the fortress. In 13 Ahau Ah Pula was killed, when it was six years short of the end of 13 Ahau, the year-count was in the east, [the day] 4 Kan had passed, and [the month] Pop had come; the eighteenth of Zip, 9 Imix, was the day that Ah Pula was killed. That year that passed may be known in a count of numbers, as 1536 years. This happened sixty years after the destruction of the fortress [i.e., Mayapan].

The count of 11 Ahau was not over when the officers of the Spaniards arrived; they came from the east when they arrived here in this land. Christianity began in 9 Ahau; baptisms took place. It was in this katun that the first bishop arrived, named Toral. This year that went by was 1544.

It was in 7 Ahau that the first bishop, [Diego] de Landa, died; in the katun 5 Ahau the first padre settled at Mani; this year was 1550.

It was in this year that went by that the padre settled on the river: 1552.

It was in this year that went by that the *oidor* (judge) came and the hospital was built: 1559.

It was in this year that went by that Doctor Quijada, the first governor here, arrived: 1560.

It was in this year that went by that hangings took place: 1562.

It was in this year that went by that the governor marshal came and the reservoirs were made: 1563.

It was in this year that went by that the great sickness took place: 1609.

It was in this year that went by that men of Tekax were hanged: 1610.

It was in this year that went by that the cah was written down [recorded in a census] by Judge Diego Pareja: 1610.

8.4. Excerpt from the Testimony of an Unbaptized Mixtec Priest During the Inquisitorial Trial of Yanhuitlan, 1544[4]

In 1544, the Inquisition investigated alleged idolatries in Yanhuitlan. The trial elicited testimony on native religious practices and responses to Christianity. Three Mixtec lords from Yanhuitlan, in the heart of the Mixteca Alta, were accused of reverting to ancient religious practices and attempting to subvert the faith. Dozens of Spanish and native witnesses testified to alleged practices, including native priests who described their ritual ceremonies and sacrifices in considerable detail. One of the four priests of Yanhuitlan who appeared in the trial, an unbaptized native noble from Molcaxtepec, was named Caxaa (1-Eagle, according to the 260-day sacred calendar, which was the basis of everyone's name in the Mixteca). Caxaa admitted to having guarded the image of Dzahui, *the rain deity. His testimony of 1545 is given here. After testifying, he was arrested and placed in chains. His description reveals patterns of behavior observable in other parts of Mesoamerica. For example, sixteenth-century Nahuatl manuscripts from central Mexico state that children were sacrificed to Tlaloc (the Nahua rain deity); just as described in this Mixtec account, the Nahua Tlaloc was associated with mountaintops and caves, and he was smeared with burned rubber by Nahua priests.*

Caxaa, native of the pueblo of Molcaxtepec, a *sujeto* (subject settlement) of the pueblo of Yanhuitlan, who is not a baptized Christian, was interrogated and declared the following:

To the first question, he said that he has known them [the accused lords of Yanhuitlan] for a very long time because he is now very old, and he is a

---

4   Translated from Spanish by Terraciano and Sousa. The original document is in AGN-Inquisición, 37, 7: f. 204. The priest's Mixtec-language testimony was translated into Spanish. See Terraciano (2001: Chapter 8) for a discussion of this testimony and the Inquisition trial in Yanhuitlan.

native of the said pueblo of Yanhuitlan. He has heard them called by their Christian names.

To the second question, he said that he has been a priest for four or more years in the pueblo of Yanhuitlan, and that he has in his charge the idols of the said pueblo, together with three other priests. One is named Cagua, the other Cahuizo, and the other Caguiyo. And this witness especially took care of the devil of water that they call Dzahui. He arranged feasts, sacrifices and ceremonies throughout the year, just as they had done before the Christians came to this land.

To the third question, he said that when he was a child he was ordered by the cacique of Yanhuitlan, who is now deceased, to go to live with the priests who were in charge of the idols of the pueblo, and he has always resided in the house of the devils, which is in Tamaxcaltepec. And he has never seen Christians or priests or a church. He took charge of the devil of water upon the death of the one who had been in charge of him. He informed his pregnant wife, named Xaco, [that he would be leaving her] when he assumed this position. And the witness was asked about the type of life that he and his fellow priests lead, and he said that all four lived together in one large house, and that each priest was in charge of a devil, and that each of them had his own chamber, and that each one was in charge of serving his idol . . .

And the witness was asked how he took care of and sacrificed to his devil, and he said that when it did not rain he took out his stone idol and he placed it before him with much reverence. He squatted before the image and he offered him [the rain deity] copal incense and feathers. He told him that the commoners were suffering from hunger and drought. He promised him that he would sacrifice doves, quail, dogs, parrots, and a person, as he wished. This witness sprinkled water from a small bowl (*jícara*) on top of the offerings. Then he took a rubber ball and bounced it on the ground. He burned the ball and smeared resin from it onto the idol. The lords of Yanhuitlan provided all the offerings, including a person who was to be sacrificed, and this witness made sure he provided everything that he had promised the idol. The lords of Yanhuitlan always had a reserve of children for sacrifice.

This witness was asked how many people he killed in the time that he was priest. He said that he ordered to be killed and he killed four children because the rains had not come. He was asked how they did it. He said that he went to the highest hill with his idol and the person who was to be sacrificed. He set the idol down in a suitable place, burned offerings of copal smoke before it, and spoke with the idol for a while. Then he placed the child before him and they sacrificed him. They did not offer adults to this devil of water, only children. He sacrificed the child by cutting out the heart from the chest and then he placed it before the idol. He remained there for two days or more; then, he burned the heart and placed the ashes with the other offerings to the idol. He made a bundle of all the offerings for the idol and guarded it . . .

8.5. Nahuatl Decree Against Dancing with Feathers Around the Crucifix, Issued by the Cabildo of Tlaxcala in 1550[5]

This stern warning against taking feathers from the church properties and dancing with them around the cross reveals that Tlaxcalans are using feathers in the church, a Mesoamerican form of veneration, and that they are dancing around the crucifix with the feathers, another non-Christian practice. Presumably, local friars instructed the cabildo to stop this activity. The proposed fine, eighty pesos, was a large sum of money in this period.

In the loyal city of Tlaxcala, on the 28th day of the month of the year 1550, the very honorable lords, the governor, *alcaldes ordinarios*, and *regidores* determined in the cabildo that a litter be made, a proper litter for the Holy Sacrament. And so that it will be done, the altepetl will make it.

And it is to be ordered that no one take away, take down, or dance with the precious feathers and other kinds of feathers that are attached to all the church properties, the litter, and the case for covering the cross. And they ordered that whoever gives them to people and whomever receives them are each to pay a penalty of eighty pesos, which will be divided into two parts. One part will belong to the treasury and exchequer of His Majesty, and an equal amount will belong to the judge.

Lucas García, Juan Jiménez, Pablo de Galicia, don Juan Maxixcatzin, don Julián Motolinia, Gaspar de Luna, don Juan Xicotencatl, don Francisco de Mendoza, don Diego de Paredes, don Juan Martín, don Francisco de Tapia, Antonio Flores, Feliciano Ceynos, don Martín (Coyolchiuhqui). Before us, the notaries of the cabildo: Fabián Rodríguez, Diego de Soto, notary.

8.6. Letter to the King of Spain from Maya Rulers of the Canul and Other Rulers in the Calkiní Region on the Subject of Spanish Priests, 1567[6]

In 1562 the provincial or head of the Franciscans in Yucatan, fray Diego de Landa, led a violent anti-idolatry campaign. Thousands of Mayas were tortured, hundreds

---

5 Translated from Nahuatl by Sousa and Terraciano, based on the transcription and translation in Lockhart, Anderson, and Berdan (1986: 70–71).

6 Translated from Yucatec Maya by Restall. These letters are taken from a series of ten, two of which have survived in the AHN and eight in the AGI. Following Restall's numbering of the letters (1998: 228), the two reproduced here are (i) and (viii). Letter (i) is in AHN, *caja* III, although a very similar letter from Motul is in Restall (1998: 156–57). Letter (viii) is in AGI-México, 359 and a slightly different version of this translation was previously published in Restall (1998: 160–65; transcriptions and translations of about a sixth of this letter were published by William Hanks [1986: 731, 736–38; 1996: 286, 288–90], who kindly shared a photocopy of the original letter, his transcription of it, and his translation of about half the letter).

died, and hundreds more were publicly humiliated in the Inquisition ritual of the auto da fé. Just five years later, dozens of batabob *or Maya town governors met to draw up joint letters to the Spanish king requesting that more Franciscans be sent to the province. Because most of the letters are very similar to each other (document 8.6 is an example), they flatter the friars so blatantly, and Landa's infamous campaign was so recent, scholars have been tempted to conclude that Franciscans wrote them and obliged* batabob *to sign them.*

However, although the letters represent almost all the cahob *or Maya towns in the colony, conspicuously absent are the communities that bore the brunt of Landa's zeal (indeed, the Xiu of Mani sent an anti-Franciscan letter instead). Ancient regional animosities, still alive in the 1560s, explain why the Canul nobles (document 8.6) and the Pech nobles (document 8.7) might perceive the misfortunes of the Cocom and Xiu as a political opportunity. Furthermore, the letters reveal a distinctly Maya set of priorities – political, economic, and religious – that help explain why these* batabob *may have chosen to ally themselves with the Franciscans. In particular, the second letter here (document 8.7) reveals various motivations behind the denunciation of the secular clergy (priests who were not members of the Franciscan or other orders). The Mayas call them* ek padresob, *"black padres," a reference to the dark robes favored by seculars but with an insult implied, for these priests are depicted as not even deserving of the Spanish title of "clergymen" (*clerigo*).*

Note that the frequent self-references of the letter-writers to their poverty, poor understanding, and common status are part of the ritualized humility required of petitioners in Mesoamerican culture. In document 8.7, the batabob *evoke an image of such poverty that even the plaster is gone from the walls of their wattle-and-daub houses. In fact, these men were among the most important Maya nobles in the province, and they knew it; hence their conviction that they might write to the King of Spain and contribute to the making of colonial religious policy.*

Holy Catholic Royal Majesty.

Because all of your subjects – you, O ruler – understand that it is wished that all is done so that we be saved; for this reason, you, O ruler, would be sure to have within your kingdoms the guides who might illuminate and enlighten and teach those who know nothing. Although we are distant and far from the kingdom of Castile, we nevertheless understand that you are concerned, O ruler, as though we were close by, and that you are also concerned that it be spoken in your ear, that which is truly necessary to us – as befits our low level of reason and our material impoverishment on this earth. For this reason, we are informing you – you, O ruler – that from the beginning of our believing in Christianity, Franciscan friars have taught us the doctrines; and they, with their doctrines and their poverty, preached to us and preach to us the spoken word of God; and truly we love them like true fathers and they love us too like true sons. But through sickness and illnesses and the opposition of the devil, they have really abandoned us and very seldom have come here to this land, and also others have not come out from the land of Castile because it is far and distant. For this reason we are petitioning you – you, O ruler – to have mercy on our souls and decide to send us Franciscan friars to guide us and teach us the way of God. There are some in particular who were here in this land and went to the land of Castile; there were several of them; they really know our language now, having previously preached to us and taught us. Their names are fray Diego de Landa, fray Pedro Gumiel of the province of Toledo – especially that fray Diego de Landa, through whose really great kindness and his goodness in the eyes of our lord God we truly owe to him alone our Christianity – and fray Miguel de la Puebla, and the other padres that have served you – you, O ruler. And because we understand that it is not in vain that we have entered into your service, we now address you – you, O ruler – to bring all our wishes to your Christian heart. And we are confident that we shall be quickly assisted by you – you, O ruler. Our lord God enlightens and continues to glorify you in his service. Here, Yucatan, on the 11th day of February, the year 1567.

Your humble subjects and servants kiss your blessed hands, you, O ruler.

> don Gonzalo Che, cacique of Calkiní
> don Juan Canul, cacique of Nunkiní
> don Francisco Ci, cacique of Kucab
> don Pedro Canul, cacique of Tah Halalch'o
> don Francisco Chim, cacique of Tecpakam
> don Lorenzo Canul, cacique of Kalahcum
> don Diego Canul, cacique of Kinlacam
> don Miguel Canul, cacique of Mopila
> don Francisco Canul, cacique of Panbilch'en
> don Francisco Uicab, cacique of Çiho

8.7. Letter to the King of Spain from Maya Rulers of the Pech and Other Rulers in the Merida Region on the Subject of Spanish Priests, 1567

Because we who are gathered together, we common men, understand our lord God, and you who are the great lord ruler, we wish you to implement something that is necessary, for you too. For truly we are humbled, all of us, beneath your foot, beneath your hand, however many of us there are – we batabob and our principal men who are here in this province of Yucatan. For here in our land, this is where we have our homes. We wish to recount something in your ear, you, O ruler, so that you may take the necessary means. Here then we speak. There is truly a great need here in the province of Yucatan for Franciscan padres for us, so that they might tell us the word of God, which is the Christian doctrine, as it is called, and so that they might say mass for us to watch, and so they might preach to us in the language of here the word of our creator, which is the gospel, as the Spaniards call it. Because it is truly necessary that they come into our districts, for it happened that since the arrival of the bishop whom you sent, named fray Francisco Toral, he brought and distributed black[-robed] padres; they are falsely named clergymen. He then appointed them to take care of the towns within our district, that they might speak the word of God to us, and also so that they might say mass for us to watch. Meanwhile, they preach to us through interpreters because they do not know this language here. There are really no Franciscan padres for us, because they have gone far away; they have scattered. Thus it is truly necessary for us – it really is necessary – that they truly settle here among us. For a very long time ago there came here those who knew our Maya language really well; at that time they preached to us – they were wise men too. Therefore nowadays, many times each day, we remember them. And although, because we are just commoners, we did not really understand the nature of their thinking and were driven out of our minds in the past by the Franciscan padres, they nevertheless verified their words to all us common people; they appointed themselves to be judges of the cah, so as to put a lid on our wickedness. For previously we were truly suffocating under the pressures of the devil; for many times we traveled along the ancient path of our ancestors, which is our path too. We shall never learn our lesson while we speak with the devil, while we go along absorbed in the devils – which are common clay pots worshipped by us in our imaginations, while we make use of *balche* (native wine). For there is no life in our heart when the forest people do not once see those padres. Truly did they soon give life to our hearts and also gave us the love of their preaching to us to prevent sin. Thus today we frequently remember them. For those clergymen never have anything to say; but the Franciscan padres speak well to us, truly and clearly preaching to us, and that is what we now wish for today. For many times they expressed a wish to learn our language here. Now they also baptize our children and baptize us too. Thus those ones that travel to us are really good, for they wish to join us to the son of God and also deliver us from guilt and from living in carnal sin. May your children be cherished, you, great ruler! Now too will they love us while truly giving us from their hearts a true understanding of the faith, you, king (*halach uinic*) that is here [i.e., the governor of Yucatan], for this is not yet known. Now too are these clergymen seen; their doctrine has the same meaning as that of the Franciscan padres, yet – and we are not insulting them – they do not love us nor are we in their hearts. Furthermore, we are not accustomed to being among them; we have spoken to them only a few times, to see this or say that. Neither do they know our language here, nor do we know their Castilian language. Nor do they really devote themselves to us, although we need them; thus do we engage them in vain. So now we are acquiring an understanding of the ways of the black padres. They often do not know how to trade, as they have their commerce with the Spaniards there; they will have no commerce with us. There are men with goods to sell, who have gone before a judge so as to be given a license in order to trade with whomever they meet. [But the clergy] don't take them; they travel a great deal, and so they are not able to; they really do not want different goods, because they would thus pile up every day too many things. Whereas the Franciscan padres are not used to doing that kind of thing; nor does anything arrest their hearts. But these oppressive clergymen get really angry at us while forcing us to work in their homes, [doing] whatever they tell us to. For those black men [the secular clergy] have their own homes and servants, and their own horses and rabbits. Furthermore, as they have settled in our cahob, we are providing them with food and household goods; they have neither paid a thing, nor do we ask them to. For they are ashamed of us and afraid of us, too, although they are the cah guardians and are given the responsibility, and are asked, to go to each cah. And as they are not paid by the bishop's cah [Merida], the burden of it is given to us; but there is no salary. So now we give them much food, and they do not pay us. We now pay them, well and fully, to be guardians of many cahob. Meanwhile, may you reimburse us, you, great reigning ruler, with whatever the bishop that is here in the province of Yucatan orders. May you, the governor, don Luis Céspedes de Oviedo, see that we do not have many things, for we are always being robbed. This is the very reason why there is discord with the bishop that is here in this province and discord with all the black padres. Thus we are unhappy and tortured by them; and we are locked up in jail just for not going along with the authority created by your magistrates, so we may be charged whatever money we have in our hands. This is the price we pay for our own homes. We do not know any reason for us to be tortured and damned by your magistrates and the other Spaniards, which we have lamented from the depths of our hearts. Thus what we have in our hands is not much, only our burial [clothes] and our tribute [goods]; we have now told of it all. We people that are here in this province, therefore, do not have the word; we truly need the doctrine, for we do not have it. For it to be born in our hearts, there must be Franciscan padres [here], for they all truly love us. They do not torture, but do good deeds; may they travel, then, to us today. For there are magistrates of good appearance; should they travel here, whatever tortures we may lament, there will be magistrates to help us. For whatever may be needed, these ministers of our lord God – and they are your ministers too, you, our great reigning ruler – would be truly good, if you sent them, you, our lord. May you allow the condemnation of that which we lament, the frequent sight of discord among them, so they may help us. This is truly very necessary, therefore, that you, chief ruler that is here, bring them too; it would be good for you to give them your license to really help us. And our cah cries out to you to order Franciscan padres to be sent to us, so that they may come and finish guiding the doctrine that they wished for us. For they do it really well; truly and consistently do they do it well; their walk is really good. Having said this, we are recounting their ways because we really want to go there to heaven, from the depths of our hearts. This then is the reason why we now wish for them to be fathers to us, for they truly love us, and we love them too. This is the reason why we wish there to be many of them. It would be good for you to order their elders, the provincial [head of the Franciscans], to send them a second time. These ones should be those who go, because they really know us, they who were here previously; and they really had just taken to speaking Maya; and because they know what we need in order to be worthy before God. And it would be good for the rest of them to come too, to be distributed among us. So who will now be given to us, who truly wishes to teach in our language here? Because they should come every day, it would not be good for them to desire money. It should not be the black-clothed padres; they really take money; they really ask and ask for a great deal of money; they drive us mad over money. Therefore, these words that we say to you, they are not lies; for this is really the truth. We will now prove it. For there were many black padres, twenty-one, that came with the Spaniards, and not one of them knew our language here; only one of them did, but that padre that entered did not teach. For at that time there were no elders, really just boys; they traded in the other cahob. Moreover, they wished to say little, the black padres; those black ones, they hated us. We are now recounting their ways to you, for every time they piled up a lot of money, much cloth, and household goods which God understands belong to us. For all these reasons, he truly understands that one Franciscan padre is better than many black padres. He does not speak, but nevertheless he understand us. The way of fray Francisco de la Torre, provincial here today, is very good; he knows the language here; we truly love him, and he preaches to us often. When he was taken ill with no small [attack of] consumption, our hearts were saddened. And he has no substitute. It is now six years since he traveled the road, since the *oidor* Loaysa came to count us here (take a census); very many of our people had died, and he really understood that you, don Luis, gave your license today so that he count us. It is really a mercy given by God that he count us a second time, for those from the cahob have brought themselves before the chief ruler so that he be merciful and lighten their tribute. Now he makes use of your license so that we shall truly be given mercy; it is for this reason that we now jointly present ourselves to you, so that you give us mercy regarding this our tribute to those lords and what we give to you. The striped walls, really the sticks, is all we have. And now there are coming those who are not accustomed to us. Truly we are afflicted. We have no property. Therefore you, the governor that is here, truly do not make blind the way forward here in the cah by placing the affairs of your cah subjects in the care of those who do not wish to walk to the cah. So that the way not be closed, give your license and authority for the coming of whatever good Christians that will come quickly to respect us. We ask this so that we people here will not be blinded. Truly the space between our cahob is great, but in the end we quickly go the same way. For there are many cahob here in Yucatan, truly so many hundreds of leagues of land here. This is the reason now we truly present ourselves to kiss [you]; we are beneath your feet, beneath your hands, you, O ruler; may you be quickly merciful to us. The power of the governor is great over your officers, chief ruler. Thus we ask that quickly you give us a statement that is truly good. We ask you, chief ruler, for [someone] who truly wishes us good; who truly loves us; who truly will bring us happiness to the bottom of our hearts; who is from God and from you, O ruler; who understands that we are not accustomed to having what we have turned upside down, that our hearts are truly good; who we may truly love, because he loves us. Here then is our statement. We wish for our protectors, those defenders, to give their signatures, so that you may know that truly, coming from our hearts, do we petition you and the governor; so that he may understand that which will truly help us; so that you may know of the anxiety in our cah, you, great reigning ruler. This is the end. Here in the city of Merida, Yucatan, on the 19th day of the month of March of the year 1567. May God truly guard you for many years in your kingdom. This is our statement, all of us batabob. Your humble subjects and servants kiss your blessed hands, you, O ruler.

Don Juan Pech; don Francisco Ucan; Francisco Chel; Francisco Chel;
Pedro Ek; don Pedro Canche; don Andrés Uitz; Diego Balam;
Juan Euan; Juan Tun; Andrés Chel; Pedro Che; Juan Pool;
Pedro Tzul; Juan Ake; Luis Pech; Pedro Cauich; Francisco Pech;
Francisco Mutul; Juan Chim; Francisco Ucan; Juan Maçun;
Pedro Huchim; Juan Mutul; Pedro Poot; Francisco Uicab.

8.8. Ecclesiastical Dispensation for a Mixtec Marriage, 1622[7]

A gathering of nobles from Chalcatongo and Miltepec arranged a marriage by church dispensation between don Diego de Velasco y Arellano and his cousin doña Micaela de la Cueva. The meeting generated a lengthy text on the hereditary qualifications of the caciques, who sought to legitimate their careful dynastic arrangements with a dispensation from the church. The marriage of two high lords, a male and a female ruler, from separate communities or ñuu resulted in the Mixtec arrangement known as the yuhuitayu. Priests presided over the ceremony with the assistance of the native fiscal and the notary, who drew up the document inside the entrance to the church. The document employs the term "tiñomi ñaha Diablo" for the devil, combining tiñumi (owl) and ñaha (person) with the Spanish loan word diablo. This "owl-person" is the equivalent of the Nahua tlacatecolotl, from tlacatl (person) and tecolotl (owl). In Nahua lore, the owl-person was a malevolent creature of the night that possessed the

7   Translated from Mixtec by Terraciano. The original case is in AGN-Tierras 637, 1: ff. 66–73. For a discussion of Mixtec-Christian terminology, see Terraciano (2001: Chapter 8).

ability to change shape and to bring sickness and death. It is possible that Christian concepts first developed in central Mexico were brought to the Mixteca by Nahuas or by the friars themselves. By contrast, the owl-person may have been a widespread Mesoamerican belief. In any case, it is clear that friars relied on this native term, one of many pre-Conquest spirits, to represent the Christian concept of the devil in the early colonial period.

Today, Saturday, the 14th of May, 1622, appeared don Felipe de Velasco, cacique of this *yuhuitayu* of Santiago Ndaanduhua (Miltepec), accompanied by his son, don Diego de Velasco y Arellano. He presented his son to the noble priest, fray Antonio Hernández. He said to the priest that he had come to confirm the statement made by the great lord provincial friar, Benito de Vega, that he had been granted a license of dispensation, so that his son don Diego de Velasco could be married to doña Micaela, the daughter of his nephew, don Cristóbal de la Cueva, from Ñusaha, for they were closely related. Thus he is accompanied by Francisco Pérez, Luis Pérez, and Luis Velásquez, *toho* (nobles) who will serve as witnesses, and all the nobles of Ñundaya (Chalcatongo) and the *ñuu* (community) of Santa Cruz Yucutnoñuhu Ytnodusa.

Then the priest declared: "the duty will be performed by Juan Felipe, the fiscal; the nobles will present themselves and when they have completed their statements they will be admonished three times inside the church of the ñuu, every Sunday, so that the statement will be known, so that nobody should obstruct it when he declares that they will be truly married, but that it will be done by the authority of and according to the order of the Holy Mother Church of Rome." This is what the priest declared.

Today, Saturday, the 14th of the month of May. I, Juan Felipe, the fiscal, am here inside the doorway of the church of this yuhuitayu Santiago Ndaanduhua. Before me appeared don Felipe de Velasco, cacique *yya toniñe* (lord ruler) of this yuhuitayu of Santiago Ndaanduhua. He brought Francisco Pérez, Luis Pérez and Luis Velásquez, the three elder nobles; they came to serve as noble witnesses, to tell the truth and to make statements [as to what they have seen], so that the Holy Church will truly declare that his son named don Diego de Velasco y Arellano can marry his niece, doña Micaela, daughter of his *primo hermano* (first cousin), don Cristóbal de la Cueva, *yya* (lord) of the yuhuitayu of Santa María Ñusaha.

I, the fiscal, completed the duty of giving the oath to Francisco Pérez, Luis Pérez, and Luis Velásquez; the three nobles were presented by don Felipe de Velasco, to be witnesses and to speak the truth. Then I, the fiscal, said to them: "Listen you three, kiss this cross, so that you respond truly and correctly to every word that I ask you. Let there be no dishonesty on your chest or in your heart from the words you speak. If you lie, the owl-person, the devil will take your souls to hell, and in hell your souls will burn, suffer, and be tormented. If you speak truthfully, God will save your soul and will protect your soul in heaven, and there you will be content and joyous forever," I said. The three nobles responded, they said "amen," they said "it will be done." Then they placed their right hands on the holy cross, which was on top of the staff of justice; the three nobles extended their hands and kissed the cross. The three nobles swore to the oath and kneeled.

Before me, the fiscal, today, Saturday, the 14th day in the month of May, 1622.

Juan Felipe, fiscal, don Gabriel de Mendoza, scribe.

8.9. Nahuatl Testament of Angelina from San Simón Pochtlan, Azcapotzalco, 1695[8]

Angelina's testament is especially interesting for her bequest of images of saints, which she expects to be served by her heirs. Then she gives lands to those saints, so that the proceeds of the lands will be used for the upkeep of the image, its altar, and presumably for a feast on the saint's day in the Christian calendar. Finally, she leaves houses to saints, admonishing others not to touch the saints' houses. In general, there seems to be a ratio of one image to one house. The accommodation of saints in separate houses is reminiscent of the santocalli, *the Nahua term in the colonial period for a saint's house that was usually part of the larger* calli *or house complex. This practice may be related to an older tradition of guarding a household deity, which by the end of the seventeenth century had become a local, native Christian practice.*

Jesus, Mary, and Joseph.

I am Angelina, my *tlaxilacalli* (subunit of an altepetl) is here in San Simón Pochtlan. I declare that now God my deity and ruler has issued his sentence upon me. My earthly body is very heavy, but my spirit is aware. Thus, now it is with all my heart and my will that I order my testament; let no one dispute what I shall say. It is to be carried out and done.

First, I declare that I have a grandchild named Tomás de los Santos, and I declare now that I am giving to him [the image of] my precious, revered mother of Candelaria; he is to serve her if God gives him strength. This is my statement, it is to be carried out and done.

Second, I declare that there is a piece of land of forty [brazas] here behind [the church of] my precious, revered father Santo Domingo, and now I declare that I am also giving it to my precious, revered mother of Candelaria; with it my grandchild whom I mentioned, named Tomás de los Santos, is to serve her with it if God gives him strength. This is my statement, it is to be carried out.

---

8   Based on translation from Nahuatl by Lockhart (1992: 463–67), modified by Sousa and Terraciano with Lockhart's consent. See also an earlier transcription and translation in Anderson, Berdan, and Lockhart (1976: 68–71).

Third, I declare that as to [the image of] the heavenly virgin Santa Catalina, I am giving it to a second grandchild of mine named Teresa de Jesús, who is to serve her if God gives her strength. This is my statement, it is not to be invalidated; it is to be carried out and done. And there is a piece of land of sixty [brazas] that I am giving to my precious mother Santa Catalina; with it my grandchild whom I mentioned named Teresa de Jesús is to serve her. This is to be carried out and done.

Fourth, I declare there are two small children, the first named Jacinto Ventura, the second named Josefa de la Encarnación; and I declare now that there is a piece of land here next to the house, fourteen brazas long, eleven wide, that I am giving to my aforementioned grandchildren named Jacinto Ventura and Josefa de la Encarnación. It belongs to them; they are to take it as their own. This is my statement, it is to be performed and carried out.

Fifth, I declare that there is a small house facing Tacuba (south); I am giving it to the one named Josefa de la Encarnación. It belongs to her; no one may take it from her. This is my statement, it is to be carried out and done.

Sixth, I declare there is a small house here. And I declare that I am now giving it to my grandchild at Tianquiztenco, Nicolasa Jacinta; with it she is to serve [the image of] my precious, revered mother of the Rosary. It belongs to her; no one is to take it from her. This is my statement, it is to be carried out and done.

Seventh, I declare that the house is on land ten and a half brazas long toward Tacuba (north to south), and eight and a half brazas wide toward the woods. It is flat land. And now I leave there my son-in-law named Tomás Pérez and his wife Francisca Jacinta. No one may take it from them; it belongs to them. This is my statement, it is to be done and carried out.

Eighth, I declare that as to the house in front, facing toward the woods, I am just leaving there the image of the heavenly virgin Santa Catalina. It is to be just her home; no one may take it away from her. This is my statement, it is to be done and carried out.

Ninth, I declare concerning the church of San Nicolás, where they observe Palm Sunday, that they are to perform a sung [high] mass dedicated to [the souls of] the dead. This is my statement, it is to be done and carried out.

With this I end my statement. I have nothing more; I have mentioned everything here, for I am a poor person. In the presence of the witnesses, the first named Josef Andrés, the second named Juan Matías, the third named Pedro de los Angeles, the fourth named Juan Andrés, and the women Ana de la Cruz and Petronilla.

Before those of us who are in charge of the holy church, including the fiscal, the sick person's testament was made; we heard her statement. To attest to it we place here our names and signatures, today, Tuesday, on the 16th of August of the year 1695.

Don Diego Juárez, fiscal of the holy church, Juan Domingo, church *topile* (constable).

Before me, don Nicolás Felipe, royal notary of the court.

8.10. Excerpt from the Nahuatl Story of the Apparition of the Virgin of Guadalupe, 1649[9]

Some time during the sixteenth century, a shrine was dedicated to the Virgin of Guadalupe at Tepeyacac, a little north of Mexico City, on a site where there had been a temple of the pre-Conquest goddess Tonantzin ("Our Mother" in Nahuatl). For a long time the shrine had a reputation only in and around Mexico City. Both native peoples and local Spaniards were devoted to it. Guadalupe remained a Mexico City phenomenon until the middle of the seventeenth century, when the cult spread throughout central Mexico among both Spanish-speaking and native-speaking people. Chapels were erected and images of the Virgin proliferated in churches and homes.

Mexicans took a shrine, modeled on Spain, and made it their own. The shrine of Guadalupe in Spain was the country's most renowned; the image of the Virgin was very similar to the one in Mexico. Mexican Spaniards appropriated this apparition from the Catholic tradition in Spain; even the story of the Virgin's apparition is modeled on the Spanish one, down to a sick relative who is miraculously healed. The main difference in Mexico is that the Virgin appears to a humble native commoner, Juan Diego, rather than to a shepherd as in the original Spanish version.

Although local Spaniards had their impact on the Guadalupe devotion, the Nahuas also contributed a great deal, including a site already associated with a female deity and the hero of the apparition account – Juan Diego, to whom the Virgin appeared and on whose cloak the miraculous image was imprinted. The Nahuas also reinterpreted the Virgin by calling her "our precious mother," much like a pre-Conquest divinity, and not just "our lady" or "the mother of God" as the Spaniards called her. Despite this reinterpretation, the Nahuas were spiritually attached to a local but regional image that appealed to Spaniards, mestizos, and indigenous people. By the end of the colonial period, the devotion had spread beyond the Nahuas to other native groups outside of central Mexico.

The devotion to Guadalupe took off in the second half of the seventeenth century, after the publication of two different but similar apparition stories; the first published in Spanish in 1648 and the second published a year later in Nahuatl. By this time the Virgin was venerated by both groups, and came to represent the cultural and spiritual convergence of two cultures. Later, in the twentieth century, the Virgin would be seen as a mestiza, Mexican redeemer more than as a Spanish saint or native goddess. Below is an excerpt of the beginning of the Nahuatl version of the story, followed by a brief summary of the remainder.

---

9   Based on the translation from Nahuatl by Sousa, Stafford Poole, and Lockhart (1998), modified slightly by Sousa.

†
HERE
IS RECOUNTED
AND TOLD IN AN ORDERLY FASHION
HOW BY A GREAT MIRACLE THE
IMMACULATE VIRGIN SAINT MARY,
MOTHER OF GOD, OUR QUEEN,
FIRST APPEARED AT
TEPEYACAC, CALLED
GUADALUPE.

First she revealed herself to a humble commoner named Juan Diego, and afterwards her precious image appeared in the presence of the first bishop, don fray Juan de Zumárraga. And here are related all the miracles she has worked.

It had been ten years since the altepetl of Mexico had been conquered and the weapons of war had been laid down, and peace reigned in the altepetls all around; likewise the faith, the recognition of the giver of life, the true deity, God, had begun to flower and bloom. In the year of 1531, just a few days into the month of December, there was a humble commoner, a poor ordinary person, whose name was Juan Diego. They say his home was in Cuauhtitlan, and [he went to] Tlatelolco for spiritual matters (to worship). It was Saturday, still very early in the morning, and he was on his way to attend to sacred matters and to his errands. When he came close to the hill at the place called Tepeyacac, it was getting light. He heard singing on top of the hill, like the songs of various precious birds. Their voices burst forth, and it was as if the hill kept on answering them. Their song was very agreeable and pleasing, entirely surpassing how the bell bird, the trogon, and the other precious birds sing. Juan Diego stopped to look, saying to himself, "Am I so fortunate or deserving as to hear this? Am I just dreaming? Am I sleepwalking? Where am I? Where do I find myself? Is it in the land of the flowers, the land of plentiful crops, the place of which our ancestors used to speak? Is this the land of heaven?"

He stood looking toward the top of the hill to the east, from where the heavenly, precious song was coming. When the song had subsided and silence fell, he heard himself being called from the top of the hill. A woman said to him, "Dear Juan, dear Juan Diego." Then he stepped forward to go where he was summoned. His heart was not troubled, nor was he startled by anything; rather he was very happy and felt fine as he went climbing the hill, heading toward where he was summoned.

When he reached the top of the hill, he saw a lady standing there; she called to him to go over next to her. When he came before her, he greatly marveled at how she completely surpassed everything in her total splendor. Her clothes were like the sun in the way they gleamed and shone. Her resplendence struck the stones and boulders by which she stood so that they seemed like precious emeralds and jeweled bracelets. The ground sparkled like a rainbow, and the mesquite, the prickly pear cactus, and other various kinds of weeds that grow there seemed like green obsidian, and their foliage like fine turquoise. Their stalks, their thorns and spines gleamed like gold.

He bowed before her and heard her very pleasing and regal words, as if inviting and flattering him, saying to him, "Listen, my youngest child, dear Juan, where are you going?" He answered her, "My patroness, my noble lady, my daughter, I am going to your home of Mexico-Tlatelolco to pursue the sacred matters that the representatives of the lord our Lord, our friars, give and teach us."

Then she spoke to him, revealing to him her precious wish. She said to him, "Know, rest assured, my youngest child, that I am the eternally immaculate virgin Saint Mary, mother of the very true deity, God, the giver of life, the creator of people, the ever present, the lord of heaven and earth. I greatly wish and desire that they build my temple for me here, where I will show and make known, and give to people all my love, compassion, aid, and protection. For I am the compassionate mother of you and of all you people here in this land, and of the other various peoples who love me, who cry out to me, who seek me, who trust in me. There I will listen to their weeping and sorrows in order to remedy and heal all their various afflictions, miseries, and torments. And so that my act of compassion which I am contemplating may come to pass, go to the bishop's palace in Mexico and tell him how I am sending you to inform him how I very much wish that he build me a house, that he erect a temple for me on the level ground here. You are to relate every single thing that you have seen and beheld, and what you have heard. And rest assured that I will be very grateful for it, and I will reward it, for I will enrich you and make you content for it. You will attain many things in return for your efforts and labors on my behalf. And so, my youngest child, you have heard my message. Get on your way, make every effort."

Then he bowed himself before her, saying to her, "My patroness, O Lady, now I am going to carry out your message. Let me, your humble subject, take leave of you for a while." Then he came back down [the hill] in order to carry out his errand, taking the causeway that comes directly to Mexico.

When he got inside the altepetl, he went straight to the palace of the bishop, whose name was don fray Juan de Zumárraga, a Franciscan friar and the very first priestly ruler to come [to Mexico]. As soon as he arrived, he attempted to see him; he begged his servants and dependents to go tell him. After a long time they came to tell him that the lord bishop had given orders for him to enter. When he came in, he knelt and bowed low before him. Then he informed and told him the heavenly Lady's message, his errand. He also told him everything that he had beheld, what he had seen and heard. But when he [the bishop] had heard his whole statement and message, he did not seem to be completely convinced. He answered, telling him, "My child, do come again, and I will hear you at length. First I will thoroughly look into and consider your wish and desire." He came out [of the bishop's palace] grieving, because his errand had not been carried out.

He came back right away, on the very same day, to the top of the hill and found the heavenly Lady in the same place where he first saw her, waiting for him. When he saw her, he bowed low before her and threw himself to the ground, saying to her: "My patroness, O personage, Lady, my youngest child, my daughter, I went to where you sent me, I went to carry out your instructions. Although it was difficult for me to enter the quarters of the priestly ruler, I did see him, and I informed him of your message as you ordered me to do. He received me kindly and heard it out, but when he answered me, he did not seem to be satisfied or convinced. He told me, 'You are to come again, and I will hear you at leisure. First I will thoroughly look into your wish and desire.' I could easily see from how he answered me that he thought that perhaps I was just making it up that you want them to build your temple there for you, and that perhaps it is not by your order. I greatly implore you, my patroness, noble Lady, my daughter, entrust one of the high nobles, who is recognized, respected, and honored, to carry and convey your message, so that he will be believed. For I am a poor ordinary man, I carry burdens with the tumpline and carrying frame, I am one of the common people, one who is governed. Where you are sending me is not my usual place, my daughter, my youngest child, O personage, O Lady. Pardon me if I cause you concern, if I incur or bring upon myself your frown or your wrath, O personage, O my Lady."

The revered immaculate Virgin answered him, "Listen, my youngest child. Be assured that my servants and messengers to whom I entrust to carry my message and carry out my wishes are not high ranking people. Rather it is very necessary that you yourself be involved and take care of it. It is very much by your hand that my will and wish are to be carried out and accomplished. I strongly implore you, my youngest child, and I give you strict orders that tomorrow you be sure to go see the bishop once again. Instruct him on my behalf, make him fully understand my will and wish, so that he will build my temple. And be sure to tell him again how it is really I, the ever Virgin Saint Mary, the mother of God the deity, who is sending you there."

Juan Diego answered her, saying to her, "My patroness, O Lady, my daughter, let me not cause you concern, for with all my heart I will go there and carry out your message. I will not abandon it under any circumstances; although I find the road difficult, I will go to do your will. The only thing is that I may not be heard, or when I have been heard I may not be believed. However, tomorrow, late in the afternoon, when the sun is going down, I will return whatever answer the priestly ruler gives to your message. Now, my youngest child, my daughter, O personage, O Lady, I am taking leave of you; meanwhile, take your rest." Then he went home to rest.

On the following day, Sunday, when it was still very early in the morning and dark everywhere, he left his home and came directly to Tlatelolco to learn sacred things and to be counted [by the friars, who took attendance at mass], and also to see the priestly ruler. It was about ten o'clock when they were finished with hearing mass and taking the count, and all the commoners dispersed again. Then Juan Diego went to the palace of the lord bishop; when he got there, he made every effort to see him, but it was with great difficulty that he saw him again. He knelt down at his feet, and he wept and grieved as he told and presented the message of the heavenly Lady, because he wondered if perhaps the immaculate Virgin's message and wish that they build and erect a temple for her, in the place where she specified, would not be believed. The lord bishop asked and interrogated him about very many things: where he saw her and what she was like. And he told the lord bishop everything. Although he told him the exact truth about her, and all that he had seen and beheld, and that she really seemed to be the immaculate Virgin, the precious, revered mother of our redeemer, our lord Jesus Christ, still he was not immediately convinced. He [the bishop] said that it was not by his [Juan Diego's] word and request alone that what he asked for would be done and carried out. Some additional sign was still very much needed so that it could be believed that it was really the heavenly Lady herself who sent him. When Juan Diego heard that, he said to the bishop, "O personage, O ruler, consider what kind of sign it is to be that you request of her, and then I will go ask it of the heavenly Lady who sent me here." And when the bishop saw that he was entirely convinced, that he had absolutely no second thoughts or doubts, he then sent him off.

And when he was on his way, he [the bishop] ordered some of the people of his household whom he trusted to follow him and keep close watch where he went, whom he saw, and to whom he talked. But it so happened that then Juan Diego came straight along the causeway, and those who followed him lost sight of him at the place where the ravine comes out near Tepeyacac, next to the wooden bridge. Though they kept searching everywhere, they did not see him anywhere; they returned empty handed. Not only did they go away vexed because of the loss of time, but it frustrated them and made them angry. They went to tell the lord bishop about it, preparing him not to believe him; they told him that he was only lying to him, only making up what he came to tell him, or that perhaps he only dreamed or saw in sleep walking what he told him and asked of him. They insisted that if he should come again, if he should return, they would seize him on the spot and punish him severely, so that he would never lie and disturb people again.

The story goes on to recount how Juan Diego returns to the Virgin, who tells him to pick some roses that had miraculously bloomed in a barren place, and to bring them to her. She takes the roses, places them in his cloak, and instructs him to take them directly to the bishop without allowing anyone to see what he is carrying. After getting by the palace attendants, who want to know what he is carrying so secretly, he appears before the bishop, opens his cloak, and the roses cascade to the floor. Imprinted on the cloak, where the roses had been, is a beautiful image of the Virgin. The bishop acknowledges the image as a miraculous sign from the Virgin, and agrees to build a church at Tepeyacac. Juan Diego dedicates his life entirely to the shrine, which becomes his new home.

Today, Tepeyac is a major pilgrimage site, Juan Diego is a saint, and the Virgin of Guadalupe is the patron saint of Mexico and many Mexican Americans.

9

RHETORIC AND MORAL PHILOSOPHY

The documents in this chapter shed light on Mesoamerican conceptions of morally appropriate behavior – codes of conduct ranging from royal demeanor to the fidelity of a married man or woman to the behavior of children. Many of the speeches that were recorded in the early colonial period accompanied life-cycle rituals, such as birth, coming-of-age, and marriage. What is most noticeable about this discourse on proper behavior is the honorific, high language that it employs. Many of the reverential expressions and words were probably more archaic, elite forms that reinforced distinctions between nobles and commoners. But it was more a manner of speaking properly and respectfully than a separate language or vocabulary that was unintelligible to commoners.

The most famous high speech is the Nahuatl *huehuehtlahtolli* or "old speech," preserved in sixteenth-century texts such as the Bancroft Dialogues or in Book VI of the Florentine Codex. As shown here, Nahuatl reverential speech contained countless metaphorical expressions, many of which combined two separate nouns or verbs imparting a particular meaning when joined as a pair. For example: *cuitlapilli*, "tail," and *atlapalli*, "wing," indicated a "commoner." To be in "someone's lapfolds," *cuexanco*, and "someone's backpack," *mamalhuazco*, meant "to be the responsibility of, or to be governed by, someone." Some expressions are simply polite ways of saying something, such as the term *tlalticpaciaoiuh*, or "earthly pleasure," for sexual intercourse. The speeches rely on repetition and a fair share of humility. Many morals invoke the lore of revered ancestors and deities. The nobles cultivated this lordly speech in their *calmecac* or schools for men and women. The huehuetlahtolli of central Mexico is renowned for its elegance, but this type of rhetorical, honorific speech was also common among the Mayas and Mixtecs and there were probably forms of it in use throughout Mesoamerica; for Yucatec Maya examples of honorific speech, see documents 8.6 and 8.7, whereas document 9.4 below features the heavy use of metaphor that was characteristic of Maya literature.

The friars were especially interested in collecting these high-minded, moralistic, and admonishing speeches so that they could infuse them with

Christian concepts and use them in their sermons and their Christian *doctrinas* or catechisms. Supposedly, fray Bernardino de Sahagún collected more than a hundred of these speeches during his lifetime. Apparently, this prestigious, "flowery" speech of the nobility had begun to wilt by the end of the sixteenth century, as the nobility underwent significant changes.

The first three documents are excerpts from mid–sixteenth century Nahuatl sources, which present pre-Conquest–style discourses on the idealized behavior of sons and daughters that are to some degree influenced by Christian concepts. The second section preserves speeches that female midwives gave to mothers and their newborn children. The third section presents a conversation between an old woman and a mother about raising children and the "good old days" before the Conquest. The last item (document 9.4) appears at first to be a prophecy about the coming of the Spaniards, but soon reveals itself to be a discourse on the morality of rulers that is partially divorced from any particular historical moment. All these documents preserve notions about what types of behavior make a society civil – in a sense, what makes a civilization.

9.1. Nahuatl Speeches from Book VI of the Florentine Codex[1]

As discussed in Chapter 3, the Florentine Codex consists of twelve books written in Nahuatl from the 1540s to the early 1570s by nobles who came primarily from Tlatelolco, which were collected and compiled by the Franciscan scholar, fray Bernardino de Sahagún. Book VI is titled "Rhetoric and Moral Philosophy." Of the forty-three chapters in this sixth book, we present excerpts of three here in document 9.1 and two more in document 9.2. The following three speeches in document 9.1 were to be delivered by parents to youths, counseling them on their need to act responsibly and on their obligations to others, including their ancestors. The first speech is that of a ruler to his son, which gives us a sense of the great respect and responsibility that such a position entailed. The second is that of a lord to his grown daughter. The third comes from the mother of the same daughter. These particular speeches and many others of this type articulate idealized Nahua cultural concepts and ways of speaking, especially those promoted by the nobility. The speeches also show Christian influences in, for example, their repeated references to the one omnipresent lord, the omnipotent Christian God. Monotheism was applied to Nahua morality. But specific Christian influences on the treatment of marriage and sexuality, for example, are less clear, and these speeches probably represent a convergence of many Nahua and Christian moral ideals that were shared by each culture. The emphasis on monogamy is likely Christian, as

---

1   Translated from Nahuatl by Sousa and Terraciano, based on the translation in Anderson and Dibble (1950–1982). We are grateful for Stafford Poole's assistance with the final translation of these three speeches.

maoon mattinemj, maco
njtimjctinemj injnemja, inj
qujcaianq, auhinjuctsia: a
uhmaic valchocas, maic
oal mellaquaoas inoiquac
itla ipan choloto, innoma
lauh, innomotecujnj. A
motzontecotzin anozl ozj
qujuhtzin njqueoa: tleä
qujmoma chitia, ma amech
motlamatca tlalili mjo. auh
maximotlacotiliean, maxi
motequjttilican, maxicmo
nana mjqujlican inttoq̄, in
naoaque, injoalli, in ehecatl.

¶ *Capitulo deziesiete,*
del razonamjento, lleno
de muy buena doctrina
en lo moral, que el señor
hazia a sus hijos, quãdo
ya auja llegado a los a-
ños de discrecion: exor-
tandolos a huyr, los vi-
cios, y a que se diesen,
a los exercicios de noble
za, y de virtud.

¶ Iccax tolli omome ca
pitulo, vncan mokeneoa
centlamatli cenca qualli, te
nonotzalistlatolli, nenemj
liztilonj: injc qujn nonotza
ia, ipilhoan tlatoanj: inj
quac ie ixtlamati, ietlaca
quj, qujntlaquauh ma
caia, injc quj tlalcahujs
que, injxqujch maqualli,
innaiectli. Auh injcqujtla
quauhtzitzqujsque, impilte
qujtl, intlatocatequjtl: auh
injxqujch qualli iectli.

it was an obsession of the friars, but the warnings against adultery would not have been new to Mesoamericans, who had an established tradition of marriage and strict prohibitions against infidelity. If the friars' teachings and the circumstances of the Florentine Codex's production had already begun to affect the writings of these select nobles, it is also true that the speeches were among the most traditional and conservative genres of the Mesoamerican oral tradition (along with songs), and still convey a wealth of information on elite Nahua conceptions of right and wrong.

Seventeenth Chapter [of Book VI of the Florentine Codex]

Seventeenth Chapter, where is related a very good speech of admonition, rules of conduct, with which the ruler advised his children. When they attained use of reason and understanding, he urged them to abandon all that is bad and impure, and to grasp the duties of nobility, the duties of rulership, and all that is good and pure.

"Come forth, my children. Listen, for you are my children; for I am your mother, I am your father. Often, I commit errors, make mistakes for the altepetl. And as I guard it for the people of the altepetl, I do that which is laughable, which is foolish. And I govern poorly on the reed mat, the reed seat (the rulership), the place of honor of the omnipresent lord.

"And here you stand, you the older brother, you the firstborn; and here you stand, you the second child and you who follows; and here you stand, you the youngest child. Thus I weep, I am sad, I am afflicted when I reflect on he who is my lazy one, on one who cannot speak.

"And who will emerge? Who will show humility before our lord? Perhaps one of you will attain, will merit the rulership, the governed. Or perhaps not. Am I bringing it to a close? Is that all? Is it now this way? Has our omnipresent lord declared it? Will the structure, my reed enclosure, which I put together, where I await the word of our lord, which was completed with difficulty and misery, will it crumble, will it fall apart? Will the land be conquered? Will it go to waste here? Will it happen here? Will my glory, my fame disappear? Will nothing of my legacy remain, nothing of my glory continue on earth? Will I disappear completely?

"Listen how there is life on earth, how compassion is shown by the omnipresent lord. It is only the weeper, the griever, who is required: he who sighs, he who is anguished. And the devout one; he is concerned with one thing, he welcomes, he dedicates himself entirely, and he holds vigil for the sweeping, the cleaning, the ordering of things. It is the pleasure of our lord. And he takes care of, he takes charge of and holds vigil over the incense burner, the offering of copal incense.

"In this manner there is entering near, next to the omnipresent lord, where his bosom is revealed, where he recognizes people, shows mercy on people, takes pity on people. He rewards people, he gives people things. Perhaps he rewards people with the heroic deeds of the eagle warriorhood, the ocelot warriorhood. There he takes, there he recognizes as his friend the one who truly summons him, the one who really prays to him. He puts him in charge of the eagle throne, the jaguar throne. He places in his hands the eagle vessel, the eagle tube.

"It is he who becomes the mother, the father of the sun. He serves drinks to those among us, he serves drinks to those in the place of the dead. And the eagle warriors, the ocelot warriors honor him; they take him as their mother, they take him as their father. Because in truth our omnipresent lord has declared it, has ordered it; it was not fabricated, it was not made up.

"And perhaps he causes him to merit, endows him with, the rulership, the governed. He places in his hands the blue water, the yellow water with which the commoners are bathed.

"And he places him on the left, he provides him with the obsidian sandals of the mother of the gods, the father of the gods, who is in the navel of the earth, who entered the turquoise enclosure, in the waters of the lovely cotinga, enclosed in the clouds. It is Huehueteotl, Ayamictlan Xiuhtecutli.

"Perhaps he assigns him the position of Tlacatecutli, or perhaps the position of Tlacochtecutli. Or perhaps he causes him to merit some humble rulership, so that he sets things in order; he makes him the mother, the father of people. He is honored. Perhaps he causes him to merit some precious thing, he provides him with commoners, the lordship, the rulership. Now I dream, I leap from bed, it is not my desert, it is not my merit.

"Perhaps our lord has mistaken me for someone else. Did I array myself? Did I create myself? Did I say 'Let me be this'? For it is the word, the mercy, the compassion of our lord; it is the property, the belongings of our lord, for it comes from him. For no one says in vain 'May I be this.' For no one merely takes the governed upon himself. For our lord creates people, disposes of people; he does with people as he pleases.

"Listen some more. It is because of this that I weep, I am anguished, I am sad, I am unhappy at midnight, in the middle of the night. Wherever my heart is, it sinks and rises. I am not pleased with any one of you; none of you pleases me. Here you are, the oldest; but in vain are you the oldest, in vain are you the firstborn. What is it with which you lead? Still you appear only childish; you show nothing of being the oldest, the firstborn.

"Here you stand, you who are the second, you who are the youngest. You have achieved only being the second one; you have achieved only being the youngest. Do you destroy yourself, do you fail to understand what is needed? Our lord has sent you second, at the end; will you therefore destroy yourself?

"Listen, please. What will you do on earth? Why were you born? You were born by means of our lords, who are the lords, the rulers who have already gone to be over there; for it was not in the place of plants, in the place of trees, that you came to life, that you were born. What will you do? Are you careful with the staff, the packframe? Do you now work only the furrows, the ditches? Are you now careful with the plants, the trees?

"Listen: here is your duty. Take care of the drum, the rattle: you will awaken the altepetl, and you will bring pleasure to the omnipresent lord, so that you will be informed of things. Then you will take from his lap, from his throat; they are the prayers with which our lord is supplicated, the counsel with which one is counseled.

"And be responsible for artisanship, the art of the worker, the knowledge; in times of the humble nobility's suffering, it will be an enclosure, a shelter, for there is food, there is drink.

"And especially take care of the furrow, of the ditch. Sow and plant the fields. It will not be up to you, you will not grow and nourish the maize. Thus those who departed, who left you, those by means of whom you were born, the lords, the rulers, they took care of and looked after the furrows, the ditches; they went planting on the fields, they went arranging everything. They went saying: 'This is what they went giving and entrusting to us.' They went saying: 'If you dedicate yourself exclusively to nobility, if you do not look after the furrows, the ditches, how will you feed people? What will you eat? What will you drink? Where have I seen nobility that [simply] rose and slept?'

"Listen, the sustenance has really benefited us. Who is said to have called, to have named, the sustenance 'our bones, our flesh'? It is our daily sustenance; it is the walking, the moving, the rejoicing, the laughing, that is already to live in sustenance. Very truly it is said of one who rules, who governs, who conquers: where have I ever seen one who has no stomach, who is not an eater, who rules, who governs? Where have I seen one without provisions who conquers? It is by sustenance alone that the earth exists, that the world goes on living, that we go about filling up the world. The sustenance is our hope.

"And in the fields plant the maguey, the nopal cactus, the trees. The elders went saying that he will refresh the little ones. And you are a little child, do you not also desire the fruit? How will it be there if you do not plant the fields?

"Here, with this, my words come to an end. Hold them in your hearts, guard them, place them in the chambers of your hearts. Inscribe them in your hearts. There are not many words. Where, in truth, shall we arrive? How much, in truth, shall we say? Here are just two words to be guarded, to be remembered, which they left upon going, bequeathed to us as they went, entrusted to us as they departed, which they went along leaving us.

"The first statement: enter near to, close to our omnipresent lord, who is the lord, the night, the wind. Give entirely to him your heart, your body. Do not let your feet go astray. Do not speak within yourself, do not say something within yourself, do not blaspheme in your defiance; for our lord sees and hears things inside wood and stone. . . .

"The second statement: live peacefully among people. Do not be silly, do not pant. May all people have your esteem, your respect. Do not in any way offend people, and do not rise up against someone for something. Do not act impatiently; let whatever is said of you be said. Let yourself be destroyed however you are to be destroyed; do not seek vengeance on people. Do not be a serpent. Do not act impatiently, do not rise up against people, do not blow like the wind against people. Rather, embrace him, just have mercy, for our lord is watching you. For he will be angry with you, he will take vengeance. Just live, for already you are so; already you are arrayed.

"The third statement: Do not know things in vain, do not doubt things in vain on earth. Do not waste the night, the day; they are as essential as our bones, our flesh, our strength and sustenance. Sigh to, request it from, our lord. Ask of our lord that which we wear around our necks, and on our legs. Go to speak with him about it night and day. Do not be negligent.

"Already, this is everything with which I perform my duty for you. Perhaps you will cast it aside; perhaps you will not listen to it. Already you know that I have fulfilled my duty.

"And which of you will benefit? You who are the firstborn, the oldest brother? You who are the second? Or perhaps you who are the youngest? Will it be you, the observant one, will it be you, the one who listens attentively? Will it be you who, it is said, has a divine heart? Will it be you, divine-hearted person? Take it, seize it, keep it, place it and inscribe it in your heart; for you will benefit from it, for you will do yourself well, for that is how you will live on earth."

Eighteenth Chapter [of Book VI of the Florentine Codex]

The eighteenth chapter, where it is told how the rulers would advise their daughters when they reached the age of reason, at which time they urged them to prudence and virtue, whether before people or not before people. They would place before them and show them, the nobility, the rulership, the honor, so that they should in no way blacken, dirty, or degrade the lineage. The words with which they would advise them were very good.

"Here you are, my dear child, my necklace, my feather, my offspring, my progeny, my blood, my color, my blood relation. Now please understand, please listen for you came to life, you were born, for our omnipresent lord, the maker, the creator, has sent you here to earth.

"And now that you already see, that you observe how things are, that there is not contentment, there is not happiness, but that there is torment, there is pain, there is weariness; out of it comes misery, torment, and pain. It's difficult on earth; it is a place of weeping, a place of suffering, where affliction and hardship are common. And a cold, chill wind comes up and passes through. It is truly said that the wind cools the sun's warmth for people. It is a place of thirst and hunger. That's just the way it is.

"Listen carefully, my daughter, my child, the earth is not a good place. It is not a place of joy, it is not a place of contentment. It is said that the earth is simply a place of happiness with fatigue, of suffering with joy; this is what the elders went along saying. So that we commoners might not always go about weeping, so that we might not die of sadness, our lord gave us laughter, sleep; and so it is the fruits of the earth that is our strength, our force, and also earthly pleasure so that seeds will be planted.

"Life on earth makes everyone drunk, so that nobody goes along weeping. Although this is the way it is, indeed, this is how things are on earth, for this reason has it been heard, has it been feared, have people been going along weeping? But on earth life goes on; one becomes a lord, a ruler, a noble, an eagle warrior, an ocelot warrior. And who says that this is how it is on earth? Who is just finished by death? For there are things to be done, livings to be made, homes to be built, work to be done, marriages to be arranged, marriages to take place, women to get married, men to get married.

"And now, my daughter, please listen carefully, look at it closely; here is your mother, your ruler. From her womb, from her throat, you were born. It is as if you were an herb, a plant, you sprouted, you blossomed, you bloomed. It is also as if you were sleeping and you woke up.

"Look around, listen, and know what it's like on earth. Live, just live, follow along a little. How are you to live, how are you to follow along a little? They say the earth is a dangerous place, a frightening, dangerous place, my daughter, dove, little one. Know that you come from people, you have descended from people, you were born by means of people; for you are the spine, the thorn, of our lords who left us, the lords, the rulers who already have gone to be over there, those who came to guard the rulership, and who came to give fame, who came to give renown to the nobility.

"Listen. I declare to you, especially, that you are a noble. Consider yourself as a precious person. Although you are a woman, you are a green stone, you are a turquoise. You were cast, you were pierced. You are blood, you are color (highborn), you are a spine, you are a thorn. You are one's hair, one's fingernail (of noble origin), you are illustrious, of noble birth. And so now I say to you: do you no longer listen very well? Is it true that, it is said that, you pile up earth, potsherds? Are you on the surface of the ground? For already you understand a little, you observe a little. Do not, just of your own accord, bring dishonor upon yourself. Do not do something to bring shame upon our lords, the lords, the rulers who have gone leaving us. Do not become a commoner; do not lower yourself.

"Thus are you to live on earth among others, for you are truly a woman. Here are your tasks that you are to do: be devout night and day. Sigh many times to the night, the wind. Plead with, speak to, cry out to it, stretch out your arms to it, especially at your resting place, at your sleeping place. Do not practice the pleasure of sleep; awake and arise quickly in the middle of the night; with your elbows and knees move quickly, get up. Bow your head and neck. Summon, cry out to the lord, our lord who is the night, the wind; for he rejoices to hear you at night, and then he will have pity on you, he will give you your desert, your merit.

"And if your desert, your merit, which you were given at night, with which you were adorned, when you came to life, when you were born, were not good, then it will be made good, it will be made favorable. The lord, our lord, the omnipresent lord, will change it.

"And at night be lively, get up quickly, get up and stretch your arms, get up, wash your face, wash your hands, wash your mouth. Seize the broom: take care of the sweeping; do not be lukewarm, do not be feverish. Wash peoples' mouths. Especially do not neglect the incense, for in this way our lord is petitioned, it is how his mercy is requested.

"And when it is so, when you have prepared yourself, what will you do? What will you take on as your woman's work? Is it the drink, the grinding stone? Is it the spindle whorl, the weaving stick? Look well to the drink, the food; how it is prepared, how it is made, how it is made well; the essence of good drink, good food, the essence of what is called one's birthright. This is the property that belongs to our lords, the rulers.

"Thus it is called, it is named, one's birthright, the food of rulers, the drink of rulers, the food of nobles, the best drink, the best food. Observe well, open your eyes well, apply yourself well to how it is done, for this is how you are to live and to take care of the land, and thus you will be esteemed, regardless of where our lord assigns you.

"Even if the humble nobility is in misery, look after it well, dedicate yourself well to the very womanly task, the spindle, the weaving stick. Open your eyes wide as to how to become an artisan, how to be a feather worker, how to make designs by embroidering, how to choose colors, how to apply colors, like your sisters, your ladies, our ladies, the noblewomen. Observe closely, apply yourself well to the combing, the warping, the measuring. Do not fail to know, do not be negligent, do not be careless.

"Now is the proper time, it is still a good time because your heart is still a precious green stone, still a precious turquoise. It is still lively, nothing harms it. It lives, it is in no way twisted. It is completely pure; it is still perfect; it is not tainted.

"And we are still here, we who have esteemed you so very much. You who are our child, do you say 'let me make myself, let me be born'? For it is our wrongdoing, we have afflicted you; but this is the way things are on earth. Was it said thus? For our lord declared, arranged the propagation, the multiplication of people on earth.

"We are still here; it is still our time. The club, the rock (punishment) of our lord has still not fallen. We do not die yet, we do not perish yet. Please know it well, my youngest child, dove, little one.

"When our lord has hidden us (when we die), you will live by means of others. The plants, the trees, the strands of chili, the cakes of salt, the soil are not your desert, not your inheritance; you are not to waste time at other people's doorways. Because you are a noble, look carefully to the spindle whorl, the weaving stick, food and drink.

"When it is inconceivable, when it is not yet spoken, someone will point you out, will take care of you. If it is impossible, how will it be? Not for this reason will we have it thrown in our faces. And if our lord has hidden us, not for this reason will we be disparaged; we will not be hidden in the land of the dead. And as for you, you will not suffer punishment, you will distance yourself from it.

"But if now you look very carefully at where the reprimand came from, not in vain will you leave a good memory with people, you will aggrandize yourself, you will make yourself proud, as though you will be in the place of the mat (order) of eagles, the place of the mat of ocelots. You are to go along bearing your shield; perhaps all the little shields will be in your hands.

"Also, because of you we will raise our heads high; you will make us great. But if you do nothing well, perhaps it will be said of you that you have lice. Seldom will you bathe. And which of the two ways does our lord want for you?

"And especially here is how I address you, cry out to you, you who are my creation, you who are my child. Take heed, you should not dishonor our lords from whom you have emerged. Do not cast dirt and filth on their heritage. Do not dishonor the nobility in any way.

"Do not desire earthly things. Do not seek to know things, as it is said, that are in the place of excrement, in the place of filth. If you turn yourself around, will you become a goddess? Do not quickly destroy yourself. Rather, very calmly and peacefully raise yourself up.

"If our lord knows it to be so, if someone should say it is so, it will be said of you, you are not to throw it way, to kick aside the message of our lord. Grasp it. Do not refuse; do not retreat twice, do not retreat three times; you are not to resist.

"Although we are your parents, and although you are born of good parents, you are not to count too much on it; you will offend our lord. For that, he will pelt you with dust, filth, debauchery; one will only be deluded, presumptuous.

"Do not trade, do not deal as if in the market place. And do not, as in the summertime, go picking out the best. Do not languish from desire. However it is, in any case, do not reject the one sent by our lord. If you do not consent, you will be mocked, for truly he deludes; he will turn you into a pleasure-giver.

"Meanwhile present yourself well, look well to your enemy that no one will mock you. Do not give yourself to the wanderer, to the restless one who is given to pleasure, to the evil youth. Nor are two, three to know your face, your head. When you have seen the one who will endure with you to the end, do not abandon him. Grab him, hang on to him even if he is a poor person,

9.1b A Nahua mother (center) advising her daughters on proper behavior and morality. From Chapter 19 of Book VI of the Florentine Codex. Courtesy of the Archivo General de la Nación. Facsimile edition Sahagún 1996, Book VI: f. 80.

even if he is a poor eagle warrior, a poor ocelot warrior, even if he is a poor warrior, of poor offspring, or one who struggles for existence. Do not detest him. Our lord, the wise one, the maker, the creator, will make arrangements for you.

"This is all I give you of my speech to comply with my duty, before our lord. Perhaps somewhere you will reject it. You already know it. Meanwhile, I do my duty. O my daughter, my child, dove, little one, pay close attention. May our lord let you be in peace."

Nineteenth Chapter [of Book VI of the Florentine Codex]

The nineteenth chapter, where it is told how, when the father had spoken, the mother then responded. And with very tender words she told her daughter to guard well, to place well within her, her father's words; to consider them as precious, as valuable. And she told her how to live well, how to stand up, how to speak, how to look at people, how to walk, and how not to be engaged in another's life, and how not to slander someone. This speech should be memorized if it is intended for instruction, for it is a very good speech; but that which is not necessary should be modified. It is especially necessary for young men and young women.

"O dove, little one, child, my dear daughter, you have taken, you have grasped the breath of your child, the master, your lord [your father]. You have taken the incomparable, the ungiveable, which lies numb, which lies folded on his stomach, on his neck. But you are not mistaken for another, for you are the blood, the color, the reflection of the master. Although you are a woman, you are his image.

"And of this, what more shall I say? What more shall I tell you? How much more can I give you? For his speech has ended; for he has everywhere supported you, for he has everywhere made you complete. He has left nothing out.

"And this is all I have to say. I fulfill my obligation. Do not reject the breath, the words of your lord, for they are precious, marvelous; for the breath, the words of our lords come forth only as precious things because they are the words of rulers. They are like precious green stones, they are known as round, reed-like precious turquoises.

"Take them, guard them, place them by your heart, inscribe them on your heart. If you are to live, with them [the words] you will raise and instruct children. You will give them to people; you will tell them to people.

"And here is the second statement which I give you, which I say to you, my dear child, little one. Look to me, for I am your mother who carried you for so many months. And when they were ended, I was putting you to sleep. I lay you in the cradle; I was placing you on my thigh. Indeed, through my nursing, I fattened you.

"Thus I say this, for we are your mothers, we are your fathers who speak to you, who cry out to you. Take our words, grasp them, guard them. In order to live prudently, you are not to dress yourself or to wear finely worked clothing, with elaborate design, for it causes flamboyance. Nor are you to wear rags; you are not to wear the goods, the property of commoners, for it brings about ridicule. You are to clothe yourself well, not in gaudiness or in vanity.

"And as to your speech: it is not to come forth quickly, you are not to sweat, not to rush, not to be uneasy. Your speech is to come forth evenly and gently. You are not to raise or lower much [your voice]. When you speak, when you address people, when you greet people, you are not to shriek, not to squeal. Your speech is to come forth directly; it is to come forth in medium voice; you should not embellish it.

"And as to how you walk, do it prudently. You are not to go in a great hurry, nor are you to amble, for it brings about pompousness, it means brazenness. You should just go deliberately; your feet are just to move along the road. But when you find it is the appropriate time, go along alertly, be content. Run swiftly when it's your time to run so that you will not become sluggish, slow.

"And as how you are to go, to walk, to come upon the road, you should not lower or raise your head; it means imprudence. You are to go directly. Also, you are not to act shamefully or to cover your mouth. You are not to stare or to become a firefly. Walk with great tranquility. Go, walk very peacefully.

"And next, behold, you are truly a noble. As to how you are to live, you are not to look here and there, not to look from side to side, not to stare up or to be looking down. You are not to look angrily; you are not to have anger on your face. Look joyously at everyone. And also, so that no one will disdain you, speak angrily [only] when necessary. And behold, never care too much about words; let what is said be said. Do not speak with others; pretend that you do not hear it. The words will end with you.

"And never desire, never want dyes (cosmetics), adornments, the darkening of the teeth, the coloring of the teeth, the coloring of the mouth; for it indicates deprivation, it means drunkenness. These are the belongings of the vagabonds, the shameless ones, the wicked women; that is the property of those who have become drunk, who have laid waste to the land; that is the work of those who go drinking, who go eating jimson weed; that is the life of those who go drinking bad pulque. These are the ones called the women of pleasure.

"So that your servant (spouse) will not hate you, pay attention to yourself, bathe yourself, wash yourself, but only when it is necessary, so that it is not said, you are not called Tepepetzton, Tinemachxoch.

"Behold the road you are to follow; in this way you are to live. This is how you were raised by your lords, our lords, the noble women, the old grandmothers, the white-haired ones, the white-headed ones. Did they leave absolutely everything? For they gave, they left, they said only one word; but that is their only statement. 'Listen. The earth is a place of learning, a place of prudence.' Listen to and guard these words, and with them lead your life, your works. We travel along a precipice, we live on earth. Over here is an abyss, over there is an abyss. If you go over here, or if you go over there, you will fall in. Only in the middle does one go, does one live.

"Place well these words, my dear daughter, dove, little one, within the chambers of your heart. Guard them well. Do not forget them; for they will become your torch, your light, all the time that you live on earth.

"Here is another thing with which I conclude my speech. If you are to live, if you are to continue a while on earth, do not make friends in vain somewhere with your body, my youngest child, dear child, dove, little one. Do not give yourself thoughtlessly somewhere to another.

"If you are still not pure, if already you are a woman who has been persuaded somewhere, you will never be at peace with people, for it will always be remembered of you; it will always cause your misery, your suffering. Never will you achieve peace or tranquility. Your servant, your spouse, will always be suspicious.

"My youngest child, dove, if you are to live on earth, do not let two men know your face, your head. Behold and listen well, guard it carefully as your strict obligation: if already you are with someone somewhere, do not consider it in vain, do not imagine it in vain. Do not still divert your heart without cause, do not look somewhere in vain. Never at any time abuse your servant, your husband. Never at any time betray him; as it is said, do not commit adultery.

"This, my youngest child, my daughter, is the bottomless, endless abyss on earth; it has no return, it has no remedy. If you are seen, if you are known [to commit adultery], you will be fallen along the road, you will be dragged on the road, your head will be struck with a stone, your head will be fractured. It is said that you will get a taste of the stone; you will be dragged. Because of you fear will descend, people will become fearful.

"And then you will make them famous, you will make them infamous. You will go dishonoring our lords, the lords, the rulers by whom you were born, from whom you have descended. You will scatter dust, trash upon their memory. You will dishonor them. The memory of you will perish there. No longer will you be recognized as a noble. It will be said of you, you will be called, you will be named: 'You wallow in the dust.'

"And listen: even if no one sees you, even if your servant, your husband, does not see you, beware, for the omnipresent lord sees you. He will become angry, he will make the commoner angry, he will take vengeance. He will require of you what he wants, perhaps paralysis, or blindness, or rottenness. And you deserve your worn clothes, your rags; there it will come to an end on earth. For truly you have abused the commoner [your husband]. Perhaps then our lord will step on you, he will kill you, he will send you to our common home, the place of the dead.

"And the master, our lord, is a compassionate one. But if you have come to this, if you have done it, if you have betrayed your servant, and the omnipresent lord does not expose you at that time, no longer will you be in peace, no longer will you live in peace. Our lord will inspire the man only to be angry; he will be furious.

"And this, my youngest child, my dear daughter, my little child, little one: live peacefully and calmly on earth. If you are to continue on for a while, do not in any way disgrace yourself upon dying. And in no way raise up the heads of your lords, the rulers from whom you are descended. And as for us, may we gain glory through you; may we gain renown.

"Please know it, my youngest daughter, my dear daughter, little one. Enter with our omnipresent lord."

9.2. Excerpts from the Midwife's Speeches from Book VI of the Florentine Codex[2]

These speeches are among the very few parts of the Florentine Codex in which women were consulted for their expertise, because no man could pretend to know the speeches of a midwife. Midwifery was the prerogative of women in Mesoamerican society;

2 Translated from Nahuatl by Sousa and Terraciano, based on the translation in Anderson and Dibble (1950–1982).

women also acted as curers and healers and, in fact, these speeches refer to the midwife with the Nahuatl word tiçitl, *the general term for a curer or medical practitioner. What is clear from these brief excerpts is that women were esteemed and honored for giving birth, and that the labor was likened to other heroic and arduous deeds, such as fighting on the battlefield. It is said that women who died in childbirth were accorded the same status as warriors who died in battle. The speeches also set forth idealized gender roles and responsibilities for boys and girls and give us a glimpse of Mesoamerican birth rituals, such as burying the umbilical cord by the hearth, that are still practiced in some places today.*

Thirtieth Chapter [of Book VI of the Florentine Codex]

Where it is told how the doctor [hereafter referred to as the midwife] exhorted the baby who had been born, and what she said to it, all the loving words.

And here is told what was the fate of each one when [the baby] was born; as they said, in the beginning such was the design of the gods. And the midwife inquired about the fate of the baby who was born.

When the pregnant one already became aware of [pains in] her womb, when it was said that her time of death had arrived, when she wanted to give birth already, they quickly bathed her, washed her hair with soap, washed her, adorned her well. And then they arranged, they swept the house where the little woman was to suffer, where she was to perform her duty, to do her work, to give birth.

If she were a noblewoman or wealthy, she had two or three midwives. They remained by her side, awaiting her word. And when the woman became really disturbed internally, they quickly put her in a sweat bath. And to hasten the birth of the baby, they gave the pregnant woman cooked *ciuapatli* (literally, "woman medicine") herb to drink.

And if she suffered much, they gave her ground opossum tail to drink, and then the baby was quickly born. That one already had all that was needed for the baby, the little rags with which the baby was received.

And when the baby had arrived on earth, then the midwife shouted; she gave war cries, which meant the woman had fought a good battle, had become a brave warrior, had taken a captive, had captured a baby.

Then the midwife spoke to it. If it was a boy, she said to it: "You have come out on earth, my youngest one, my boy, my young man." If it was a girl, she said to it: "My young woman, my youngest one, noblewoman, you have suffered, you are exhausted.

"Your father, the master, the omnipresent lord, the creator of people, the maker of people, has sent you. You have come to arrive on earth, where your relatives, your kin suffer fatigue and exhaustion; where it is hot, where it is cold, and where the wind blows; where there is thirst, hunger, sadness, despair, exhaustion, fatigue, pain.

"My youngest one, perhaps you will live for a while, perhaps you are our reward, our merit. Perhaps you will know your grandfathers, your grandmothers, your kin, your lineage. And perhaps they will come to know you. And how were you dressed? How were you arrayed? How has your mother, your father, Ome Teuctli, Ome Cioatl, arrayed you, outfitted you? How do you come, for what purpose are you dressed? Perhaps something is our fate, something is our merit; perhaps something will be yours. Perhaps our omnipresent lord will value you, will favor you. Or perhaps there is no reward, no merit. Perhaps you were born as a measly ear of maize. Perhaps filth, trash is your merit, your reward. . . .

"You have suffered exhaustion, you have suffered pain, my youngest one, my precious noble, necklace, feather, precious one. You have arrived. Rest, relax. Here are gathered your beloved grandfathers, your beloved grandmothers who wait for you. You have arrived here in their hands. Do not sigh, do not be sad. What is to be done of your arrival, of your coming. Truly, you will suffer exhaustion, you will suffer fatigue and pain. Truly, our lord has ordered, has determined that there will be suffering and pain. Sustenance is your affliction, work, and labor. Eating, drinking, and wearing clothes is toil, fatigue, and hard work. Truly, you will suffer exhaustion, truly you will suffer fatigue.

"My youngest one, my precious noble, you have suffered exhaustion, you have suffered fatigue. May the omnipresent lord who is your mother, your father cherish you, dress you. And we parents, are we deserving of you? Perhaps you are all done; the revered parent will call you, will summon you. Maybe you have [only] passed before our eyes, perhaps we have seen you before us [for a while]. My precious child, let us wait still for the word of our lord.

"And then the midwife cut the umbilical cord; she took the umbilical cord from the baby. And she removed the mother's placenta, in which the baby came dressed, in which the baby came wrapped. She buried this in the corner [of the house]. The umbilical cord of the baby was saved, it was dried. Later they left it in battle [if it was the umbilical cord of a boy]."

Thirty-first Chapter [of Book VI of the Florentine Codex]

Where are told the words which the midwife said to the baby when she cut the umbilical cord.

"Thus she told him that it was all suffering, hard labor, that would befall him on earth, and that he would die in battle, or perhaps he would become a captive to be killed as an offering to the deities. And she left his umbilical cord with the warriors, those wise in war, to bury it there in the middle of the plains where war was waged. So she told him that he could go off to make war everywhere. And as to the umbilical cord of the baby girl, she just buried her umbilical cord there by the hearth; thus she signified that the woman was to go nowhere. Her only real task was the home life, by the fire, life by the grinding stone.

"My precious son, my youngest one, behold the decree, the example which your mother, your father Ihualtecutli, Ihualticitl, have established. I take, I cut the umbilical cord from your side, from your middle. Know, listen; your home is not here, for you are an eagle, an ocelot, a roseate spoonbill, a troupial, a serpent, a bird of the omnipresent lord. Here is only the place of your nest. You have only been hatched here; you have only come, arrived. You have only emerged on earth here. Here you bud, blossom, sprout. Here you become the chip, the piece [of your parents]. Here are only your cradle, your cradle blanket, your head's resting place: only your place of arrival. You belong out there; out there you have been chosen. You have been sent into warfare. War is your reward, your task. You will give drink, nourishment, food to the sun, the lord of the earth. Your real home, your property, your fate is the home of the sun there in the sky. You will praise, you will bring joy to Totonametl. Perhaps you will receive the gift, maybe you will merit death by the obsidian knife, the flowery death of the obsidian knife.

"And this which is lifted from your side, which comes from your middle, I take from you; it is the gift, the property of Tlalteuctli, Tonatiuh. And when the battle has begun, has been waged, it will be introduced into the hands of the eagle warriors, the ocelot warriors, the brave warriors. They go giving it to your mother, your father, Tonatiuh, Tlalteuctli; they go entering into the center, the middle, of the plains. And thus you have been assigned, you have been entrusted to the sun, to Tlalteuctli; thereby you deliver yourself to him. And thus there within the battlefield, your name will be written, will be registered so that your renown will not be forgotten, will not be lost. The precious thing removed from your side is your thorn, your maguey, your reed, your special plant (acxoyatl) with which you are to do penance (autosacrifice). Your vow is to be fulfilled. And now let us hope for something; perhaps we shall deserve, we shall merit something. Work, my precious son; may the omnipresent lord give you life, provide for you, array you."

And if [the baby] were a woman, the midwife said to her when she cut the umbilical cord: "My dear young lady, my dear noblewoman, you have endured fatigue. Our lord, the omnipresent lord, has sent you. You have come to arrive at a place of weariness, a place of anguish, a place of fatigue where there is cold, there is wind. And now listen: from your side, from your middle I take it, I cut it. Your mother, your father, Ihualteuctli, Ihualticitl, order it, request it. You will be in the heart of the home, you will go nowhere, you will nowhere become a wanderer, you become the smoldering fire, the hearth stones. Here our lord plants you, buries you. And you will become fatigued, you will become tired; you are to provide water, to grind maize, to work hard; you are to sweat by the ashes, by the hearth."

Then the midwife buried the umbilical cord of the noblewoman by the hearth. It was said that by this she signified that the little woman would

9.2 Illustration accompanying the midwives' speeches in Book VI of the Florentine Codex, showing the women ritually bathing the child and presenting him with the clothing and belongings of a Nahua male. Courtesy of the Archivo Gereral de la Nación. Facsimile edition Sahagún 1996, Book VI: f. 170.

nowhere wander. Her dwelling place was only within the house; her home was only within the house. It was not necessary for her to go anywhere. And it meant that her very duty was drink, food. She was to prepare drink, to prepare food, to grind, to spin, to weave.

9.3. Excerpts from the Nahuatl Tetzcoco Dialogues, c. 1570s[3]

The Tetzcoco Dialogues represent a selection of sample speeches among Nahua men and women of different age and social status in the great altepetl of Tetzcoco, in the Valley of Mexico, probably in the 1570s. Apparently, the dialogues were recorded by a Franciscan friar who relied on native nobles from Tetzcoco to supply the material. The speeches resemble those of the Florentine Codex in their mastery of elaborate metaphors and honorific conventions, typical of Nahuatl huehuehtlahtolli. The speech of an aged woman to the mother of two children presents a nostalgic, idealized view of the way things used to be in the good old days. Their conversations about the disciplining of children are reminiscent of a part in the Codex Mendoza on the prescribed work routines and punishments for boys and girls. Her speech resonates with the words of anybody who reflects nostalgically on the distant past and worries about present and future generations, especially "kids these days." By contrast, consider the changes that this woman had experienced in her lifetime. She would have lived through the arrival of Europeans, the fall and destruction of Tenochtitlan, the scourge of successive epidemics, and the demise of many indigenous traditions under Spanish rule.

An old woman congratulates a mother on her two sons having turned out well.

My lady, how fortunate you are in that the giver of life, our engenderer and creator, has given you these precious jewels and jade! The creatures of our lord are growing very big. Consider our home Mexico-Tenochtitlan, the place of the dike, or the palaces in all the other places; hardly anyone who is born grows up, they just die. It is the same in Tlacopan, Azcapotzalco, and Itztapalapan, wherever there have been nobles. Here in our home of Tetzcoco, your birthplace, things are also coming to an end. There were countless rulers and nobles who were relatives of the former lord Acolmiztli Nezahualcoyotl, and also the son Acamapichtli Nezahualpilli and the Chichimeca nobles. Back when I was growing up there was an infinite number of them. And how many noble houses there were, the palaces of the former nobles and rulers! It was like one big palace. There were countless nobles and relatives, and one could not count the commoners who were dependents, or the slaves; they were like ants. But now everywhere our lord is destroying and reducing the land, we are coming to an end and disappearing. Why? For what reason? Perhaps we have incurred his wrath and offended him with our sins and wrongdoing. But what are we to do? Since we are his creatures and entirely in his hands and he is our engenderer and creator, let us await his command as to what he wants us to do in the future. Let us do all we can to raise children; let parenthood flourish. Let our children, our offspring, be made to look after the proper and good so that they will truly fear and serve our omnipresent lord, and so that they can live peacefully among other people. Today, especially, they really need to be looked after, because evil and bad behavior are greatly growing, increasing, and hardening in them; hardly are they born when they begin not to care about anything, not to obey, not to have any shame.

She continues and tells how children were raised in the old days, in pre-Christian times.

Back when I was raised, the boys who were children of rulers were taught and raised at the Tlacatecco (a temple); the lord Tecuepotzin, the Cihuacoatl, and the senior priest, the great priest, themselves took care of them, and also the Quetzalcoatl (a priest). The adults got them up right at midnight; the children sprinkled and swept everywhere. Next they left for the edge of the woods and carried fir and ferns with which they adorned the temples. Now was that already the house of our lord? They were still just demons' temples, of Tezcatlipoca, Huitzilopochtli, or Tlaloc, and of other demons who were false gods. Next they washed and bathed themselves, even though it was very cold. And by the time it had cleared and become full day, they had prepared the adornment everywhere. Then the adults threw an old tortilla on the ground to each of the children, or perhaps two each if they were a little larger; they treated them like little dogs. And when they had eaten breakfast, the adults began teaching them how to live, how to obey, and how to honor people, to give themselves to the good and to relinquish and avoid evil, bad behavior, and excess. How much wisdom and prudence they absorbed there.

And as to how they were punished, if they did the least thing wrong, it was very frightening; they hanged them up, they set them in the smoke of burning chiles, they hit them with nettles and beat them with switches on their calves and elbows, they stuck maguey spines in their ears, they put their heads close to the fire and scorched them. And likewise, at midday, when the sun was very hot, they sent them to the edge of the woods; the children carried wood, bark, and kindling. They ran vigorously, no one idled or went along shoving people down; all ran prudently and went with fear and respect, and in a very short while they returned. And when the children had arrived again, the adults fed them the same way, they just threw down on the ground to them one or two old tortillas each, for their midday meal. And when they had eaten, right away the adults began teaching them again: to some how to do battle, or how to hunt, how to shoot a blowgun or how to hurl stones; they were taught all about the shield and the handsword, and how to hurl spears and darts with a spear thrower; also about netting and snaring.

Others were taught the different crafts: featherwork, how small feathers and plumes were arranged; also mosaic work, goldsmithery, jewel cutting, and metal polishing; and also codex painting, woodworking, and the various other crafts. Others were taught song composition and oratory and the study known as "the drum and the rattle" (music), and also the study of the heavens, how the sun and moon and stars, called the nine levels, move; and then what are called divine codices which talked about the all-pervasive, the creator of humanity, though they also were about the former false gods with whom people used to fool themselves, for it was still the time of darkness, and the light of our lord, the [Christian] faith, had not yet reached them. And indeed, some they took to the fields or the flower gardens to teach them how to sow seeds, to plant trees and flowers, and to cultivate and work the land. They taught them all that they needed to know by way of service, knowledge, wisdom, and wise living.

Likewise within the houses, where the ladies were in their quarters, the girls were taught all the different things women do: sweeping, sprinkling, preparing food, making beverages, grinding maize, preparing tortillas, making tamales, all the different things customarily done among women; also the art of the spindle and the weaver's reed and various kinds of embroidery; also dyeing, how rabbit down or rabbit fur was dyed different colors. And in the same way as with the boys, those who did something wrong or did not take care were severely punished. And they were all well cared for; no men, no matter who it was, entered there; taking care of them was the exclusive domain of the elderly noblewomen.

And every eighty days they went to the Tlacatecco and heard the eighty-day speech of the lord ruler Acolmiztli Nezahualcoyotl, and there the lord Tecuepotzin admonished them and cautioned them. And the commoners were raised in the same way; the youths were raised in the school at the youths' house, and the girls at the women's temple, where the female penitents were enclosed and fasted. This is how the ancients who left us behind lived and ordered things; they took very great care. But how we raise our children today is a very different thing; bad behavior is no longer feared, for they no longer fear adultery, theft, drunkenness, and other kinds of bad behavior, because it is no longer punished as it used to be punished long ago, when they forthwith strangled and destroyed people. For I still saw it myself, it happened before my eyes, when the daughter of the lord Axay-acatl, ruler of Mexico-Tenochtitlan, committed adultery with Maxtla of the house of Tezonyocan and with Huitzilihuitl; it was done on a grand scale and countless people were punished, strangled, and crushed with stones, along with the lady; some stewards, some artisans, and some merchants, and also the ladies-in-waiting and dependents of the lady. All the world assembled, people came from the altepetls all around to see it; the ladies brought along their daughters even though they might still be in the cradle, to have them see. Even the Tlaxcalans, and the people of Huexotzinco and Atlixco, although they were our enemies, all came to see; the whole roof of the house of the Cholulans was full of people. And as to how the lord ruler Nezahualpilli fed people, there were all the containers, the reed baskets, and the sauce bowls, by which the Mexica were very much put to shame.

And likewise I saw how they strangled the lord Huexotzincatzin, who was the eldest son of the lord ruler Nezahualpilli; he was punished just for composing songs to the lady of Tula, his stepmother, one of the wives of the lord. And Nezahualpilli came back and shut himself up in his palace; the lord Nezahualpilli named the palace "the place of tears," because he wept greatly over the death of his beloved son. Likewise I saw how Quauhiz-tactzin, younger brother of Huexotzincatzin, was punished just because he built himself a residence of his own, not by order of the lord. And I saw other noblemen and ladies whose wrongdoings were punished, as well as the rulers of altepetls (subject to Tetzcoco). Tzotzomatzin of Quauhtitlan was punished for drunkenness. If I mentioned all of them here, it would be a very long time before I finished telling it. And so, my lady, let our grandchildren be very well taken care of, for the world is a difficult place; they will fall into misdeeds and descend into the abyss, or they may make friends with some delinquent boys and they will be accused of something and punished. Make every effort, my mistress and lady, precious person.

The mother answers the old woman.

Your little subjects owe you thanks. What will be the will of our lord? Perhaps they will be able to grow up; but perhaps the remembrance of our lord, illness, will strike us, perhaps in that way he will destroy and remove them from view. I exert all my effort to take care of them, and the noblewoman (the grandmother of the children) also exerts all her effort. And Antonio Coatecatl, your ancestor, has really taken them upon himself; he goes about looking after them and taking good care of them, for raising children is his special domain. How many of my noble uncles did he raise? And also he raised my younger brother. But especially the little first-born concerns me somewhat; he's quite mischievous and afraid of nothing at all; he flies out of the house, he runs howling and shouting as though he were a Chichimec. He stops nowhere, and right away goes running off. Sometimes they catch him in Tetzcoco, or even somewhere in places farther away. Though I skin his hide with a rope and stick him in chile smoke or mistreat and afflict him even more and leave him practically dead, he won't listen at all.

The old woman replies.

Such is not his destiny, my lady, it bothers you needlessly; perhaps he takes after his great-grandfather, the lord Ixtlilxochitl, for he was just like that.

9.4. A Prophesy on Morality, from the Maya Book of Chilam Balam of Mani[4]

One of the principal ways in which Mayas made sense of the past and how it lead to the present was to construct prophecies. These were descriptions of events couched in the

---

4   Translated from Yucatec Maya by Restall, using the photostat of the original manuscript in TLH, Codex Pérez, pp. 70–72. An earlier version of this translation appeared in Restall (1998: 138–40).

rhetoric of prediction and warning, ostensibly made before events but usually written down, if not composed, after the fact. The prophesy here, credited to a pre-Christian priest named Ah Xupan Nauat, warns of the moral and civil breakdown that will accompany the Spanish invasion. In a sense, the prophecy is a mirror image of the old Nahua woman's lament for the passing of the good old days (document 9.3). She complains, for example, of how common "evil and bad behavior" has become among children, whereas Nauat warns that children will become "lazy . . . disrespectful and bellicose." She looks back from the 1570s, he looks forward to how things will decline after the eighth year of the katun *or calendrical cycle named 13 Ahau – 1527 in the Christian calendar, the year of the first Spanish invasion.*

The chief stylistic characteristic of the Maya prophecy – and indeed of much of the Chilam Balam *literature (see document 8.3 for another excerpt from this text) – is the heavy use of metaphor. The plumeria flower is used as a metaphor both for the passing of the years and for female sexuality. People with certain characteristics are represented as animals – bad governors as vultures, for example. Ambiguous Maya phrases or terms are used to convey paired meanings. Because the phrase* hokol ich *can mean both "to show one's face" and "to germinate seedlings or grow crops in," a double meaning is intended to suggest that bad governors will both appear in the wrong places and do the wrong things. Tree symbolism played a role in Mesoamerican rulership imagery, so the trees mentioned near the end of the passage can also be taken as rulers.*

Another term that becomes ambiguous when written here is na. *In the colonial period, Mayas wrote both* na' *("mother") and* na *("house") simply as* na, *enabling the term to be used here to convey a double meaning; the term is used earlier in the passage to refer to the Virgin Mary and also to the houses of pre-Conquest Ichcansiho (or Tiho, the Maya city upon which Spaniards founded Merida). Thus, the end of the paragraph that predicts the arrival of Christianity in Tiho is able simultaneously to evoke the introduction of the worship of the Virgin (holy mother) in the new church (holy house, built to replace the temple atop the old pyramid of Chuncaan).*

Finally, although this text was composed in Maya for Maya audiences, it was written alphabetically in colonial times and there was thus a certain risk in including provocative or incendiary political or religious material. The problem is easily avoided by the author, who uses traditional animal metaphors to predict – and thus, indirectly, incite – a Maya revolt of "tight-lipped brothers" against the rule of Spaniards and their usurping native allies.

The statement of the priest Xupan Nauat.

The prophecy of the priest Ah Xupan Nauat. My elder brothers, my younger brothers, prepare yourselves! Our elder and younger brothers the white men, the white-faced noblemen, will be coming now. In the time of the eighth year of katun 13 Ahau of the Maya rule the thirteenth idol will come; on the day 13 Cauac of 13 Ahau will it be established; its seat will come. The jaguar and the great eagle will be made into shoes by the white man, who will come wearing a visor, with a large mouth, thick lips, and bloody teeth and fingernails. There will come a great plague of ants. There will come too the burden of quarrelling. There also will come the substituting of your white clothes; your white clothing will be permanently replaced. Baptism will come. The tribute solicitors shall come hopping along, coming to bring an end to the wishes in people's hearts. Crazy children, lazy children, will be disrespectful and bellicose; be warned that they will come to disrespect you. Hairless dogs and vultures shall come to assume the town governorship; they shall come and show their faces/grow crops in woodlands and on stony ground; they shall come wearing visors, seated on carpets, slumped down, with sleepy faces; they shall be motionless as though they were sick.

The priests and prophets, the great priests and great prophets, will be replaced by nine wise men who shall appear on the nineteenth day of the katun 11 Ahau. The foundation of the province, its center and gateway, will from this day forth be the Virgin Mother – the Holy Virgin Mother is her name. Thus it is written in the book of generations, these documents given to the priests to revere, to look at, to deduce the katun count. It was given to them because, according to the words of the book of Ah Uuc Satay, it was at Chuncaan, and from Chuncaan it was taken, from inhabited Ichcan-siho [Merida]. The reason why this great aid, the seven-generation book, was given to them to revere was because Hunab Ku had collected the plumerias there; he received each plumeria there. Among the houses that are seen there, the houses of thatch and the houses of stone, the rule of the virgin will be established. The people do not know these things, but at the thirteenth plumeria, they will behold the Holy Mother/house; it will be done to the flute and the trumpet.

[The day] 10 Cauac is the start of the katun 11 Ahau; together with the year-bearers there is the serpent; this second force will reach ears at the center of the province and, facing westward, invade – it is war. There will come nine nights tied together, nine of them before the coming too of much madness, much lust – the time for the plumeria to open. Children will be conceived late; old women will conceive them, old women of the plumeria; and old men shall conceive sons, old men of the plumeria. This will be possible because there will be no youth. Children will now come to take notice of this, to speak about it; our sons, you will be shipwrecked; you will be at sea, your ship will list to the side, waterlogged, powerless with only two or three oars, and it will turn over. One will be asked to go without sandals, to have sore feet, to get used to bruises that are not small; one will be asked to immediately stop wearing Maya-style trousers, to burn the trousers; we will be asked to have no more of them. We will cease following the trail of the urraca, the bird with the blue arrow feathers. We will become tight-lipped, so that our brothers be strengthened for the time when the lineage will fight the serpent, when the green lizard will be taken on with force, when the jaguar will take on the weasel, when the jaguar lineage will do likewise with the leopard, with the puma. The trees/rulers will be snatched, the rule of the cahob will be snatched in 11 Ahau; in the time of 11 Ahau, the jaguar and the leopard will bite and claw each other; in the ninth year of the katun 6 Ahau the jaguar and the puma – the puma that is a lion, the supreme rulers [*halach uinicob*], shall claw each other.

GLOSSARY

Key:

[Sp] Spanish
[Na] Nahuatl
[Mx] Mixtec
[My] Maya

Adelantado (Sp). Title of nobility
Albacea (Sp). Executor of a testament
Alcaide (Sp). Jailor
Alcalde (Sp). A rank of judge and a cabildo member
Alcalde mayor (Sp). Chief magistrate in a given area, appointed from outside; generally the chief Spanish judicial and administrative official in a jurisdiction embracing several native communities; often used interchangeably with corregidor
Alcalde ordinario (Sp). Same as alcalde
Alguacil (Sp). Constable
Almehen (My). Maya nobleman
Almud (Sp). Dry measure, a twelfth of a fanega
Altepetl (Na). Nahua municipal community, equivalent to cah and ñuu
Aniñe (Mx). "Place of royalty," lord's palace
Arroba (Sp). Measure, usually of liquid
Audiencia (Sp). Spanish High Court and its jurisdiction; also used by notaries to refer to a cabildo session or the room or building where the meetings took place
Azteca (Na). People from Aztlan; term applied variously to the Mexica and Nahua of central Mexico; Aztecs in English
Barrio (Sp). Subdistrict of municipality
Batab (My). Cah governor (batabil: governorship)
Braza (Sp). Among Spaniards, a unit of measure equal to a fathom; also used for the larger, regionally variable unit predominant among the indigenous population
Cabecera (Sp). Head town of a Spanish administrative district
Cabildo (Sp). Spanish-style municipal council, body of political officers
Cacique (Sp). Indigenous ruler derived from Arawak term; Nahua tlatoani, Mixtec yya toniñe or Maya batab; in late colonial Spanish, any prominent indigenous person
Cacica (Sp). Female indigenous ruler or spouse of cacique
Cah (My). Maya municipal community (cahob in the plural)
Cahnal (My). Cah resident and member
Caja (Sp). Community treasury chest that indigenous cabildos used to pay expenses and tribute; also spelled "caxa"

227

Callalli (Na). "House-land," a household's central agricultural plot, associated with its residence; similar to Spanish "solar"

Calpolli (Na). Subdistrict of an altepetl; often spelled "calpulli"

Chibal (My). Patronym-group

Chilam Balam (My). Mythical Maya prophet and reputed original author of Maya-language books copied alphabetically in colonial period

Chinampa (Sp). Artificial raised plot for intensive agriculture built up in shallow water; derived from Nahuatl

Cihuacalli (Na). "Woman house," possibly a common room; sometimes owned by a woman, sometimes not

Cihuapilli (Na). Noblewoman, lady

Cihuatlalli (Na). "Woman-land," land held by a woman in her own right, often brought with her into a marriage as her inheritance

Cofradía (Sp). Lay religious brotherhood

Comadre, compadre (Sp). Ritual co-parent; refers to the relationship between the true parent and the godparent

Congregación (Sp). Forced resettlement to central site

Corregidor (Sp). Often used as a synonym for alcalde mayor, although at times indicating a higher rank

Despoblado (Sp). Literally "uninhabited"; Spaniards' misnomer for the "unpacified" (unconquered) southeastern regions of the Yucatan

Diputado (Sp). Deputy, person delegated, name of various secondary offices

Don, doña (Sp). High-ranking title prefixed to first name; like English "sir" and "lady"

Dzul (My). Foreigner, non-Maya, including Spanish Yucatecans

Encomendero (Sp). Holder of an encomienda

Encomienda (Sp). Grant (nearly always to a Spaniard) of the right to receive tribute and originally labor from the population of an altepetl, cah, ñuu, and so on through their existing mechanisms

Escribano (Sp). Notary, clerk

Estancia (Sp). A private landholding most often devoted to livestock; another meaning, in Spanish administrative language, was an indigenous sociopolitical subunit of a larger entity that was separated from or at least noticeably outlying in relation to the main body of the unit

Fanega (Sp). Unit of dry measure; often considered equivalent to one and a half bushels

Fiscal (Sp). In this context, church steward, the highest indigenous ecclesiastical official in a district

Fray (Sp). Title for a friar, member of a mendicant order of the church

Gobernador (Sp). Governor; in this context, an indigenous person filling the highest office of the native cabecera, exercising many of the powers of the preconquest ruler

Hacienda (Sp). Spanish estate

Halach uinic (My). Preconquest regional ruler (literally, true man)

Henequen (Sp). Plant and the fiber it produces, used for making cordage

Hidalgo (Sp). A Spanish word for a person of nobility

Huahi ñuhu (Mx). "Sacred house," term adopted for a church, presumably based on pre-Conquest temple

Huehuetlalli (Na). "Old land," patrimonial or inherited land

Huehuetque (Na). "Old men," elders, usually referring to municipal authorities or ancestors

Huipil (Sp). Indigenous woman's dress (from Nahuatl, huipilli)

Indio (Sp). Spanish term for all indigenous people, who did not use it in reference to themselves

Indio hidalgo (Sp). Category of indigenous nobility recognized by Spanish authorities and exempt from tribute

Kax (My). Forested land; also used in some cahob for cultivated land

Ladino (Sp). Spanish-speaking or acculturated indigenous person

Lienzo (Sp). Early post-Conquest indigenous pictorial writing on cloth

Macehualli (Na). Term for a common person or nonnoble, which in the colonial period came to mean any indigenous person; term adopted by Maya as macehual and by Spaniards as macehuale

Maestro (Sp). Teacher, choirmaster; official in charge of liturgy and catechism

Maestro de capilla (Sp). Choirmaster

Maguey (Sp). Agave, source of the drink pulque and of fibers for various uses; derived from Arawak word

Manta (Sp). Length of cotton cloth, used as an indigenous tribute unit

Marqués (Sp). Spanish noble title, same as "marquis"; Hernando Cortés became the Marqués del Valle de Oaxaca and often was called the Marqués

Matl (Na). "Arm, hand"; one of the terms for the principal indigenous unit for measuring land, sometimes apparently equal to a quahuitl, sometimes a fraction of it

Mayordomo (Sp). Majordomo, steward, name for an official with various organizations

Mesoamerica. Term used mainly by scholars for the area from central Mexico south to Guatemala containing "high" cultures with a great many common elements

Mestizo (Sp). Person of mixed Spanish and indigenous ancestry

Metate (Sp). Grinding stone, mainly for maize; derived from Nahuatl "metlatl"

Mexica (Na). Nahuas from the altepetl of Mexico-Tenochtitlan, which became the basis of Mexico City; sometimes referred to as "Tenochca"

Mulatto (Sp). Person of mixed African and European descent; used in the sixteenth century for mixtures of Africans with any other group

Nahuas. Nahuatl-speaking indigenous central Mexicans

New Spain. The large jurisdiction centered on Mexico City and embracing much of present-day Mexico and Central America; also used more broadly for the whole general or greater Mexican region

Ñandahi (Mx). Mixtec term for a commoner; called macehuales in Spanish (from the Nahuatl term macehualli)

Ñudzahui (Mx). "Place of rain" or "place of Dzahui," the rain deity: term used by the Mixtecs for themselves and for their language

Ñuhu (Mx). Land, as a lot or in general

Ñuu (Mx). Mixtec community, equivalent to cah and altepetl

Obraje (Sp). Any factory-like shop, here specifically an establishment for manufacturing textiles

Oidor (Sp). A judge of an audiencia (in the sense of the Spanish imperial High Court and its jurisdiction, such as those of Mexico City and Guatemala)

-ob (My). Yucatec Maya plural suffix

Peso (Sp). Primary monetary unit, consisting of eight reales or tomines

Petate (Sp). Reed mat; derived from Nahuatl "petatl"

Petlatl icpalli (Na). "Reed mat and seat," and by extension royal throne; considered in central Mexico a symbol of high authority

Pilli (Na). Noble (pipiltin in the plural)

Pochtecatl (Na). Professional indigenous merchant active in interregional trade

Pueblo (Sp). Spanish term for an indigenous municipality (altepetl, ñuu, cah), applied to any autonomous or separate settlement

Pulque (Sp). The main alcoholic drink in central and southern Mexico, produced from the juice of the maguey (an agave); derived from an Arawak term

Principales (Sp). Indigenous community elders or prominent men

Quahuitl (Na). Unit of measure, literally "stick" after the measuring stick, often in the range of seven to ten feet

Quetzal (Na). A tropical bird with long, spectacular blue-green tailfeathers

Real (Sp). A silver coin worth one-eighth of a peso

Regidor (Sp). Councilman, cabildo member

Repartimiento (Sp). A grant of temporary labor of Indians to a Spaniard; often amounted to coerced labor and forced purchase of goods

Siña (Mx.). Term for subentity of a Mixtec ñuu in the Yanhuitlan area; equivalent of Nahua calpolli; local units that Spaniards called barrios

Siqui (Mx). Term for subentity of a Mixtec ñuu in the Teposcolula area; see also "siña"

Solar (Sp). House-lot

Sujeto (Sp). Outlying subject hamlet; term used by Spaniards for communities that were designated as belonging to a cabecera

Teccalli (Na). Lordly house, establishment, with a lord, related nobles, dependents, and lands; contains "teuctli" and "calli," "house"

Tecpan (Na). "Where the lord is," palace, establishment of a ruler or lord; see also "teccalli"

Teniente (Sp). Lieutenant; office attached to Maya cabildo

Teocalli (Na). "God house" or "sacred house"; a pre-Conquest temple or a Christian church or chapel

Tequitl (Na). Rotary draft labor for the altepetl

Teuctli (Na). Lord, titled head of a lordly house (teccalli) with lands and followers (pl. teteuctin)

Tilmatli (Na). A man's cloak; cloth in general

Tithe. An obligatory ecclesiastical tax, formally one-tenth of the increase of goods each year, in fact collected only on certain things, mainly staple crops and livestock

Tlalli (Na). Land

Tlatoani (Na). Dynastic ruler of an altepetl

Tlaxilacalli (Na). A more common name for a "calpolli" or altepetl constituent, especially as a territorial unit

Tlayacatl (Na). In this context, a subaltepetl with its own tlatoani inside a complex altepetl, usually lacking a single dominant ruler

Tniño (Mx). Rotary draft labor and public service (including office) for the ñuu or yuhuitayu

Toho (Mx). Noble not entitled to rule a yuhuitayu

Tomín (Sp). A coin worth one-eighth of a peso; also a generic term for coin or money

Toniñe (Mx). Dynastic rulership based on direct descent from high lords, called yya toniñe

Topile (Na). "One with a staff," constable, official in any of various lower-level supervisory posts

Vara (Sp). A Spanish unit of measurement close to a yard; also a staff carried by alcaldes of the cabildo

Vecino (Sp). Nonindigenous resident

Viceroy. "Vice-king," highest executive officer in New Spain

Visita (Sp). Inspection tour, visit, also by extension a district church visited periodically by a priest from the main parish church

Yuhuitayu (Mx). "Reed mat and ruling couple or throne"; the establishment of a Mixtec ruling lord and lady who unify two dynastic lines in marriage, and the place or places that are considered part of that united patrimony

Yya (Mx). High lord, applied to rulers and sometimes important Spanish officials; "yya dzehe" refers to a female lord (lady)

Yya toniñe (Mx). Mixtec ruling lord; called cacique by Spaniards and tlatoani by Nahuas; yya dzehe toniñe refers to a female lord

Yum (My). Father, lord; used reverentially

REFERENCES AND READINGS

References and abbreviations of archives cited in the notes

AGEY   Archivo General del Estado de Yucatán, Merida
AGI   Archivo General de las Indias, Seville
AGN   Archivo General de la Nación, Mexico City
AJT   Archivo Judicial de Teposcolula, Oaxaca City
ANEY   Archivo Notarial del Estado de Yucatán, Merida
AHN   Archivo Histórico Nacional, Madrid
CAIHY-CCA   Centro de Apoyo a la Investigación Histórica de Yucatán, Colección Colección Carrillo y Ancona, Merida
CDI   Colección de documentos inéditos relativos al descubrimiento, conquista, y organización de las antiguas posesiones Españolas en América y Oceania, Madrid
TLH   Tozzer Library, Rare Manuscripts Collection, Harvard University, Cambridge
TULAL   Tulane University, Latin American Library, Rare Manuscripts Collection, New Orleans

References of published works cited in the notes

Anderson, Arthur J. O., and Charles E. Dibble, trans. 1950–82. *The Florentine Codex: General History of the Things of New Spain*. 13 parts. Salt Lake City and Santa Fe: University of Utah Press and School of American Research, Santa Fe.

Anderson, Arthur J. O., Frances Berdan, and James Lockhart, eds. 1976. *Beyond the Codices: The Nahua View of Colonial Mexico*. UCLA Latin American Studies. Berkeley and Los Angeles: University of California Press.

Carrasco, Pedro P., and Jesús Monjarás-Ruiz, eds. 1976, 1978. *Colección de documentos sobre Coyoacan*. 2 vols. Mexico City: Instituto Nacional de Antropología e Historia.

Cline, S. L., and Miguel León-Portilla, eds. 1984. *The Testaments of Culhuacan*. Nahuatl Studies Series 1. Los Angeles: UCLA Latin American Center.

Dieseldoff, Erwin P. 1931. "A Kekchi Will of 1583," in *The Maya Society Quarterly* 1:1 (December): 65–68.

Edmonson, Munro S. 1982. *The Ancient Future of the Itza: The Book of Chilam Balam of Tizimin*. Austin: University of Texas Press.

Edmonson, Munro S. 1986. *Heaven Born Merida and Its Destiny: The Book of Chilam Balam of Chumayel*. Austin: University of Texas Press.

García, fray Gregorio. 1981 [1607]. *Origen de los indios de el Nuevo Mundo e Indias Occidentales*. México: Fondo de Cultura Económica.

Hanks, William F. 1986. "Authenticity in the Text: A Colonial Maya Case," in *American Ethnologist* 13:4: 721–44.

Hanks, William F. 1996. *Language and Communicative Practices.* Boulder, CO: Westview Press.

Hinz, Eike, Claudine Hartau, and Marie-Luise Heimann-Koenen, eds. 1983. *Aztekischer Zensus: Zur Indianischen Wirtschaft und Gesellschaft im Marquesado um 1540.* 2 vols. Hanover: Verlag für Ethnologie.

Karttunen, Frances, and James Lockhart, eds. 1987. *The Art of Nahuatl Speech: The Bancroft Dialogues.* Los Angeles: UCLA Latin American Center Publications.

Kellogg, Susan, and Matthew Restall, eds. 1998. *Dead Giveaways: Indigenous Testaments of Colonial Mesoamerica and the Andes.* Salt Lake City: University of Utah Press.

León, Nicolás, ed. 1933. *Códice Sierra: Traducción al español de su texto náhuatl y explicación de sus pinturas jeroglíficas.* México: Museo Nacional de Antropología.

Lockhart, James. 1991. *Nahuas and Spaniards: Postconquest Central Mexican History and Philology.* Stanford and Los Angeles: Stanford University Press and UCLA Latin American Center Publications.

Lockhart, James. 1992. *The Nahuas After the Conquest: A Social and Cultural History of the Indians of Central Mexico, Sixteenth Through Eighteenth Centuries.* Stanford: Stanford University Press.

Lockhart, James. 1993. *We People Here: Nahuatl Accounts of the Conquest of Mexico.* Berkeley and Los Angeles: University of California Press.

Lockhart, James, Frances Berdan, and Arthur J. O. Anderson. 1986. *The Tlaxcalan Actas: A Compendium of the Records of the Cabildo of Tlaxcala (1545–1627).* Salt Lake City: University of Utah Press.

Martínez Hernández, Juan. 1926. *Crónica de Yexkukul.* Merida: Nuevos Talleres de la cia. Tipográfica Yucateca.

Recinos, Adrián, ed. 1950. *Memorial de Sololá: Anales de los Cakchiqueles; Titulo de los Señores de Totonicapan.* Mexico City: Fondo de Cultura Económica.

Restall, Matthew. 1995a. "'He Wished It in Vain': Subordination and Resistance among Maya Women in Post-Conquest Yucatan," in *Ethnohistory* 42:4 (Fall): 577–94.

Restall, Matthew. 1995b. *Life and Death in a Maya Community: The Ixil Testaments of the 1760s.* Lancaster, CA: Labyrinthos Press.

Restall, Matthew. 1997. *The Maya World: Yucatec Culture and Society, 1550–1850.* Stanford: Stanford University Press.

Restall, Matthew. 1998. *Maya Conquistador.* Boston: Beacon Press.

Restall, Matthew. 2000. "The Telling of Tales: A Spanish Priest and His Maya Parishioners," in *Colonial Lives: Documents on Latin American History, 1550–1850*, Richard Boyer and Geoffrey Spurling, eds. New York: Oxford University Press, pp. 18–31.

Roys, Ralph L. 1933. *The Book of Chilam Balam of Chumayel.* Washington, DC: Carnegie Institution.

Roys, Ralph L. 1939. *The Titles of Ebtun.* Washington, DC: Carnegie Institution.

Sahagún, fray Bernardino de. See Anderson and Dibble.

Sahagún, fray Bernardino de. 1996. *Historia Universal de las cosas de Nueva España: Codice Laurenziano Mediceo Palatino 218, 219, 220.* Florence: Giunti.

Scholes, France V., and Ralph L. Roys. 1948. *The Chontal Maya Indians of Acalan-Tixchel.* Washington, DC: Carnegie Institution.

Schroeder, Susan, James Lockhart, and Doris Namala. N.d. *Annals of His Time: Volume Three of the Codex Chimalpahin.*

Sousa, Lisa, Stafford Poole, C. M., and James Lockhart, eds. and trans. 1998. *The Story of Guadalupe: Luis Laso de la Vega's Huei tlamahuiçoltica of 1649.* Nahuatl Studies Series, 5. Stanford and Los Angeles: Stanford University Press and UCLA Latin American Center Publications.

Sousa, Lisa, and Kevin Terraciano . 2003. "The 'Original Conquest' of Oaxaca: Late Colonial Nahuatl and Mixtec Accounts of the Spanish Conquest." *Ethnohistory*, 50:2: 349–400.

Terraciano, Kevin. 1998. "Crime and Culture in Colonial Mexico: The Case of the Mixtec Murder Note." *Ethnohistory*, 45:4: 709–45.

Terraciano, Kevin. 2000b. "El Contexto Histórico del Códice Sierra." In *Codices y documentos sobre Mexico: tercer simposio*. Edited by Constanza Vega Sosa. México: Instituto Nacional de Antropología e Historia.

Terraciano, Kevin. 2001. *The Mixtecs of Colonial Oaxaca: Ñudzahui History, Sixteenth through Eighteenth Centuries*. Stanford University Press.

Torre, Mario de la, Josefina García Quintana, and Carlos Martínez Marín, eds. 1983. *El Lienzo de Tlaxcala*. Mexico City: Litógrafos Unidos, SA.

Zimmermann, Günter. 1970. *Briefe der indianischen Nobilität aus Neuspanien an Karl V und Philipp II um die Mitte des 16. Jahrhunderts*. Beiträge zur mittelamerikanischen Völkerkunde 10. Hamburg: Hamburgischen Museum für Völkerkunde und Vorgeschichte.

Additional sources and suggested readings

Altman, Ida, and James Lockhart, eds. 1976. *Provinces of Early Mexico: Variants of Spanish American Regional Evolution*. Los Angeles: UCLA Latin American Center Publications.

Alvarado, fray Francisco de. 1962 [1593]. *Vocabulario en lengua mixteca*. Edited by Wigberto Jiménez Moreno. México: Instituto Nacional de Antropología e Historia.

Anderson, Arthur J. O., and Susan Schroeder, eds. and trans. 1997. *Codex Chimalpahin: Society and Politics in Mexico Tenochtitlan, Tlatelolco, Texcoco, Culhuacan, and Other Nahua Altepetl in Central Mexico. The Nahuatl and Spanish Annals and Accounts Collected and Recorded by don Domingo de San Antón Muñón Chimalpahin Quauhtlehuanitzin*. 2 vols. Norman: University of Oklahoma Press.

Andrews, J. Richard. 1975. *Introduction to Classical Nahuatl*. Austin: University of Texas Press.

Arana Osnaya, Evangelina, and Mauricio Swadesh. 1965. *Los elementos del mixteco antiguo*. México: Instituto Nacional Indigenista e Instituto Nacional de Antropología e Historia.

Boone, Elizabeth Hill. 2000. *Stories in Red and Black: Pictorial Histories of the Aztecs and Mixtecs*. Austin: University of Texas Press.

Boone, Elizabeth Hill, and Tom Cummings, eds. 1998. *Native Traditions in the Postconquest World*. Washington, DC: Dumbarton Oaks.

Borah, Woodrow. 1943. *Silk Raising in Colonial Mexico*. Ibero-Americana, 20. Berkeley and Los Angeles: University of California Press.

Borah, Woodrow. 1983. *Justice by Insurance: The General Indian Court of Colonial Mexico*. Berkeley and Los Angeles: University of California Press.

Borah, Woodrow, and S. F. Cook. 1960. *The Population of Central Mexico, 1531–1570*. Ibero-Americana, 43. Berkeley and Los Angeles: University of California Press.

Bradley, C. Henry, and Barbara E. Hollenbach, eds. 1988–92. *Studies in the Syntax of Mixtecan Languages*. 4 vols. Dallas: Summer Institute of Linguistics and the University of Texas at Arlington.

Burkhart, Louise. 1989. *The Slippery Earth: Nahua-Christian Moral Dialogue in Sixteenth-Century Mexico*. Tucson: University of Arizona Press.

Burkhart, Louise. 1996. *Holy Wednesday: A Nahua Drama from Early Colonial Mexico*. Philadelphia: University of Pennsylvania Press.

Carmack, Robert. 1973. *Quichean Civilization: The Ethnohistoric, Ethnographic, and Archaeological Sources*. Berkeley: University of California Press.

Carrasco, Pedro, and Johanna Broda, eds. 1976. *Estratificación social en la Mesoamérica prehispánica*. México: Centro de Investigaciones Superiores, Instituto Nacional de Antropología e Historia.

Chance, John. 1972. *Race and Class in Colonial Oaxaca*. Stanford: Stanford University Press.

Chance, John. 1989. *Conquest of the Sierra: Spaniards and Indians in Colonial Oaxaca*. Oklahoma: University of Oklahoma Press.

Chance, John. 1996. "The Caciques of Tecali: Class and Ethnic Identity in Late Colonial Mexico." *Hispanic American Historical Review* 76:3: 475–502.

Chance, John. 2000. "The Noble House in Colonial Puebla, Mexico: Descent, Inheritance, and the Nahua Tradition," in *American Anthropologist*, 102:3: 485–502.

Cline, S. L. 1986. *Colonial Culhuacan, 1580–1600: A Social History of an Aztec Town*. Albuquerque: University of New Mexico Press.

Cline, S. L., ed. 1993. *The Book of Tributes: Early Sixteenth-Century Nahuatl Censuses from Morelos*. Nahuatl Studies Series 4. Los Angeles: UCLA Latin American Studies Center Publications.

Collier, George, Renato Rosaldo, and John Wirth, eds. 1982. *The Inca and Aztec States*. New York: Academic Press.

Doesburg, Bas van. 2000. "Origin of the Lienzo de Tulancingo: New Facts about a Pictographic Document from the Coixtlahuaca Region," in *Ancient Mesoamerica* 11: 169–83.

Doesburg, Sebastián van. 2001. *Códices Cuicatecos: Porfirio Díaz y Fernández Leal. Edición facsimile, contexto histórico e interpretación*. 2 vols. Mexico: Editorial Porrua.

Farriss, Nancy M. 1984. *Maya Society under Colonial Rule: The Collective Enterprise of Survival*. Princeton, NJ: Princeton University Press.

García Icazbalceta, Joaquín. 1954. *Bibliografía mexicana del siglo XVI: Catálogo razonado de libros impresos en México de 1539 a 1600*. México: Fondo de Cultura Económica.

Gerhard, Peter. 1972. *A Guide to the Historical Geography of New Spain*. Cambridge: Cambridge University Press.

Gibson, Charles. 1952. *Tlaxcala in the Sixteenth Century*. New Haven, CT: Yale University Press.

Gibson, Charles. 1964. *The Aztecs Under Spanish Rule: A History of the Indians of the Valley of Mexico, 1519–1810*. Stanford: Stanford University Press.

Glass, John B, 1975. "A Survey of Native Middle American Pictorial Manuscripts," in Robert Wauchope, gen. ed., *Handbook of Middle American Indians*, 14 (Guide to Ethnohistorical Sources, part 3, ed. by Howard F. Cline): 3–80. Austin: University of Texas Press.

Glass, John B., and Donald Robertson. 1975. "A Census of Native American Pictorial Manuscripts," in Robert Wauchope, gen. ed., *Handbook of Middle American Indians*, 14 (Guide to Ethnohistorical Sources, part 3, ed. by Howard F. Cline): 81–252. Austin: University of Texas Press.

Gosner, Kevin. 1992. *Soldiers of the Virgin: The Moral Economy of a Colonial Maya Rebellion*. Tucson: University of Arizona Press.

Greenleaf, Richard E. 1969. *The Mexican Inquisition of the Sixteenth Century*. Albuquerque: University of New Mexico Press.

Gruzinski, Serge. 1993. *The Conquest of Mexico: The Incorporation of Indian Societies into the Western World, 16th–18th Centuries*. Translated by Eileen Corrigan. Cambridge: Polity Press.

Gruzinski, Serge. 1989. *Man-Gods in the Mexican Highlands*. Stanford: Stanford University Press.

Harvey, H. R., ed. 1991. *Land and Politics in the Valley of Mexico: A Two Thousand Year Perspective*. Albuquerque: University of New Mexico Press.

Harvey, H. R., and Hanns J. Prem, eds. 1984. *Explorations in Ethnohistory: Indians of Central Mexico in the Sixteenth Century*. Albuquerque: University of New Mexico Press.

Haskett, Robert S. 1991a. *Indigenous Rulers: An Ethnohistory of Town Government in Colonial Cuernavaca*. Albuquerque: University of New Mexico Press.

Haskett, Robert S. 1991b. "Our Suffering with the Taxco Tribute": Involuntary Mine Labor and Indigenous Society in Central New Spain." *Hispanic American Historical Review* 71:3: 447–475.

Haskett, Robert S. 1996. "Paper Shields: The Ideology of Coats of Arms in Colonial Mexican Primordial Titles," in *Ethnohistory* 43:1: 99–126.

Haskett, Robert S. 2005. *Visions of Paradise: Primordial Titles and Mesoamerican History in Cuernavaca*. Norman: University of Oklahoma Press.

Hassig, Ross. 1985. *Trade, Tribute, and Transportation: The Sixteenth-century Political Economy of the Valley of Mexico*. Norman: University of Oklahoma Press.

Hernández, fray Benito. 1567, 1568. *Doctrina en lengua misteca*. México: Pedro Ocharte.

Hill, Robert M. 1987. *The Pirir Papers and Other Colonial Period Cakchiquel-Maya Testamentos.* Nashville: Vanderbilt University Publications in Anthropology, no. 37.

Horn, Rebecca. 1997. *Postconquest Coyoacan: Nahua-Spanish Relations in Central Mexico, 1519–1650.* Stanford: Stanford University Press.

Jansen, Maarten E. R. G. N. 1982. *Huisi Tacu: Estudio interprativo de un libro mixteco antiguo: Codex Vindobonensis Mexicanus I.* 2 vols. Amsterdam: Centrum voor Studie en Documentatie van Latijns Amerika.

Jansen, Maarten E. R. G. N. 1994. *La Gran Familia de los reyes mixtecos: Libro explicativo de los códices llamados Egerton y Becker II.* Austria, España, y México: Akademische Druckund Verlagsanstalt (Vienna), Sociedad Estatal Quinto Centenario (España), and Fondo de Cultura Económica (México).

Jansen, Maarten, and Luis Reyes García, eds. 1997. *Códices, Caciques, and Comunidades.* Cuadernos de Historia Latinoamerica, no. 5. Netherlands: Asociación de Historiadores Latinoamericanistas Europeos.

Jones, Grant. 1989. *Maya Resistance to Colonial Rule: Time and History on a Colonial Frontier.* Albuquerque: University of New Mexico Press.

Karttunen, Frances. 1983. *An Analytical Dictionary of Nahuatl.* Austin: University of Texas Press.

Karttunen, Frances. 1985. *Nahuatl and Maya in Contact with Spanish.* Texas Linguistic Forum, 26. Austin: Department of Linguistics, University of Texas.

Karttunen, Frances, and James Lockhart. 1976. *Nahuatl in the Middle Years: Language Contact Phenomena in Texts of the Colonial Period.* University of California Publications in Linguistics, 85. Berkeley and Los Angeles: University of California Press.

Karttunen, Frances, and James Lockhart. 1978. "Textos en náhuatl del siglo XVIII: Un documento de Amecameca, 1746," in *Estudios de Cultura Náhuatl,* 13: 153–75.

Karttunen, Frances, and James Lockhart. 1980. "La estructura de la poesía náhuatl vista por sus variantes," in *Estudios de Cultura Náhuatl,* 14: 15–65.

Kellogg, Susan. 1995. *Law and the Transformation of Aztec Culture, 1500–1700.* Norman: University of Oklahoma Press.

Kicza, John E. 2003. *Resilient Cultures: America's Native Peoples Confront European Colonization, 1500–1800.* Upper Saddle River, New Jersey: Prentice Hall.

Landa, fray Diego de. 1982 [1566]. *Relación de las Cosas de Yucatán.* Mexico: Editorial Porrúa.

Leon-Portilla, Miguel. 1961. *The Broken Spears: Aztec Account of the Conquest of Mexico.* Boston: Beacon Press.

Leon-Portilla, Miguel. 1969. *Pre-Columbian Literatures of Mexico.* Translated from the Spanish by Grace Lobanov and the Author. Norman: University of Oklahoma Press.

Leon-Portilla, Miguel, and Earl Shorris, eds. 2001. *In the Language of Kings: An Anthology of Mesoamerican Literature, Pre-Columbian to the Present.* New York: W. W. Norton.

Lockhart, James. 1999. *Of Things of the Indies: Essays Old and New in Early Latin American History.* Stanford: Stanford University Press.

Lockhart, James. 2001. *Nahuatl As Written: Lessons in Older Written Nahuatl, with Copious Examples and Texts.* Stanford and Los Angeles: Stanford University Press and UCLA Latin American Center.

Lockhart, James, ed. and trans. 2001. *Grammar of the Mexican Language, with an Explanation of its Adverbs (1645), by Horacio J. Carochi, S. J.* Stanford and Los Angeles: Stanford University Press and UCLA Latin American Center.

López Austin, Alfredo. 1988. *The Human Body and Ideology: Concepts of the Ancient Nahua.* 2 vols. Translated by Thelma Ortiz de Montellano and Bernard Ortiz de Montellano. Salt Lake City: University of Utah Press.

Maxwell, Judith, and Craig Hanson. 1992. *Of the Manners of Speaking That the Old Ones Had: The Metaphors of Andrés de Olmos in the TULAL Manuscript Arte para Aprender la Lengua Mexicana 1547.* Salt Lake City: University of Utah Press.

Molina, Alonso de. 1992 [1571]. *Vocabulario en lengua castellana y mexicana y mexicana y castellana.* Mexico: Editorial Porrua.

Mundy, Barbara. 1996. *The Mapping of New Spain: Indigenous Cartography and the Maps of the Relaciones Geográficas*. Chicago: University of Chicago Press.

Munro, Pamela, and Felipe Lopez. 1999. *Di'csyonaary X:tèe'n Dìi'zh Sah Sann Luu'c* (San Lucas Quiaviní Zapotec Dictionary / Diccionario Zapoteco de San Lucas Quiaviní). Los Angeles: UCLA Chicano Studies Research Center.

Oudijk, Michel. 2000. *The Historiography of the Benizaa: The Postclassic and Early Colonial Periods (1000–1600 A.D.)*. Leiden: Research School of Asian, African, and Amerindian Studies.

Pastor, Rodolfo. 1987. *Campesinos y reformas: La mixteca, 1700–1856*. México: El Colegio de México.

Patch, Robert W. 1993. *Maya and Spaniard in Yucatan, 1648–1812*. Stanford: Stanford University Press.

Peterson, Jeanette. 1993. *The Paradise Garden Murals of Malinalco: Utopia and Empire in Sixteenth-Century Mexico*. Austin: University of Texas Press.

Poole, Stafford. 1995. *Our Lady of Guadalupe: The Origins and Sources of a Mexican National Symbol, 1571–1797*. Tucson: University of Arizona Press.

Restall, Matthew. 2001. "The People of the Patio: Ethnohistorical Evidence of Yucatec Maya Royal Courts," in *Royal Courts of the Ancient Maya, vol. 2: Data and Case Studies*, Takeshi Inomata and Stephen D. Houston, eds. Boulder, CO: Westview Press, pp. 335–90.

Restall, Matthew. 2003. *Seven Myths of the Spanish Conquest*. New York: Oxford University Press.

Reyes, fray Antonio de los. 1976 [1593]. *Arte en lengua mixteca*. Vanderbilt University Publications in Anthropology, 14. Nashville: Vanderbilt University Press.

Reyes García, Luis. 1977. *Cuauhtinchan del siglo XII al XVI: Formación y desarrollo histórico de un señorío prehispánico*. Wiesbaden: Franz Steiner Verlag.

Reyes García, Luis. 1978. *Documentos sobre tierras y señoríos en Cuauhtinchan*. Mexico: Centro de Investigaciones y Estudios Superiores en Antropología Social.

Reyes García, Luis, Carmen Celestino Solís Cayetano, Francisco García Ramírez, and Elias Pineda Mendoza, eds. 1982. *Documentos mexicanos*. AGN Serie guias y catálogos, 72. 2 vols. México: Talleres Graficos de la Nación.

Ricard, Robert. 1966. *The Spiritual Conquest of Mexico: An Essay on the Apostolate and the Evangelizing Methods of the Mendicant Orders in New Spain: 1523–72* [1933]. Trans. by Lesley Byrd Simpson. Berkeley and Los Angeles: University of California Press.

Romero Frizzi, María de los Ángeles. 1990. *Economía y vida de los españoles en la Mixteca Alta: 1519–1720*. México: Instituto Nacional de Antropología e Historia.

Romero Frizzi, María de los Ángeles, ed. 2003. *Escritura Zapoteca: 2,500 años de historia*. México: Instituto Nacional de Antropología e Historia.

Roskamp, Hans. 1998. *La historiografía indígena de Michoacan: El Lienzo Jucutácato y los títulos de Carapan*. Netherlands: University of Leiden, CNWS.

Ruiz de Alarcón, Hernando. 1984. *Treatise on the Heathen Superstitions That Today Live Among the Indians Native to This New Spain, 1629*. Translated and edited by J. Richard Andrews and Ross Hassig. Norman: University of Oklahoma Press.

Sahagún, fray Bernardino de. 1997. *The Primeros Memoriales*. Paleography of Nahuatl Text and English Translation by Thelma Sullivan. Completed and revised, with additions, by H. B. Nicholson, Arthur J. O. Anderson, Charles E. Dibble, Eloise Quiñones Keber, and Wayne Ruwet. Norman and London: University of Oklahoma Press in cooperation with the Patrimonio Nacional and the Real Academia de la Historia, Madrid.

Scholes, France V., and Ralph L. Roys. 1948. *The Chontal Maya Indians of Acalan-Tixchel*. Washington, DC: Carnegie Institution.

Schroeder, Susan. 1991. *Chimalpahin and the Kingdoms of Chalco*. Tucson: University of Arizona Press.

Schroeder, Susan, ed. 1998. *Native Resistance and the Pax Colonial in New Spain*. Lincoln: University of Nebraska Press.

Schroeder, Susan, Stephanie Wood, and Robert Haskett, eds. 1997. *Indian Women in Early Mexico*. Norman: University of Oklahoma Press.

Schwartz, Stuart B. 2000. *Victors and Vanquished: Spanish and Nahua Views of the Conquest of Mexico*. Boston: Bedford/St. Martin's Press.

Sell, Barry D., and John Frederick Schwaller, eds., with Lu Ann Homza. 1999. *A guide to Confession Large and Small in the Mexican Language, 1634, by Don Bartolomé de Alva*. Norman: University of Oklahoma Press.

Sharer, Robert J. 1994. *The Ancient Maya*. 5th ed. Stanford: Stanford University Press.

Sigal, Pete. 2000. *From Moon Goddesses to Virgins: The Colonization of Yucatecan Maya Sexual Desire*. Austin: University of Texas Press.

Siméon, Rémi. 1988. *Diccionario de la lengua náhuatl o mexicana*. Translated from French by Josefina Oliva de Coll. México: Siglo Veintiuno Editores.

Smailus, Ortwin. 1975. *El Maya-Chontal de Acalan: Análisis lingüístico de un documento de los años 1610–12*. Mexico City: UNAM (Centro de Estudios Mayas, #9).

Smith, Mary Elizabeth. 1973. *Picture Writing from Ancient Southern Mexico: Mixtec Place Signs and Maps*. Norman: University of Oklahoma Press.

Sousa, Lisa. 2002. "The Devil and Deviance in Native Criminal Narratives from Early Mexico," in *The Americas* 59:2 (October): 161–79.

Spores, Ronald. 1967. *Mixtec Kings and their People*. Norman: University of Oklahoma Press.

Spores, Ronald. 1984. *The Mixtecs in Ancient and Colonial Times*. Norman: University of Oklahoma Press.

Stern, Steve J. 1995. *The Secret History of Gender: Women, Men, and Power in Late Colonial Mexico*. Chapel Hill: University of North Carolina Press.

Taylor, William B. 1972. *Landlord and Peasant in Colonial Oaxaca*. Stanford: Stanford University Press.

Taylor, William B. 1979. *Drinking, Homicide, and Rebellion in Colonial Mexican Villages*. Stanford: Stanford University Press.

Taylor, William B. 1996. *Magistrates of the Sacred: Priests and Parishioners in Eighteenth-Century Mexico*. Stanford: Stanford University Press.

Terraciano, Kevin. 2000a. "The Colonial Mixtec Community." *Hispanic American Historical Review* 80:1: 1–44.

Terraciano, Kevin, and Matthew Restall. 1992. "Indigenous Writing and Literacy in Colonial Mexico," in *UCLA Historical Journal* 12: 8–28.

Thompson, Philip C. 1999. *Tekanto, A Maya Town in Colonial Yucatán*. New Orleans: Middle American Research Institute Pub. 67, Tulane University.

Wood, Stephanie. 1991. "The Cosmic Conquest: Late Colonial Views of the Sword and Cross in Central Mexican Títulos," in *Ethnohistory* 38:2: 176–95.

Wood, Stephanie. 2003. *Transcending Conquest: Nahua Views of Spanish Colonial Mexico*. Norman: University of Oklahoma Press.

Zeitlin, Judith F. 2005. *Cultural Politics in Colonial Tehuantepec: Community and State Among the Isthmus Zapotec, 1500–1750*. Stanford: Stanford University Press.

INDEX